THE OIL PAINTING BOOK

Materials and Techniques for Today's Artist

BILL CREEVY

WATSON-GUPTILL PUBLICATIONS/NEW YORK

A lot of people helped me in this project and I'd like to thank them for all they did. Many thanks to the editorial and production team at Watson-Guptill, especially Marian Appellof, Areta Buk, and Ellen Greene; and a very special thanks to Candace Raney for believing that I could do this book in the first place.

Thanks also for the information and professional expertise of Ed Brickner, Carl Plansky, Richard Frumess, Dominique Sennelier, Pierre Guidetti, Jim Cobb, Robert Gamblin, Jacques Blockx, Clyde Chinitz, Ron Howard, Andrew Daler, Wendell Upchurch, E. Peter Hopper, June Lee, and Jim Foster.

Also many thanks to Bob, Ellen, Jane, Rallou, Marianne, Christie, Pat, Jack, and especially Virgilia for keeping everything going when I couldn't be there.

Art on page 1:
PEARS AND APPLES
Oil on Masonite, 11 × 14" (27.9 × 35.6 cm).
Collection of Dr. Charles and Nelly Goodsell.

Art on page 5:
LANDSCAPE (detail)
Oil on panel, 20 × 40" (50.8 × 101.6 cm).
Collection of the artist.

Copyright ©1994 Bill Creevy

First published in 1994 in the United States by Watson-Guptill Publications, a division of BPI Communications, Inc., 1515 Broadway, New York, N.Y. 10036.

Library of Congress Cataloging-in-Publication Data

Creevy, Bill.
    The oil painting book : materials and techniques for today's artist / Bill Creevy.
        p.   cm.
    Includes index.
    ISBN 0-8230-3273-6
    1. Painting—Technique.   I. Title.
ND1500.C73 1994
751.45—dc20   94-26964
                                                        CIP

Manufactured in Malaysia

First printing, 1994

2 3 4 5 6 7 8 / 01 00 99 98 97 96 95

This book is dedicated in gratitude to the four women who spent a lot of their time raising me.
First of all, thanks to my mother, Frances L. Creevy, who did most of the work taking care of me in those days.
But thanks also to Thelma Lewis, my favorite aunt, and to my late grandmother, Julia Lester ("Grammy"),
who was always there for me and once even saved my life. And finally, thanks to my sister,
Kathryn Binnings, who even to this day still looks out for her little brother.

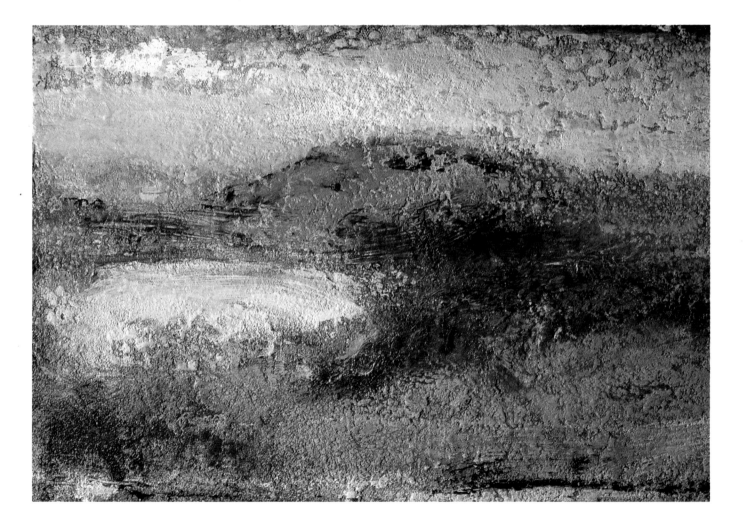

CONTENTS

INTRODUCTION

Ever since it emerged in the early 15th century, oil painting has enjoyed a reputation unsurpassed by any other artistic medium. During the last 500 years it has grown to become the most dominant form of artistic painting and the medium of choice for most of the world's greatest artists.

One significant reason oil painting has enjoyed such a timeless and universal popularity is that it is so versatile. There are a lot of ways to do an oil painting; oil techniques are myriad. Whether an artist wants colors applied flat or illusionistically, hard-edged or subtly, heavily built up or exquisitely glazed, oil paint can easily do the job. The very simple fact that it is a slow-drying medium gives the artist time to make changes and corrections and, more importantly, time to evolve ideas and discover new ones while a painting is in progress. Oil paint's technical flexibility is responsible for the growth of the stylistic individualism that has characterized Western painting since the Renaissance. Oil paint is truly the medium that has let us be ourselves. Of course, probably the main reason oil painting is so popular is that it is so incredibly beautiful. No other medium can come as close to representing the beauty of the real—or the imaginary—world.

The purpose of this book is to help those who are curious to become more familiar with the materials and techniques of oil painting. We will see how diverse a medium it is, starting with direct painting methods that include simple oil sketching and various other alla prima techniques. We will examine how to blend oil colors and how to work them into heavy impasto textures. Paint handling techniques such as drybrush, wet-on-wet, dabbing, and palette knife work are covered as well.

Beyond these direct painting methods are the more complicated indirect techniques of glazing and scumbling. Oil glazing, an approach based on oil paint's transparent nature and the one with which the medium originated, is a subject often overlooked today. This book, however, treats it in great depth, demonstrating both traditional and modern glazing techniques, from building a grisaille underpainting to choosing the colors and mediums that will help you produce mirror-smooth realistic paintings.

This book offers an extensive survey of all the oil painting materials that exist today, including descriptions of the leading professional oil paints and their unique qualities. As you will see, this is a truly international medium, with high-quality paints now coming to us from such diverse locales as Australia, Japan, and Russia, not to mention the more traditional sources of Europe and the United States.

Oil painting relies heavily on modifying substances that make the paint do different things. Some of these modifiers, or mediums, as they are called, have legendary reputations, while others are no more than a few years old. All of them are fully explained here, with an eye toward showing that today's array offers many more possibilities to the craft of oil painting than we may have imagined previously.

We will also look at the many choices of painting surfaces and grounds available. Linen, cotton, wood, Masonite, and even metal are examined in the context of their historical and contemporary use. We'll take a look as well at the various tools employed in oil painting, including brushes, palette knives, palettes, and cleaners and their multiple uses in the studio.

Exciting innovations in the chemistry of oil paints have been made in recent years. We will examine such new developments as the synthetic resin-oil paints called alkyds, as well as water-miscible oil paints and the increasingly popular oil sticks—oil paint in solid form.

Many of these recent variations on oil paint are pointing to future innovations in the medium and new directions for oil painters to take. It is hoped that this book will serve as a basic guide to the contemporary world of oil painting—a world that combines history and tradition with modern innovation.

THREE PEARS
Oil on wood,
12 × 8" (30.5 × 20.3 cm).
Private collection.

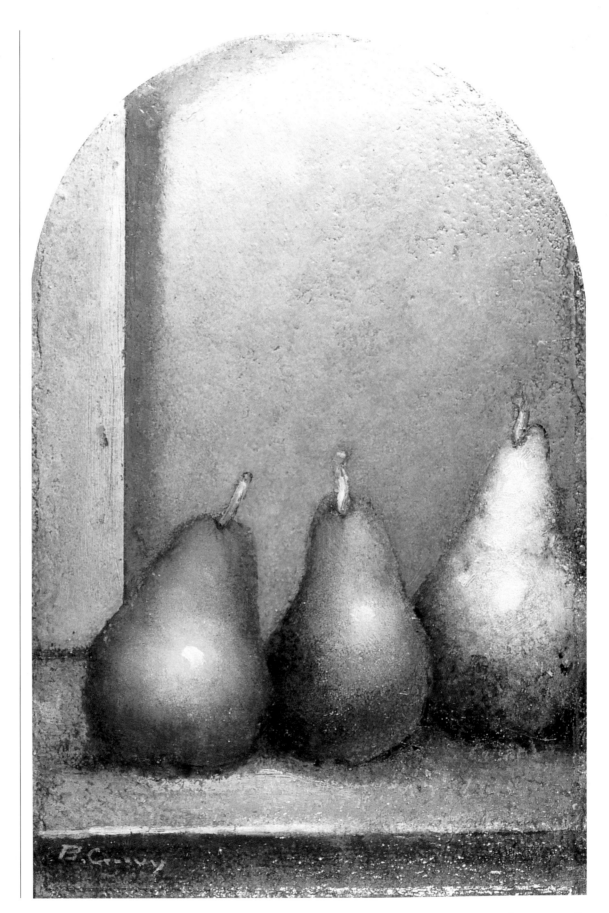

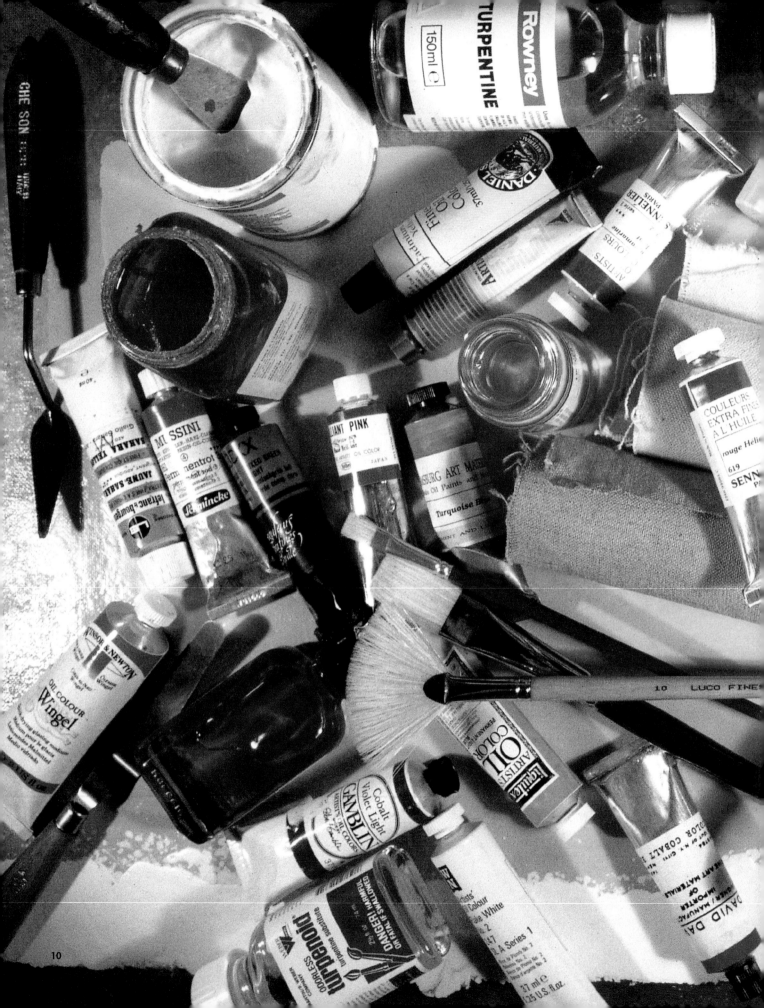

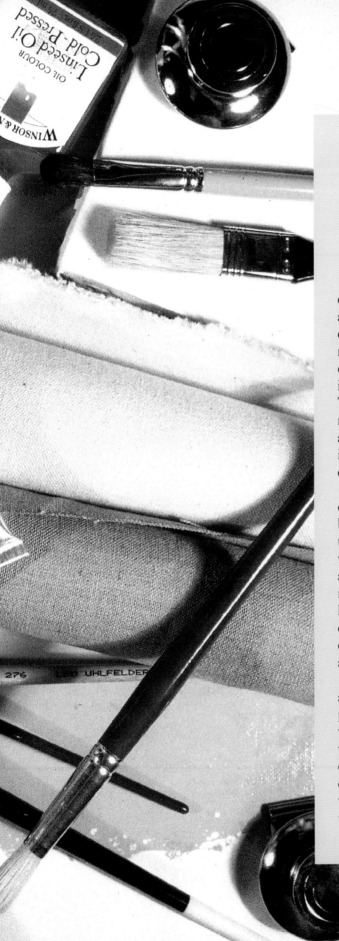

MATERIALS AND TOOLS

Here at the end of the 20th century, oil painters are in a unique and fortunate position. We are the inheritors of 500 years of oil painting experience, half a millennium's worth of scientific and technical developments built on the ambitious, often inspired experimentation of our artistic ancestors. Their legacy to us is an array of oil painting materials that today exist in greater variety and abundance than ever. And, we have come into our inheritance during a period of intense commercial competition, which keeps quality very high.

This chapter is an overview of the many brands of professional oil paints, mediums, supports, brushes, and other tools that are available to us today. Because oil painting offers a lot of technical variety and can be adapted to suit almost every artistic style, the list of materials it involves is not short. Although many of oil painting's time-honored accoutrements are still with us, our century has seen technological advances in paint chemistry that have resulted in the addition of new and improved materials to this already long list.

So a chapter like this helps you keep up. Use it as a guide to selecting materials suitable for your purposes. It will help you know more about your favorite brand of oil paint as well as introduce you to new ones. It will expand your technical expertise in the craft of oil painting with a complete presentation of paint mediums and varnishes. It will help you pick the right tool for the right job, the right brush for the right effect.

Oil Paints

The myriad brands of oil paint available to today's artist form an impressively long and diversified list. Some of these paints have been around for over a century, while others are no more than a few years old, and manufacturers range from international conglomerates to little more than artist-run storefronts. Each company has something unique to offer the oil painter and strives for its own definition of quality. Whether it's water-miscible oils, new colors, or ancient recipes, somebody out there has it all wrapped up and ready for you to use today.

Archival Oils

Archival Oils, or Archival Permanently Flexible Artists Oils, as the brand is officially titled, is a new, high-quality professional oil paint that comes from Australia. Developed in 1990 by Jim Cobb, the technical director of Chroma Acrylics, Archival was adopted within its first two years on the market as the "paint of choice" by 40 percent of all Australian oil painters. In 1993 it was introduced to the United States and the rest of the world.

Archival oils have the distinction of being the first designed specifically to overcome a problem endemic to oil paints: brittling as a painting ages. It is well known that one of oil paint's defects is that the linseed oil vehicle stiffens and becomes less flexible as it dries, unfortunately resulting in a cracked paint film. This happens because the canvas support, even under ideal conditions,

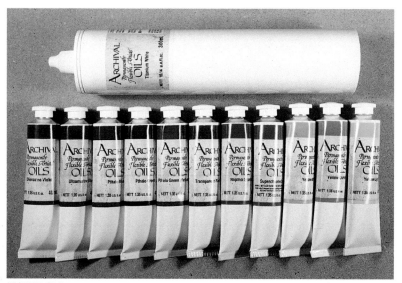

ARCHIVAL OILS

expands and contracts with changes in humidity. But with Archival oils, the dried paint film remains flexible forever. The secret is a genuine linseed oil binder that has been altered by the addition of a patented synthetic resin plasticizer, which allows the paint film to expand and contract with the canvas and thus prevents brittling and cracking. Archival is not an acrylic or an alkyd but a genuine oil paint. It dries slowly and handles just like any other oil paint, and can be mixed with all the traditional oil painting mediums and solvents, as well as with any other brand of oil paint you might want to use.

The Archival range of 43 colors is modest but choice, comprising in roughly equal number traditional colors such as cadmiums and cobalts and newer colors made from modern pigments such as arylide and quinacridone. There is an equal balance of opaque to transparent colors, making Archival oils excellent for glazing techniques.

Titanium white is the only white in the Archival line, but it comes in four versions: a regular opaque stiff type and a softer, more painterly one, as well as a fast-drying type used for underpainting and a semitransparent type called pearl white that, when mixed with other colors, converts them into shimmering pearlescents.

Because permanence is Archival's goal, the company has focused on producing paints based on the most lightfast pigments available. For example, in place of genuine alizarin crimson, Archival offers a color called permanent alizarine, which perfectly matches traditional alizarin in hue and transparency but has the additional advantage of being very lightfast.

Archival oils come in the usual flexible tubes in two sizes, 40ml and 150ml. They are also available in 300ml stiff plastic "canisters" that are designed to work with a handyman's paint gun; alternatively, you can squirt paint out through the nozzle by pushing the back end of the canister with a paintbrush handle.

Blockx Oils

Blockx is one of the oldest, most prestigious paint manufacturers in the world. This Belgian firm was founded in 1865 by the chemist Jacques Blockx and has stayed in his family for four generations. The company's goal is the same today as it was from its very inception: to make the very best oil paints possible, and only of professional quality. Such leading artists as René Magritte, Salvador Dalí, and Fairfield Porter have

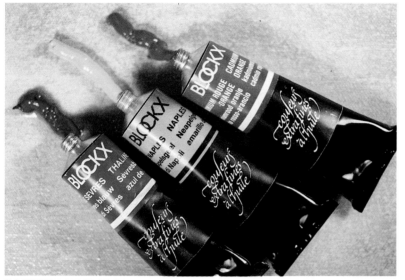

BLOCKX EXTRA-FINE OIL COLORS

lavished glowing praise on Blockx oils, a testament to the extremely high quality of these paints.

The superiority of Blockx oils can be attributed to three simple factors. The first is a careful selection of only the very best pigments and oils available. The second is powerful pigmentation. Blockx oils are made with the highest concentration of pigment possible. All fillers, extenders, and driers are excluded; the paints are nothing but pure pigment and oil. The third factor is Blockx's 150-year legacy of serious craftsmanship, from the careful grinding of pigments in old-fashioned stone mills to the exacting formulations of paint recipes.

The Blockx color range reflects quality rather than quantity. The firm offers only 60 colors, which, except for the whites, come in just one size: a sexy black 35ml tube. (Blockx's 4 different whites are available in 60ml tubes as well as 35ml tubes.) Approximately one-third of the Blockx palette consists of earth colors, whose particular beauty has made them legendary and reflects the importance of choice pigments. Blockx's range of earth colors offers several surprises. For example, there is no raw umber, but in its stead is a beautiful transparent brown; neither is there raw sienna, but two burnt siennas take its place, one dark, the other light. Another unique Blockx earth color is Capucine yellow, in both light and dark varieties. Undiluted, these colors are a rich, transparent "wood" red; when mixed with white, they produce earthy flesh tones.

Because of the heavy pigmentation, the more chromatic hues of the Blockx line really sing out.

Where necessary, Blockx's brighter and lighter colors, such as cerulean blue, are mixed with poppyseed oil rather than linseed oil to avoid any possible discoloration or yellowing. In fact, Blockx is the only paint maker to use poppyseed oil to such a great extent—in more than one-third of its color line. The firm offers the full range of cadmiums and cobalts, plus a genuinely transparent aureolin. Interestingly, Blockx does not have an alizarin crimson, but instead offers a series of rose madders made from the newer and more lightfast pigment anthraquinone. Finally, Blockx makes one of the world's few genuine vermilions, but this brilliant red is not cheap at around $80 a 35ml tube. Most painters settle for cadmium red orange.

DANIEL SMITH OILS

Daniel Smith Finest Oil Colors are perhaps the newest oil paints on the market. They are manufactured and sold by Daniel Smith Inc., a large, Seattle-based art materials supplier. Most of the world knows of this company through its fabulous catalog, which is as beautiful as it is indispensable. The whole thrust of the Daniel Smith operation is to make top-quality materials accessible to all, and its emphasis on high standards is especially evident in the materials that bear the firm's own logo.

Daniel Smith Finest Oils began to appear in the late 1980s, first just the whites, followed by the earth colors; with each succeeding catalog new colors were introduced, until 1991 when the whole line was completed. Today Daniel Smith Finest Oils are available in a range of 80 colors plus four whites, and include the world's largest selection (30) of metallic and luminescent oil colors. As if this wasn't enough, in 1993 the firm introduced Dan Smith "Autograph Series" Oil Colors, a line of superior, select-grade paints made in America that rival those produced by the oldest mills in Europe. The "Autograph Series," consisting of 44 colors manufactured with only the finest ingredients and formulated to exacting standards, represent the epitome of quality.

The color range of Daniel Smith oil paints gives today's artist the best of two worlds. On one hand it is deeply rooted in tradition, featuring a complete selection of cadmium yellows and reds, no less than seven cobalts, three ultramarines, all the Mars oxides, the chromium oxides, the phthalos, and a full spectrum of the earth and neutral colors that are the backbone of the oil palette. On the other hand it includes a large number of new colors that are just now making their appearance on the palette. Such pigments as monoazo yellow (the pigment used in Hansa yellow), diarylide orange, indanthrone blue, and quinacridone red, just to name a few, are used extensively in Daniel Smith oils. More than 20 new colors are unique to the Daniel Smith lines. Pyrrol red, for example, is an extremely brilliant, lightfast scarlet that is almost identical in hue to vermilion but is a fraction of vermilion's cost. There are seven beautiful, transparent, lightfast quinacridones that are superior glazing colors. Also offered are interesting mixed colors, such as the dark, sensuous moonglow, based on an 18th-century recipe for creating the color of landscape shadows, and phthalo turquoise, a deep blue-green that is more powerful than viridian. Daniel Smith's mixed white is a combination of zinc white, which is favored for its brushability, and titanium white, which offers opacity. There is also a stiff mixed white, which has a greater concentration of pigment and is meant for rendering textures and impastos.

Daniel Smith oil paints contain no lead pigments, and in fact Ron Howard, the chemist who formulates them, has made a tremendous effort to select the least toxic pigments possible. The overall philosophy at Daniel Smith is that the company will never stop trying to improve the paints it makes and that, in the tradition of the great paint manufacturers, it will supply its customers not only with what they want but also with the best.

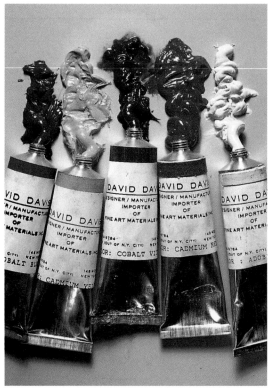

DAVID DAVIS OILS

DAVID DAVIS OILS

David Davis Fine Art Materials Inc. is a one-of-a-kind art supply dealer that manufactures most of the items it sells. The store is a living tribute to its founder and guiding force, the late David Davis, a vintage New Yorker who was so knowledgeable about quality artist's materials that it was almost inevitable that he would end up making his own products. Located in the heart of New York City's SoHo district, David Davis is world-famous for its handmade wooden easels and studio furniture. Its canvas stretchers (both precut and custom made) are probably the best in the world.

David Davis makes its own line of oil colors and oil paint mediums and controls all aspects of the paint making process, from pressing its own linseed oil to grinding pigments in its own mills. The David Davis line consists of 45 colors plus five whites. All colors come in standard 40 and 150cc tubes and are also available in pint-, quart-, and gallon-size cans. What characterizes these paints is their fundamental simplicity: They are made with the finest pigments available and David Davis's own brand of cold-pressed linseed oil. Nothing else is added—no fillers, extenders, or waxes. An incredibly large amount of pigment goes into each tube of David Davis oil paint;

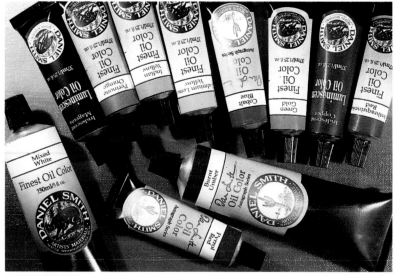

DANIEL SMITH OILS

in fact, because the pigment-to-oil ratio is so high, a tube of David Davis physically weighs more than a comparable tube of any other brand. Even a tube of the company's zinc white, an inherently lightweight pigment, has a heft to it.

The colors represented in the David Davis line are all the strong, permanent, lightfast cadmiums, cobalts, and traditional earth colors we have come to rely on. But in addition to these standard pigments, David Davis offers some exotic rarities, including two shades of a genuine lead antimony Naples yellow (Lapis Arts is the only other American source for this beautiful color in its genuine form); Milori blue, an iron-oxide blue similar to Prussian blue; and a very beautiful, buff-colored yellow called adobe yellow, a rare combination of zinc and antimony oxides that comes in two shades and is excellent for warm flesh tones.

In addition to its eponymous line of oil paints, David Davis makes a complete line of extraordinary, high-quality oil painting mediums, sparing no effort in their preparation. The gum turpentine, for example, is "triple refined" to ensure its absolute purity. The firm makes its own cold-pressed linseed, safflower, and poppyseed oils as well as a very viscous stand oil, and is the world's only commercial producer of "black oil," which is linseed oil boiled together with lead; this compound gives oil paint a lustrous body and is a perfect glazing medium. David Davis is one of but a few suppliers of a genuine Maroger Medium, the legendary "secret" painting medium of the Old Masters.

In short, for the truly professional oil painter, David Davis Fine Art Materials is a great source for the best in high-quality products at prices that are not artificially inflated. Service is provided by a staff that knows and cares about the products they sell.

GAMBLIN ARTIST'S OIL COLORS

Gamblin, based in Portland, Oregon, is a new American oil paint manufacturer that follows one of the medium's oldest traditions—namely, artists who make their own paint. As a painter emerging from the 1960s, Robert Gamblin became deeply concerned about the quality of the materials he and other artists were working with and began asking questions of the various paint manufacturers at the time. More often than not, he was referred to a chemist, prompting him to realize that scientists had now essentially replaced artists as paint manufacturers. What was needed, he felt, was for artists to reclaim control of their own materials, so in the early 1980s he began making his own paints.

For the longest time his efforts were confined only to white, which he strongly feels is the backbone of any paint line, since it is almost inevitably mixed with all other colors. Gradually, with the assistance of his wife and partner, Martha, Robert Gamblin's expertise at paint making grew to the extent that the firm currently offers a line of 70 oil colors. By the 1990s the Gamblins' reputation was such that the Smithsonian Institution's conservation department asked them to re-create the oil palettes of the 18th and 19th centuries. Using such ancient pigments as lapis lazuli, vermilion, and gamboge, the Gamblins made fresh paints exactly like those used 200 years ago. The unique and often dangerous experience of working with ancient pigments led Gamblin to the conclusion that the paints we use today are far superior to the ones our ancestors had, which were difficult to make, harder to manipulate, and often poisonous. Moreover, many were fugitive and susceptible to darkening. Modern pigments are, by comparison, brighter and far more lightfast.

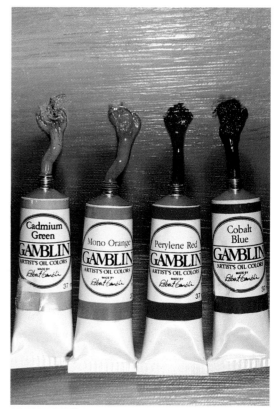

GAMBLIN ARTIST'S OIL COLORS

Balance characterizes the Gamblin oil color line, which is equally divided into the older, mineral-based pigments such as cadmiums, cobalts, and earth colors and the more modern, organic colors such as the quinacridones and phthalos. Modern organic pigments are extremely bright and powerful and have a high degree of tinting power, while the mineral colors are more subdued, more naturalistic. Gamblin's line also offers an equal balance of opaque and transparent colors, the more transparent modern colors serving as excellent glazes for underpaintings done in the relatively opaque mineral pigments. Included in the firm's color line are four excellent metallics, notably pale gold.

Perhaps the most important characteristic of Gamblin Artist's Oil Colors is the high concentration of pigment they contain in proportion to binder. Furthermore, absolutely no fillers or driers are added to these paints.

Gamblin Artist's Oils are available in standard-size tubes of 37ml and 150ml, as well as in 8 oz., 16 oz., and 32 oz. cans that offer immense savings to those who paint large canvases or use a lot of paint. Gamblin appreciates the fact that many artists don't have a lot of money to spend on quality paints, so prices are set to meet the budget of the average artist.

Gamblin offers two extremely useful paint mediums, Cold Wax Medium and Galkyd Painting Medium #1; these are discussed below.

GRUMBACHER PRE-TESTED ARTISTS' OIL COLORS

Grumbacher has been the standard and reliable brand of professional oil paint for a very long time. This company's Pre-tested Artists' Oil Colors and other painting supplies have an almost ubiquitous presence in the United States. When I started painting in the early 1960s, the first tubes of oils I bought were Grumbacher. At the time, I didn't know the name of any other brand.

Today Grumbacher is an immense art supply corporation, but its origins were quite humble. The firm was founded in 1905 by a German immigrant named Max Grumbacher, who sold high-quality, German-made brushes door to door, mostly to artists and sign painters. During the 1920s Max Grumbacher expanded his line to include imported color products that were also made in Germany. By the 1930s he entered into a manufacturing arrangement with the great German color maker Schmincke, such that Grumbacher was allowed, under the direction of German chemists, to make an American oil paint using the Schmincke formulations. At the

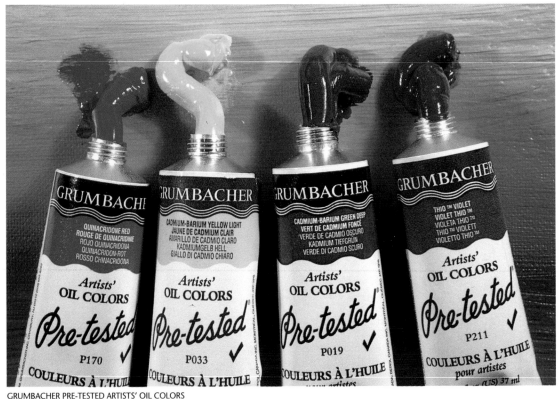

GRUMBACHER PRE-TESTED ARTISTS' OIL COLORS

onset of World War II Schmincke sold its rights to the Grumbacher family. Aided by postwar prosperity and increasing interest in painting in America, Stanley Grumbacher led his company into a period of unprecedented growth, making it one of the world's top suppliers of art materials. Today Grumbacher is owned by Koh-I-Noor Rapidograph, Inc., and under this new corporate ownership it has begun to expand the size of its oil paint selection and to develop new products, including a line of water-miscible oil paints called Grumbacher Max, which are discussed below.

Pre-tested Artists' Oil Colors are Grumbacher's traditional, professional-quality oil paints. At one time the firm produced a super high-quality (and expensive) line called "Professional," but it has since been discontinued. Grumbacher Pre-tested Artists' Oil Colors are formulated to a creamy, even texture, and all colors, regardless of their oil content or pigment characteristics, handle in a similar way. Under the Koh-I-Noor corporate umbrella, the Grumbacher Pre-tested palette has expanded in range to include 86 colors plus four whites. Many of the newer colors are made from synthetic organic pigments, are extremely lightfast, and have heavy tinting strength. Such intense colors as indanthrone blue, monoazo orange, and quinacridone red are new to the Pre-tested line, as are some interesting new neutral, mineral-based mixed colors such as unbleached titanium, nickel titanate yellow, and cobalt titanate blue. Most of the older mineral-based colors, such as the cadmiums and the cobalts, remain in the color lineup; in fact, Grumbacher is one of the few American manufacturers that still produce a flake (lead) white and a zinc yellow.

Grumbacher Pre-tested Artists' Oil Colors have never been overly expensive. Their reasonable price and easy accessibility have made them universally popular with teachers and students as well as with professional painters. Rich color, buttery texture, and an extensive range of hues make the Grumbacher Pre-tested line an excellent choice for any professional oil painting technique.

GRUMBACHER MAX

Introduced in 1993, Grumbacher Max Artists' Oil Colors represent a revolution in the formulation of oil paints. In a nutshell, Max oil colors are water miscible—even though there is no water in the paints' actual formula—and are workable with either water or oil. Neither acrylic nor mixable with acrylics, Max is a genuine oil paint that handles and dries exactly like traditional oil color

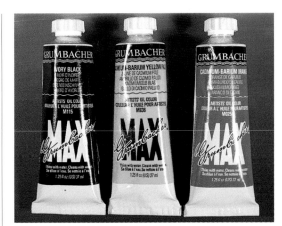

GRUMBACHER MAX WATER-MISCIBLE OILS

(such as Grumbacher's Pre-tested line) and has the same texture.

With Max oils there is no need to use traditional oil painting solvents such as turpentine or mineral spirits, as ordinary tap water will do the job of thinning and cleanup. This is a real boon for artists who have allergic reactions to standard solvents, which are often caustic. I myself am slightly allergic to turpentine; prolonged contact with it results in an annoying itch beneath my skin.

Max Artists' Oil Colors can be applied to any type of oil painting surface with virtually any brush imaginable, including the ones that you've always used with your standard oil paints. Moreover, Max oils can be mixed with any oil painting medium and used interchangeably with other oil paints as well. The trick in mixing mediums and other oil paints with Max is to keep these additions to under 30 percent. In other words, as long as 70 percent of your paint is Max, whatever mixture you make will still be "water-friendly." Otherwise, you'll have to use traditional solvents. It's almost impossible to believe until you've tried it that a combination of Max oil color with a medium as thick and viscous as, for example, stand oil, can be worked and cleaned with water.

Max oils come in 60 colors and have the same buttery consistency as the Grumbacher Pre-tested oils. They are excellent for artists who have sensitive skin and are allergy-prone—not to mention economical, due to the savings earned from no longer having to buy turpentine. Max oils are becoming increasingly popular in classroom studios, where large accumulations of solvent fumes can cause ventilation problems. Techniques for using water-miscible Max Artists' Oil Colors are discussed in the chapter on alkyds, oil sticks, and water-miscible oils.

HOLBEIN ARTISTS' OIL COLORS

Despite its European-sounding name, HK Holbein is a large Japanese art supply company with head offices in Osaka. Founded at the turn of the century, the firm took the name "Holbein" (after the 16th-century German painter Hans Holbein) in the 1930s. Today it dominates Japan's professional art materials market and has sizable influence throughout the rest of Asia as well as in Australia, South Africa, Europe, and the United States.

HK Holbein is dedicated to excellence and believes there is no substitute for quality. To achieve its goals, the company employs an immense staff, including 12 full-time color chemists who monitor paint manufacture according to rigorous standards that ensure consistent high quality in its products. This dedication to excellence is clearly evident in Holbein's Artists' Oil Colors, which are noted for being consistent in texture and working characteristics from color to color. Holbein achieves this by grinding its pigments three to five times more than necessary to compensate for differences in how individual pigments respond to the oil vehicle. The result is that all the Holbein oil colors handle in the same way.

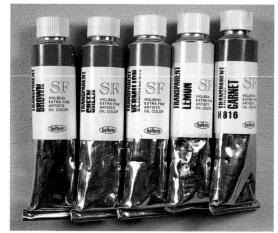

HOLBEIN TRANSPARENT OILS

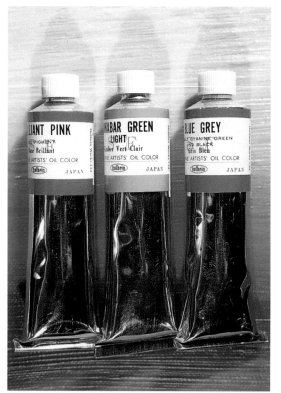

HOLBEIN ARTISTS' OIL COLORS

Moreover, each color is carefully monitored for its chromatic purity and tone.

Holbein offers one of the largest paint selections in the world. Its entire line comprises 150 colors, including an unsurpassed number of whites—11 in all. Among these are five versions of a lead white, three of which are tinted for underpainting prime coats; ceramic white, which is nontoxic and combines the best qualities of all other whites; and quick-drying white, which dries in four to six hours and is so flexible as a heavy impasto that it can be easily carved. Additionally, Holbein offers a line of 11 transparent oil colors that, unlike those found in the standard oil palette, are specially formulated to provide a full spectrum of transparents from yellow to violet, as well as a genuinely transparent black.

One reason Holbein's range is so large is that it includes 42 mixed, or "composite," colors—paints that contain a mixture of pigments. Most of these function as chromatic neutral colors, that is, as subtle variations on a base color. For example, most paint brands offer only one jaune brillant, while Holbein has four; likewise, in addition to a straight Naples yellow there are two variations plus an Italian and a French Naples yellow, not to mention 10 mixed grays. This array of mixed and neutral colors is very useful to the careful figurative or abstract painter who relies on consistently subtle nuances of tone and color in his or her work.

Holbein Artists' Oil Colors come in three tube sizes: 10ml, 20ml, and a standard 40ml. The whites come in 50ml and 110ml tubes and 330ml jars. The firm recently introduced Ecolse Oil Colors, a 42-color line of student-grade oil paints that are available in both 37ml and 150ml tubes.

LAPIS ARTS OILS

Lapis Arts typifies the emerging breed of small American paint manufacturers whose guiding principle is to make the finest oil paint possible—and sell it at prices the average artist can afford. Based in Denver, Colorado, Lapis Arts was founded in the 1980s by brothers Erik and Jon Rieger, both of whom are artists and designers.

Lapis Arts makes its superior-grade oil paints in accordance with traditional methods and recipes, using only the purest of pigments and oils. The paints are aged and milled several times to ensure an even dispersion of pigment, resulting in paint so thick and heavy that the tubes must be filled by hand.

In sharp contrast to what the larger paint manufacturers offer, Lapis Arts has only 35 colors in its product line. But these are enough. With the exception of phthalo green, there are no modern synthetic organic pigments in the Lapis Arts line; all other colors are either the basic mineral-based pigments, such as cadmium yellow, cobalt blue, and manganese violet, or genuine earth pigments such as umbers from Cyprus and red oxides from Spain. There are no "mixed" or composite colors in the Lapis range—not even a Payne's gray.

What makes Lapis Arts oils unique is that all colors are truly genuine; nothing is faked. For example, the firm's Naples yellow is a genuine lead antimony pigment—the real thing. One of its standard colors is a genuine mercuric sulfide vermilion, which is sold at a price comparable to that of cadmium red. Lapis Arts' vermilion is so powerful a color that just a pin drop of it in white will make a vibrant pink. Its signature blue, the color that gives the firm its name, is lapis blue, made from the semiprecious stone lapis lazuli, which Lapis Arts obtains from ancient mines in northeast Afghanistan. The color made with lapis lazuli is a deep ultramarine blue with an indescribable "mineral" cast to it. This is the blue of Bellini and Titian. Lapis Arts offers this rare color in a tiny, 11ml tube for around $70; other colors are sold in 37ml tubes.

In short, Lapis Arts oils are a purist's delight. This small Rocky Mountain firm may use handmade labels and may not run full-page color ads in the art magazines, but it makes oil colors the serious oil painter can trust.

LEFRANC & BOURGEOIS OILS

Lefranc & Bourgeois is an illustrious French paint manufacturer that has been making artists' materials since the early 18th century. In 1720 Charles Laclef, the direct ancestor of the Lefranc firm (the Lefranc family eventually inherited Laclef's business), opened his corner store in Paris in the very same building where Jean-Baptiste-Siméon Chardin kept his studio. In the 18th century it was still customary for painters to grind their own colors, but the ailing Chardin was grateful to have his paints personally ground in the Laclef shop and delivered to him wrapped in airtight pig bladders. Thus began the modern art supply business, as well as the Lefranc & Bourgeois tradition of working with contemporary artists to provide them with the best materials possible. The alliance of artist and paint maker gave us many of the conveniences we now take for granted, such as the screw-top flexible metal paint tube, invented and patented by Alexandre Lefranc in 1865; this made it possible to carry oil paints outdoors, leading to the development of plein air painting and Impressionism.

The partnership of Lefranc & Bourgeois, formed in 1965, led to the creation of one of the best brands of oil paint available. The 401 range of Extra-Fine Oil Colours is Lefranc & Bourgeois's world-class line of oil paints. It comprises 120 colors plus three whites, and includes a very interesting and useful range of nine transparent colors. Some of the firm's oil colors are legendary, such as its Naples yellow, which Lefranc developed at the urging of the 19th-century painter Jean-François Millet. This color had not existed since antiquity, and the artist wanted it to create highlights in his work.

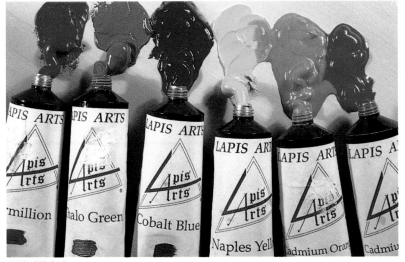

LAPIS ARTS OILS

Lefranc's reinvention gave us Millet's Naples yellow. Certain colors in the 401 range are available only from Lefranc & Bourgeois. They go by names that are as exotic as outposts of the French Foreign Legion—golden Sahara yellow, Senegal yellow, deep Breughel and Japanese reds, for example. Especially beautiful are the deep, almost midnight-dark Egypt violet and the wine-red Bayeux violet, a more lightfast alternative to the fugitive rose madder. Paints in the 401 range are characterized by their high concentration of pigment and their extremely fine texture, meaning that they handle smoothly and have great tinting power.

Lefranc & Bourgeois also produces high-quality mediums and varnishes, including the very beautiful Flemish and Venetian mediums. Both are gel mediums made from gum mastic combined with heated oil and metallic oxides. Adding Flemish medium to oils permits high-gloss painting techniques reminiscent of works by 16th-century Flemish masters; Venetian medium is similar but contains wax, allowing the artist to create more pronounced brushstrokes in the manner of the Venetian painting style. Lefranc & Bourgeois has the world's largest selection of oil varnishes—13 in all. In the 19th century Lefranc worked very closely with the fashionable and highly technical painter J. G. Vibert to develop a superior line of varnishes, and today the company's products bear this artist's name. Currently the firm offers seven gloss and four matte picture varnishes, plus two retouch varnishes as well as genuine vinyl "isolating" varnish, which is useful in certain glazing techniques.

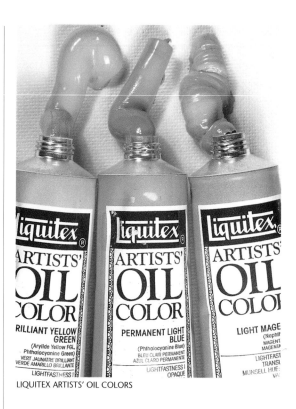

LIQUITEX ARTISTS' OIL COLORS

LIQUITEX ARTISTS' OIL COLORS

The name Liquitex is almost universally associated with acrylic paint; in fact, during the early days of acrylics—the 1960s—some artists even used this brand name generically to refer to all acrylic paints. These days, of course, almost all paint manufacturers produce an acrylic line, and Liquitex, not to be outdone, now also has its own line of oil colors.

Made in the United States by Binney & Smith Inc., the large art products manufacturer perhaps best known for making Crayola crayons, Liquitex Artists' Oil Colors are moderately priced, professional-level oil paints that are aesthetically (though not chemically) similar to their acrylic cousins, especially in the area of color. Liquitex oils and acrylics share what can only be described as a total approach to color selection and color mixing.

There are 89 colors in the Liquitex oil line, and they come in standard 37ml tubes. All the pure colors we expect to find are present—cadmium reds and yellows, ultramarine and cobalt blues, etc.—plus myriad beautiful mixed colors with highly descriptive names, such as barn red, light portrait pink, dirty green, and parchment.

Liquitex takes a truly systematic approach to color. Each color in the line can be used and appreciated individually, or it can be seen in the context of the Liquitex Color Map &

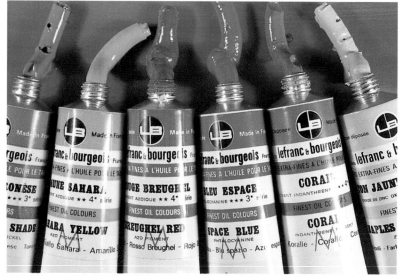

LEFRANC & BOURGEOIS OIL COLOURS

Mixing Guide. This "map" (there are two, one for acrylics and one for oils) is a very thorough color chart that offers the painter a complete system for mixing any color he could ever want. Each color in the Liquitex oil line is arranged into a section that describes its general look (for example, there is a green earth section, an aqua green section, a Naples yellow section, and so on). To help the painter determine the correct value of an individual color, each hue is rated on a gray scale consisting of Liquitex's six neutral grays plus black and white.

The labeling on the tubes carries a lot of information, specifying each color's exact value and intensity, its rating for lightfastness and degree of transparency, and the chemical names of the pigment and vehicle used in its formulation. All of the oil colors, regardless of pigment, have a smooth, even, unified texture. They are excellent for any painting techniques that require accurate color blending. Clearly, for the painter who would like to follow an absolute color system, Liquitex Artists' Oil Colors and the Color Map & Mixing Guide are just the thing.

MAIMERI OILS

Maimeri is modern Italy's most popular paint maker, offering everything from acrylics to watercolors but world-famous for its oil paints. Based in Milan, the firm is named after Gianni Maimeri, a turn-of-the-century Italian artist.

Maimeri's top-of-the-line oil paints are its Artisti Extra Fine Oil Colors, which come in 107 colors and eight series that are priced according to pigment—cadmiums and cobalts being the most expensive, of course. In recognition of the fact that painters don't use all colors in equal amounts, Maimeri Artisti oils are packaged in two unique tube sizes—20ml and 60ml—that work to the artist's economic advantage. For example, why spend over $40 for a standard-size (35–40ml) tube of an expensive color like cobalt violet when all you really need is a little bit to do an occasional glaze? Conversely, when larger amounts are needed, the 60ml tube provides the artist with a lot of reserve color.

Maimeri Artisti oils are outstanding for their color brilliance and texture. Typical of many fine, professional-grade European oil paints, all of Maimeri's whites and lighter colors are made with poppyseed or safflower oil to maintain their high key and to prevent yellowing. Because these oils are somewhat slower drying than linseed oil, Maimeri oil paints are ideal for direct, wet-on-wet painting and blending techniques. In short, artists use and trust Maimeri Artisti oils for their brilliance, color strength, workability, lightfastness, and the purity of the materials used in their manufacture.

Maimeri also makes Restauro oil colors, the world's finest for professional restoration work. Formulated in a special mastic varnish base, these paints are interesting in that they are completely "erasable." That is, they dry rapidly and permanently, but like a varnish, they can be removed with solvents, an advantage for anyone restoring an old painting. Also, the mastic varnish in Restauro oil colors gives them a lower, more golden tone that helps them blend well with the patina of paints that have aged.

In addition to these products is Maimeri's Classico line of artist's-quality oil paints. Made with less expensive pigments, all 66 colors cost the same according to which size tube you buy: 20ml, 60ml, or 150ml. The firm's popular Brera line of student-grade oil paints consists of 48 colors that are available in 150ml tubes only, at one low economical price regardless of hue.

Americans can purchase Maimeri paints in the United States at tremendous savings from The Italian Art Store (see List of Suppliers).

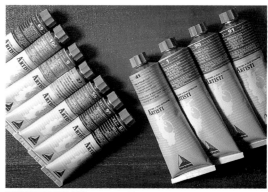

MAIMERI ARTISTI OILS

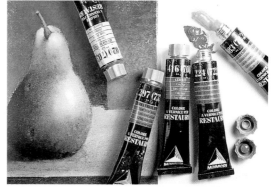

MAIMERI RESTAURO OILS

OLD-HOLLAND CLASSIC OIL COLOURS

Founded in 1664, Old-Holland is today's oldest manufacturer of oil colors. The original Old-Holland factory evolved out of a commune of artists' studios in the medieval town of Scheveningen, Holland, where for centuries artists gathered to obtain superior, properly made oil paints. Today the original Scheveningen factory is a museum, but as a reminder of the high quality of the products made there, the name is still used to describe many of the Old-Holland Classic Oil Colours.

Traditional manufacturing methods and high quality are the two guiding principles behind Old-Holland Classic Oil Colours. Only the finest genuine pigments are used, and in generous amounts. With the purest cold-pressed linseed oil, Old-Holland paints are ground slowly on stone rollers, which, unlike metal rollers, do not alter the color of the pigments. Furthermore, the Old-Holland Oil Colour Association guarantees that no fillers or waxes are added to this highly pigmented formulation. The final result is a smooth, very intense oil paint that is so dense it must be put into the tube by hand.

Old-Holland has more colors to choose from than any other brand of oil paint. Originally the Old-Holland Classic Oil Colours line consisted of 75 colors, but recently, under the direction of the paint chemist Professor Theo de Beer, the palette was expanded by creating new colors and by reinventing old, obsolete colors with new, synthetic organic pigments that are permanent and lightfast. The result is a total of 168 lightfast colors—the world's largest single selection of oil colors from one manufacturer. This vast assortment seems almost infinite in its spectral subtlety. All the colors you could ever need are here. Of special interest are many transparent glazing colors that Old-Holland calls "lakes," including some that are subtle variations of a single color. For example, instead of a single Indian yellow, Old-Holland has three: a green, a brown, and an orange Indian yellow. Colors designated "extra" are lightfast re-creations of fugitive or obsolete colors; gamboge lake extra and madder crimson lake deep extra are two such examples. Old-Holland also makes the only oil painting equivalents of the inks used in color process printing: Scheveningen yellow light, Old-Holland cyan blue, and Old-Holland magenta, all, of course, totally lightfast.

Old-Holland Classic Oil Colours are, by virtue of the large amount of pigment and slower production methods used, more expensive than most other oil paints. Nevertheless, because of their strong tinting power, they are actually economical to work with. For the artist who wants reliability, excellent texture, and a vast and subtle color assortment, Old-Holland Classic Oil Colours truly fit the bill.

REMBRANDT EXTRA-FINE ARTISTS' OIL COLOURS

Rembrandt Extra-Fine Artists' Oil Colours are moderately priced, professional-quality oil paints made by Talens in Apeldoorn, Holland. Popular in Europe since the turn of the century, they are now sold worldwide. These paints have two outstanding qualities: their texture and their color.

Rembrandts are made according to a traditional method of grinding the pigment and binder together in a three-roller mill. These ingredients are sent through the mill three to five times so as to completely disperse the pigment into its binder. The final result is an oil paint whose texture is exceptionally smooth, creamy, and even. Rembrandts respond to the brush with a full-bodied, buttery feel, an excellent characteristic for artists who are after a gestural, "painterly" look.

Rembrandt Extra-Fine Artists' Oil Colours come in a gorgeous range of 116 colors plus five whites. Because Talens uses only high-quality pigments and highly refined production methods, Rembrandt oils have a noticeable brilliance and color intensity, and almost all are lightfast. This brand is noted for its interesting and useful selection of composite colors, as

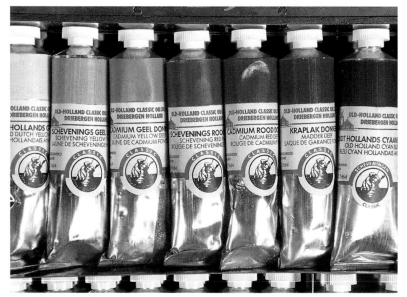

OLD-HOLLAND CLASSIC OIL COLOURS

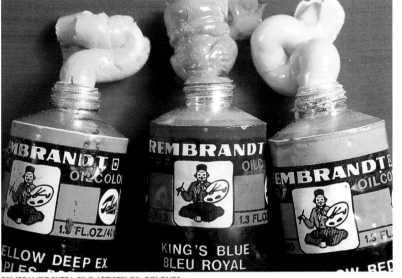

REMBRANDT EXTRA-FINE ARTISTS' OIL COLOURS

typified by caput mortuum violet, turquoise blue, four versions of cinnabar green, and three grades of Naples yellow. There is an equally balanced selection of opaque and transparent colors, and these characteristics are clearly marked on each tube—helpful information for painters fond of working in glazes and scumbles. Some particularly beautiful transparent Rembrandt colors for glazes are stil de grain brun, transparent oxide yellow, and greenish umber. As for earth colors, the Rembrandt line seems to have more than any other. These are indispensable for creating undertones that have just the right amount of warmth; and, when mixed with whites, Rembrandt earth colors produce an almost limitless assortment of luminous grays.

Reasonable price, high-quality materials, and a superior color range make Rembrandt Extra-Fine Oil Colours an excellent choice for the professional artist as well as the serious student.

ROWNEY OILS

Rowney oil paints are made in Great Britain by Daler-Rowney. Founded in the 19th century, this firm is now an international supplier of a complete universe of art materials, including, besides oil paints, watercolors, acrylics, egg tempera, and soft pastels.

Rowney oils come in two varieties: professional-quality Artists Oil Colour and good-quality, economical Georgian Oil Colour. The Georgian line consists of 53 colors, whose price is kept low by substituting inexpensive synthetic organic pigments for the costlier cadmiums, cobalts, and vermilions. The Georgian oils have a creamy texture and are excellent for artists looking to keep expenses down, especially those who paint exceptionally large works. They are also ideal for student painters.

Rowney Artists Oil Colours come in a gorgeous assortment of 97 colors made from the best pigments available, regardless of cost. All colors are permanent and lightfast and, to ensure consistency year after year, pass through a careful quality-control system before making their way to the marketplace. Some of the colors in the Artists line are legendary, notably coeruleum (after the Latin *caeruleus*, meaning dark blue, and *caelum*, meaning sky), the world's oldest cerulean blue, which Rowney first introduced commercially in 1870.

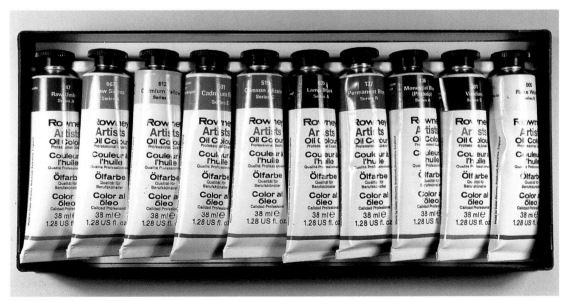

ROWNEY ARTISTS OIL COLOURS

Equally noteworthy are Rowney vermilion, one of the few genuine vermilions commercially made, as well as the firm's three Naples yellows. Particularly beautiful are transparent colors such as Italian pink, mineral violet, alizarin green, and Rowney olive.

Perhaps just as important as Rowney's oil paints are its many supporting mediums, varnishes, and solvents. This manufacturer's turpentine and retouch varnish are famous for their purity and performance, especially the spray retouch varnish, which I have found outperforms all others. Also of special note are Rowney's exceptionally clear and workable alkyd mediums and gels. (Unfortunately, Rowney does not make an alkyd paint line.)

SCHMINCKE MUSSINI FINEST ARTISTS' RESIN-OIL-COLOURS

Schmincke, founded in 1881, is a world-class German manufacturer of artists' materials. (The word *Schmincke* means owl, hence the company's emblem.) Its very unique resin-oil paints bear the brand name Mussini, after Cesare Mussini, who in the late 19th century was a professor of painting technique at the Academy in Florence, Italy.

At that time, Professor Mussini was one of the few remaining practitioners of the Old Masters' technique of working in resin-oil colors, a tradition stemming back to the very beginnings of oil painting in the 15th century. Painters from that period believed that a stronger, more lustrous oil

paint could be made by including a resinous varnish in its formulation, the idea being that replacing a portion of the fatty oil in the paint with a leaner resin would allow the paint to dry in a more "balanced" manner. In other words, the drying process would be a combination of oxidation of the oil and evaporation of the resin. Of course, getting the correct formulation of oil and resin for each individual pigment took extensive experimentation. The knowledge of these formulations was Professor Mussini's legacy to Schmincke.

Today Schmincke has transformed and developed the idea of an oil-resin paint into an outstanding line of 118 colors, all made from the finest pigments available and manufactured with painstaking care. Natural damar varnishes and the purest oils are slowly ground with the pigments on rollers made of hard vulcanite stone. This preserves the integrity of the colors while at the same time gives the paint a smooth, creamy texture. The result is an oil paint that is both strong and lustrous, making it ideal for glazing and for working in layers. The presence of natural resins in Schmincke's Mussini oils helps reduce aging and cracking. And, because of the resins' additional light-refractive qualities, these paints dry to a final brilliant luster.

Schmincke's resin-oil colors require no special handling and can be mixed with other oil paints. They are available in 15ml and 35ml tubes, with whites available in larger sizes of 55ml and 120ml.

SENNELIER EXTRA-FINE OIL COLORS

For four generations the Sennelier family has supplied France's artists with the highest-quality oil paints imaginable. These are the paints of Cézanne, Picasso, and Kandinsky. Only a handful of the world's best oils can equal those made by Sennelier; certainly none can top them.

A French institution since 1887, the firm was founded by the Parisian chemist Gustave Sennelier. The original Paris shop, which is still in operation, is located on the quai Voltaire near the Louvre and the Ecole des Beaux-Arts. Here Gustave Sennelier and his staff carefully handcrafted oil paints at the turn of the century, guided—just as the company is today—by the principles of quality materials and customer satisfaction. Even now, a century later, Dominique Sennelier, Gustave's grandson and the firm's current CEO, routinely visits the store to keep in touch with local artists and tend to their needs.

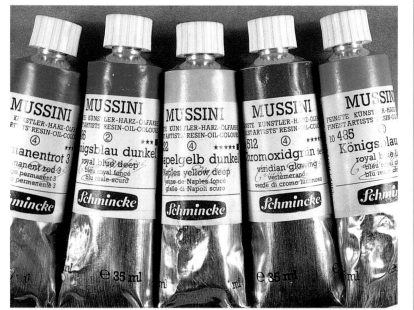

SCHMINCKE MUSSINI RESIN-OIL-COLOURS

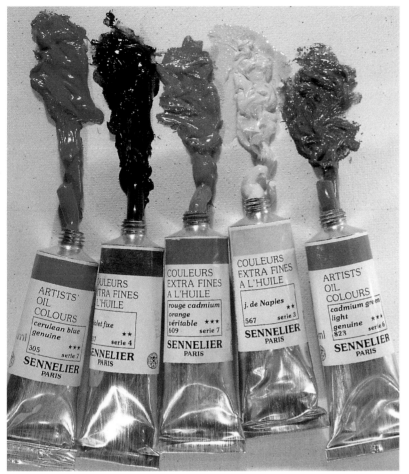

SENNELIER EXTRA-FINE OIL COLORS

Sennelier Extra-Fine Oils come in 110 colors. The range is a complete balance of opaque and transparent colors, as well as a full selection of new synthetic organic colors and older, more traditional pigments. Interestingly, Sennelier is a rare source for certain obsolete and outdated colors, such as red lead and bitume, both of which are fugitive. But for those painters who have a use for these ancient pigments, Sennelier still makes them. Of particular interest is the large selection of transparent "lake" colors, such as alizarine yellow, blue, green, red, and violet. These and others, such as deep madder lake, pink madder lake, and geranium lake, are all bright, powerfully lightfast colors made from modern synthetic pigments, and are excellent, permanent glazing colors. In addition to colors made with traditionally expensive genuine pigments like the cadmiums and cobalts, Sennelier offers some convincing, almost identical substitutes that are made from less costly pigments yet retain the texture and consistency of the originals.

Sennelier also has a particularly strong achromatic and neutral palette. This range features three blacks, four whites, and a number of interesting neutral grays and browns, including the beautiful and softly transparent Sennelier brown and the deep neutral tint. The latter two colors are wonderful for painting shadows. The company is particularly proud of its titanium white, which is considered the most opaque white ever made.

SHIVA OILS

Known for high-quality materials and innovative art products, Shiva is an American manufacturer that has been producing artists' oil colors since the early 1920s. Today it comes under the corporate umbrella of Creative Art Products Co., which produces everything from professional oil paints and oil sticks to acrylics and has the distinction of being one of the last commercial suppliers of casein paints.

Shiva's professional oil paints are its Signature oils, which come in 64 colors and are sold in 37ml tubes at a moderate price. These paints are made in a two-step process: First the oils and pigments are mixed in open vats, then each color is ground through a three-roller mill. The colors are ground for different lengths of time—anywhere from a few hours to four days, depending on the pigment. The paint that results has an even, smooth, and consistent texture.

Of course, today Sennelier is more than just a Paris shop, and Dominique's artistic contacts have expanded to include all of Europe as well as the United States, but its philosophy remains one of producing artists' materials of the highest quality.

This emphasis on quality is abundantly clear in Sennelier's oil paints. The firm makes only professional artists'-quality oils; there is no student or "economy" version. The pigments that go into these paints come from no less than eight different countries. They are ground on large granite rollers and mixed with one of three different oils: cold-pressed linseed oil for dark colors, poppyseed and safflower oils for lighter colors to prevent yellowing. The colors in the Sennelier line have a balanced, harmonious quality about them. For example, some very intense organic pigments are softened a bit so that they do not dominate the other colors. Moreover, the drying rates of certain colors have been stabilized with lead-free siccatives, so that the entire palette dries in a more even way.

The Shiva Signature palette is a balanced mix of standard mineral, earth, and synthetic pigments. Those made with synthetic pigments bear the trade name "Shiva"—Shiva blue, for example, is the familiar phthalocyanine (phthalo) blue, Shiva red is naphthol red, and Shiva violet deep is carbazole violet. Among the Signature oils are some truly unique blacks and whites, including ferrous black, which is like a Mars black but warmer in tone, and texture black, another Mars variation that dries matte and can be safely used to build up thick, black impastos without cracking—never an easy trick with the usual black oil colors. (Traditional blacks contain well over 100 percent oil to pigment, making them unreliable paint films. In impasto they dry slowly and unevenly.) Shiva's nonyellowing ultra white is a specially formulated, neutral bright white that does not alter the integrity of the colors it is mixed with.

In addition to its regular Signature colors, Shiva offers Permasol Transparent Oil Colors—a glazer's dream come true. These paints are transparent right out of the tube; no glaze medium or extra oil is needed to make them more transparent. Permasol oils offer the painter an entire "transparent" vocabulary to work with; they can be used either alone as glazes or in combination with traditional oils. They can be glazed over acrylic or casein underpaintings or painted directly over dried oil colors. With 20 hues (the world's largest range of transparent oils) to choose from, including black and white, Permasols can be combined to make any color imaginable. Permasol white is the only genuinely transparent white; made from a combination of zinc and titanium oxide, it gives a milky translucence to colors it is glazed over.

UTRECHT PERMANENT ARTISTS' OIL COLORS

When it comes to getting good oil paints for rock-bottom prices, Utrecht is almost a national institution. Because of Utrecht's low prices and marketing practices, art students and professional artists alike have for decades been able to keep their studios well stocked with paint. Officially known as the Utrecht Manufacturing Corporation, this Brooklyn-based art supplier makes its own products and markets them through six national outlet stores, as well as through its famous *Utrecht Art & Drafting Supply Catalog.* Although probably best known as a great source of artists' linen and cotton canvas and canvas stretchers, Utrecht makes everything, including its own oil paint.

Utrecht oils are heavy-bodied, full-pigmented paints that have a beautiful color tone straight from the tube. They come in 37cc "studio" and 150cc "large" sizes; whites are available in pint and quart cans. Price tags are breathtakingly low; many of the "studio"-size colors, for example, cost under $3.00. The range of 43 colors is simple and basic, and all are made from lightfast pigments. There are almost no specialized or exotic colors in the Utrecht line. Missing are many of the delicate, transparent glazing colors that grace most professional oil paint lines. Also missing are the myriad of subtle composite colors; no jaune brillant or king's blue for Utrecht. But the simple palette and economical price make Utrecht oils ideal for the artist who likes to paint very directly and in large formats, and who does a lot of searching and changing on the canvas. The low price of these paints lets the oil painter take big chances with color, and if something doesn't work, it's no big deal to scrape it off.

Utrecht also sells its own linseed and stand oil as well as a glazing gel called Flex-Gel. A fresh pint of damar varnish is yours if you buy the Utrecht make-it-yourself Damar Varnish Unit. This is as fun as it is economical. Pour a pint of turpentine into the can containing a gauze bag of damar crystals and in 36 hours you have fresh damar varnish—right before your eyes.

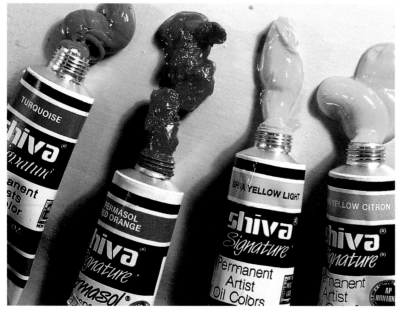

SHIVA OILS

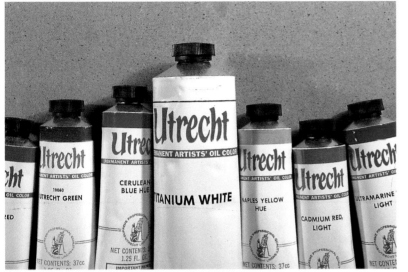

UTRECHT ARTISTS' OIL COLORS

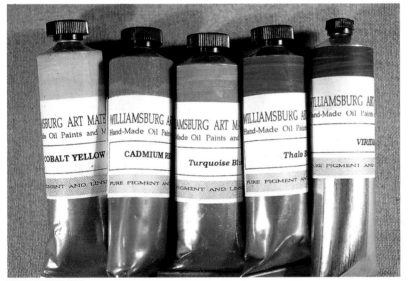

WILLIAMSBURG OILS

WILLIAMSBURG OIL PAINTS

Located in a small storefront in New York City's SoHo district and named after the location of its factory and studio across the river in Brooklyn, Williamsburg Art Materials is one of the newest and finest manufacturers of artists' oil paints. This firm has been steadily gaining an "underground" reputation among many leading professional painters in the New York City area for its high-quality paints, interesting colors, and prices the average artist can afford.

The guiding force behind Williamsburg Art Materials is its founder, the New York artist Carl Plansky. An expert paint maker for years, Plansky has an unerring instinct for locating the finest pigments. His philosophy is to use the best pigments available and keep the mixture simple.

At the moment the Williamsburg oil paint line comprises 68 colors. With a firm this young, it's likely that the number will grow as Plansky stumbles across new and interesting pigments to work with. The current color range is a strong, solid cross-section of the contemporary oil painter's palette, consisting in large part of cadmiums, cobalts, ultramarines, and earth colors. All pigments are genuine and a lot goes into each tube; their are no "hue" designations in Williamsburg paints. Moreover, all the paints are lead-free—Williamsburg does not make a flake white. A few colors are unique to Williamsburg, such as Turkey green umber, made from a rare, greenish earth pigment found only in Turkey, and zinc buff, the world's only raw, "unbleached" zinc white. This especially soft, transparent white produces a very useful opalescent pink when scumbled and glazed. Williamsburg also has several interesting composite colors, such as Payne's gray violet, a deep gray-purple, and Courbet green, one of Carl Plansky's personal favorites; it is a gorgeous, dark earthy green that's excellent for producing deep, lustrous shadows.

Williamsburg paints are ideal for artists who work large or who want a stiffer, handmade feel to their oils. They are great for anyone who paints in a very direct way. And, in spite of their high quality, Williamsburg paints are not expensive, especially when bought in large quantities. All colors are available in standard 37ml tubes, but significant savings can be realized by purchasing paints in the 8 oz. and 16 oz. cans the firm offers. Williamsburg also makes its own linseed oil, damar varnish, and painting mediums. Particularly exciting is its stand oil, which has got to be the thickest, most concentrated of its kind anywhere.

Williamsburg may have no color advertising and its labels may be handmade, but for genuine quality at a great price, these paints can't be beat. If you don't live in the New York area, you can take advantage of their prices by shopping through their small catalog (see List of Suppliers).

WINSOR & NEWTON ARTISTS' OIL COLOURS

Founded in 1832, Winsor & Newton is a very highly respected English manufacturer of artists' materials. Originally the firm devoted itself exclusively to making watercolor paints, but later began to produce oil paints as well, and today offers a selection of 113 oil colors. Winsor & Newton's preeminence in the field has been modified a bit over the last decade by the growing popularity and availability of such European brands as Schmincke, Old-Holland, and Lefranc & Bourgeois; nevertheless, this company still represents the standard of quality that most people associate with a professional-level oil paint. Winsor & Newton has many devoted followers who paint with nothing else, even though these days higher-quality paints at lower prices can be easily found.

The company prides itself on the consistency of its oil paints from one production run to another. The paints are made by constantly grinding the pigments between heavy steel rollers, producing a pressure so precise that it would be impossible to duplicate by hand. Winsor & Newton has just about everything you could want in oil paints: a palette with a balanced selection of opaque and transparent colors; beautiful earth colors; three blacks; and no less than seven versions of white. Like many other European paint makers, Winsor & Newton offers a number of colors that are highly specialized in nature and of limited appeal. Its series 6 carmine, for example, is a beautiful, extremely rare and expensive red that

is also very fugitive, meaning it will fade. But Winsor & Newton knows that some artist needs exactly this color, and so continues to make it.

Winsor & Newton Artists' Oil Colours come in standard 37ml tubes and a 21ml size that's more often found in sets. Whites are available in 120ml tubes. All colors are arranged and sold in seven price categories, with the cobalt violets at the high end at $59.95 per 37ml tube.

WINSOR & NEWTON GRIFFIN ALKYD COLOURS

Winsor & Newton is very much the innovator in oil paint technology, as exemplified by its Griffin alkyd line, the world's first and most successful synthetic oil polymer paint. In fact, Winsor & Newton is currently the only manufacturer of artists' alkyd paints.

Alkyds are made with the same pigments that are used in regular oil paints. The difference is in the binder. Just as in traditional oil paints, natural linseed oil is used, but it is altered and synthetically modified to create a new substance. This "oil-modified" binder is in many ways an improvement. The alkyd paint film dries fast and at an even rate for all colors, and the dried film is stronger and more flexible than traditional

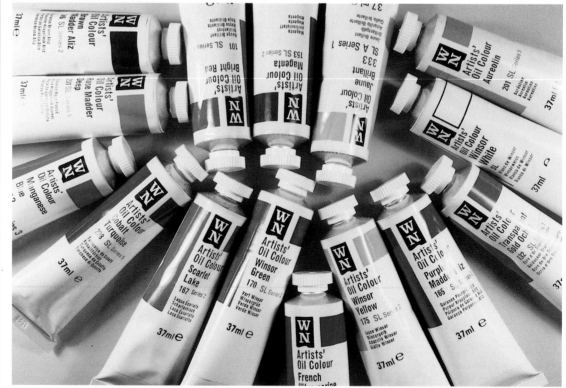

WINSOR & NEWTON ARTISTS' OIL COLOURS

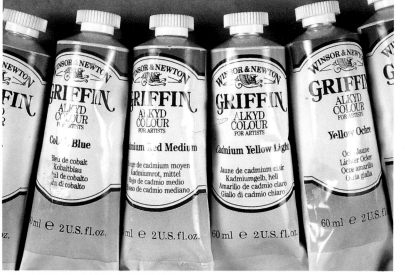

WINSOR & NEWTON GRIFFIN ALKYD COLOURS

oil paint, meaning it is less likely to crack than dried linseed oil. In addition, the general appearance of the color is more unified and more brilliant. In short, alkyds could be considered "improved" oil paints.

Alkyds are oil paints and handle just like traditional oils, with the exception that they dry more quickly. They are not as fast-drying as acrylics; alkyds remain workable and blendable for hours on the canvas and, unlike acrylics, can be easily scraped off as they dry and then sanded.

Designed to dry in less than 24 hours, alkyds are excellent to work with in one sitting. They are totally dry in two weeks and can be given a final varnish that soon. This quick-drying characteristic makes Griffins excellent glazers. Most of the colors are naturally transparent, and when modified with mediums such as Wingel and Liquin, they become even more so. The fast-drying nature of alkyds really pays off when you want to do many glazes in one sitting. Glazing with traditional oil paint can never be accomplished overnight, because the underpainting needs time to dry first.

Griffin alkyds come in 40 colors plus titanium white and flake white. Besides being interesting and beautiful, these paints are a bargain as well: All colors come in slightly larger-than-average 60ml tubes, and most cost well under $10.

YARKA OILS

During the cold war, we in the West may have wondered what kind of paints Russian artists worked with. Now we can know. Fostport Imports of Massachusetts has recently made traditional Russian artists' materials, sold under the name Yarka, available here in America. Yarka, which means bright, shining color, is actually a collection of small Russian mills and factories that have joined forces to market their products. Some of these factories have been in existence since the time of the czars.

Combining exoticism with quality and economic value, Yarka offers an entire universe of art materials, from oils to watercolors and pastels, to sable brushes and linen canvas, all made by Russian labor and from native Russian materials. This should come as no surprise, since Russia is the world's largest producer of both flax and sable, and is rich in the minerals used in paint pigments.

Yarka currently offers a limited palette of good, average professional-quality oil paints; forthcoming on the market is a top-of-the-line brand named St. Petersburg, consisting of 53 hues. Most of them are familiar, such as the cadmiums, cobalts, and umbers. But there are some interesting differences; for example, Yarka has several unusual earth colors that are available nowhere else, and exotic colors such as thioindigo black and Ladoga blue, not to mention an assortment of transparent Mars colors—an innovation unique to Yarka, since Mars colors are traditionally very opaque. Yarka oils are made using very traditional, time-tested methods. All colors are ground in pure cold-pressed linseed oil, and all the pigments are found and processed in Russia. This ready source of high-quality raw pigments helps keep Yarka paints economically priced.

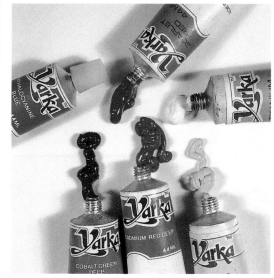

YARKA OILS

OIL STICKS

One of the 20th century's modifications of the oil medium is the invention of the oil stick, which has proven that these days not all paint comes in tubes. The oil stick is basically oil paint and wax rolled into a giant crayon. It can be used to draw and paint on all the traditional oil painting supports, including canvas, panels, boards, and paper, and is miscible in all oil mediums and solvents. (Oil sticks are made with oils that dry, such as linseed; this distinguishes them from oil pastels, which contain nondrying oils.) Until 1990 there was only one brand—Shiva. Since the early 1990s, however, the medium has really taken off, so that there are now four brands available. If anyone seriously doubts the professional integrity of oil sticks, just take a look at who puts them out: Winsor & Newton, Sennelier, and Shiva, each a prestigious manufacturer of traditional oil paints. R & F Pigment Sticks, the other brand in this lineup, are so good that their manufacturer specializes in them exclusively.

R & F PIGMENT STICKS

Of all the brands of oil sticks currently on the market, none can compare in quality and beauty to R & F Pigment Sticks. Personally developed and manufactured by New York artist Richard Frumess, R & F Pigment Sticks first appeared in the early 1990s and today are still made to his exacting standards. Frumess, the founder and producer of R & F Encaustics, had the kind of experience working with pigments and waxes in making encaustic paints that put him in the ideal position to go one step further and perfect the oil/wax paint stick. He once described paint sticks as a "bastard medium," being neither encaustic nor oil paint but in fact a combination of both. In handling and application, oil sticks are actually more like oil paints than encaustics.

Frumess once said that his goal was to create an oil crayon that was the equivalent of a brush loaded with oil paint, and he has certainly succeeded. R & F Pigment Sticks are an oil painter's dream come true: slow-drying, juicy, fully pigmented pure colors that are creamy in application, soft enough to apply to stretched canvas—a real delight to paint with. Each crayon is essentially a "stick" of pure unmixed pigment. Frumess seeks out the finest pigments available to make his oil crayons, and expertly formulates the proportions of wax and oil to allow the maximum pigment coverage possible.

The number of colors offered in the R & F line is still growing, with the count currently at 67—and that includes 10 of the most beautiful metallic and iridescent colors that exist in paint stick form. The palette is permanent and lightfast, and is built around pure cadmiums and cobalts, genuine cerulean and ultramarine; none of the colors are "faked" with less expensive look-alike pigments. R & F Pigment Sticks come in two standard sizes: a jumbo crayon the size of a small flashlight, measuring $6^{1}/_{2}$" in length and $1^{1}/_{2}$" in diameter, and a smaller size that measures 5" in length and $^{3}/_{4}$" in diameter. In addition, R & F custom-makes 751ml sticks measuring $6^{1}/_{2}$" long and 3" in diameter.

Because oil sticks are unavoidably messy to work with, none of the R & F Pigment Sticks contain lead; thus, there is no flake white. Still, caution is advised; many of the pure pigments used to make these crayons are toxic if ingested. Warnings are clearly labeled on the wrappers: In no uncertain terms, R & F Pigment Sticks are for professional use only.

SENNELIER EXTRA-FINE OIL STICKS

In 1992 Sennelier introduced its own "Extra-Fine" line of high-quality, professional-level oil painting sticks and is the first European paint maker to have done so. This is not surprising, since Sennelier, long famous for its unsurpassed soft pastels and the original

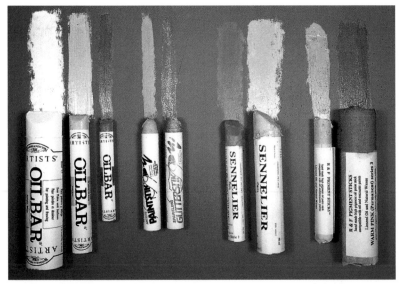

OIL STICKS. Left to right: Winsor & Newton Artists' Oilbars, Shiva Artists Paintstik and Glitterstik, Sennelier Extra-Fine Oil Sticks, and R & F Pigment Sticks.

inventor of the oil pastel, has had tremendous experience in making pigments work beautifully in a crayon format.

Sennelier's oil sticks are comparable in quality to the American-made R & F Pigment Sticks but have a much firmer feel, making them ideal for perfectly controlled execution and color handling. They are by far the cleanest of all oil sticks to work with. Colors are easily applied yet their texture is even and never out of control. Sennelier Extra-Fine Oil Sticks come in 55 colors and two sizes: 130mm long and 20mm in diameter (about $5^1/8 \times {}^3/4"$), and 150mm × 30mm ($6 \times 1^1/8"$). What makes them stand out is their brilliant, sparkling color. The palette is an equal balance of opaque and transparent hues. The presence of so many beautiful transparent colors, such as alizarin green lake, carmine red, and Sennelier brown, makes all painting techniques possible, including working in multiple layers of glazes. Only the skill and experience of Sennelier could have brought about an oil paint stick this superior.

SHIVA ARTISTS PAINTSTIKS

Shiva was the first to commercially manufacture a line of oil sticks, introducing just a handful of basic colors in the late 1970s. In those days art supply stores didn't know whether to put them in the oil paint section or with the oil pastels. But today, with a palette that has grown to some 80 colors, there can be no doubt that this medium occupies an important niche in the realm of art materials.

All the colors of the Shiva palette are available in standard-size sticks measuring $4^1/2 \times {}^5/8"$; a few others are available in the Thinline size measuring $4^1/4 \times {}^7/16"$; and 19 very basic colors are available in a jumbo size. What characterizes this brand is the seemingly infinite variety of colors it offers. Among them are the bright hues that are made from less expensive synthetic pigments and that make Shiva Paintstiks very affordable. The basic palette includes such standard colors as alizarin crimson, ultramarine blue, raw umber, titanium white, and so on, but it is also heavily keyed with mixed, "decorator" colors such as Wedgwood blue, pewter gray, and dusty rose. In addition, Shiva puts out several sets of exotic colors, such as its 16-stick set of beautiful iridescent and metallic colors and its 12-stick set of glitter-enriched colors called Glitterstiks. One might think that the main use for these colors would be the decoration of T-shirts and fabrics, but for adventurous and daring oil painters, they promise exciting, creative color combinations.

Shiva is the only brand that has a special line of student-grade oil sticks, a simple selection of 12 basic colors for the beginner. They are all nontoxic and inexpensive, and great for anyone who might like to try oil sticks for the first time.

WINSOR & NEWTON ARTISTS' OILBARS

Oilbars were invented to be the first truly professional-level oil sticks. They were originally developed and produced by a handful of Brooklyn artists who were not satisfied with the quality of existing oil sticks. Today Oilbars are distributed exclusively by Winsor & Newton and are quickly becoming the most widely used oil stick brand.

The Oilbar palette consists of 34 colors, including gold and silver (the latter is actually called aluminum). There are two whites, a cool titanium white and a warmer, "antique" version. Buff titanium is an interesting light buff-tan color that is extremely useful for blending warm colors and off-whites. Titanium yellow—a dulled yellow—is excellent for toning down brighter, more intense colors. Also present are the brighter cadmiums, cobalts, and ultramarines, as well as the standard range of earth colors. The Oilbar palette is not so much brilliant or bright as it is subdued—almost reminiscent of ancient encaustic paints. It has an overall matte "blonde" quality, rather like the matte quality of fresco. The abundance of mixed colors such as buff titanium and titanium yellow contribute to this muted aesthetic. Even the Oilbar gold and silver are more like earth colors than shiny metallics.

Oilbars come in three sizes. The standard size measures 6" in length and ${}^7/8"$ in diameter, and can be used for most types of painting. Think of it as the equivalent of a #10 paintbrush— but one that never runs out of paint. The slim size measures $4 \times {}^1/2"$ and can easily be sharpened to a point, allowing, with practice, for a surprising degree of precision—even though detail work in the usual sense is difficult to do with Oilbars. The largest-size Oilbar is called a stump, measuring a hefty 6" in length and $1^1/2"$ in diameter. Its shape is ovoid, permitting two types of wide strokes. The stump is for moving color around in a serious way, and is what Oilbars are really all about. It's a great tool for working out large forms and for filling in massive areas of color.

Oil Paint Mediums

Theoretically, oil paint is little more than microscopic, solid particles of color (the pigment) evenly suspended in a transparent liquid oil medium (the vehicle). But actually, oil paint has many more variables than this simple definition suggests. Of the two components, the pigment remains constant, while the vehicle is subject to change. Tiny particles of cadmium red will always be just what they are, but variations or modifications can be made to the vehicle in which they float to make oil paints behave in different ways. The substances that cause these changes are called modifiers or, more commonly, mediums.

Here is an overview of both traditional and modern oil paint mediums. Among these are linseed oil, alkyd gels, and waxes, all of which affect the way oil paint behaves and how it looks (as do solvents and varnishes, which are discussed subsequently). They can accelerate drying, add a gloss, create transparencies, harden, thicken, thin, dull, or even totally destroy a paint film. Knowledge of how to use oil mediums is indispensable in the mastery of oil painting technique. It enables the artist to make the paint do exactly what he wants it to do; it gives the artist control.

Linseed Oil

Linseed oil comes from the seed of the flax plant, *Linum usitatissimum*, the very same plant whose fibers are used to make linen. Flax is one of man's oldest domesticated plants and grows best in the cool, damp climate of northern Europe—small wonder, then, that oil painting was invented and flourished first in the Low Countries.

Before the 15th century linseed oil had only a very limited role in the craft of easel painting. Its main function was as a final varnish for paintings executed in egg tempera on wooden panels, but in this role it was unreliable at best, because it dried too slowly and often had to be sun-dried. Such procedures always ran the risk of cracking the wooden panels. At some point in the early 15th century (possibly even earlier), it was discovered that mixing a small amount of lead pigment with linseed oil caused it to dry much more quickly and evenly. Among the earliest to seize upon the artistic potential of adding pigments to linseed oil were the Flemish painters Jan (d. 1440) and Hubert (d. 1426) van Eyck, who, if they themselves did not invent the medium, most certainly contributed to its development.

Linseed oil thus took on the important role it has played ever since as the binder in oil paint. It is an excellent drier that forms a strong paint film, and is compatible with most pigments. Linseed oil dries by oxidation, meaning that it dries slowly and therefore remains "open"—workable—for a long time. But once dry, it cannot be reversed or reliquefied without totally destroying the paint film. Linseed oil's chief defects are that as it ages it tends to yellow and turn brittle. Thus, over time, oil paintings are almost all doomed to cracking to some extent.

Linseed oil comes in several different varieties and is used in a number of ways, as discussed here.

Cold-Pressed Linseed Oil

Cold-pressed linseed oil is linseed oil in its purest form. It is produced by crushing raw flaxseed without the facilitating use of heat— hence the term *cold*-pressed. Its basic use is as a binder in the formulation of oil paint. While there's some disagreement on this point, oil paints made with cold-pressed linseed oil are generally considered superior in handling, film strength, and textural brilliance to paints made from more refined types of linseed oil.

Because the manner in which it is produced results in a low yield, cold-pressed linseed oil is expensive. This fact almost brought about its extinction by the mid–20th century, by which time it had largely been replaced by cheaper, steam-pressed refined versions. But since then, primarily because of the demand from a younger generation of painters who wanted their paints to be the best they could be regardless of price, cold-pressed linseed oil has made a very strong comeback—so much so that today there are many commercial brands of cold-pressed linseed oil available: Daniel Smith, Gamblin, Grumbacher, and Holbein, just to name a few.

Refined or Steam-Pressed Linseed Oil

Today most of the linseed oil we find in art supply stores and use in our paint mediums has been chemically refined. In the 19th century it was discovered that steam heating flaxseeds and then pressing them resulted in a higher yield of oil. Unfortunately, steam pressing also produced a lot more than just pure linseed oil. Useless waste products and mucilage (called "foots") also came through in the pressing. To obtain an oil with any real value, these by-products had to be removed through a refining process.

The usual method of removing waste matter from steam-pressed oil is to treat it with sulfuric acid, which destroys all the foots and leaves the oil clean. But then the acid has to be removed somehow. This is done by neutralizing the acidic linseed oil with an alkali solution. The end result is what we call "alkali-refined" linseed oil.

Alkali-refined linseed oil is a very neutral, acid-free oil, and next to cold-pressed it is the preferred type for making paints. Because refining requires mass production, alkali-refined oil is abundant as well as inexpensive. This helps keep the cost of oil paint production down without skimping on the pigment content. The result is a high-quality oil paint with a strongly pigmented base at a more affordable price.

SUN-THICKENED LINSEED OIL

The primary uses of cold-pressed and refined linseed oils are as binders in the manufacture of oil paint. But when it comes to using linseed oil as an independent painting medium, better results are obtained by turning to one of its "bodied" forms. A bodied linseed oil is one that has been transformed and thickened through the application of heat.

Sun-thickened linseed oil, which uses sunlight as its heating agent, is among the best and purest of these bodied painting mediums. Equal amounts of linseed oil and water are mixed together in a container and left exposed to strong sunlight for several weeks. The oil and water eventually separate, of course, with the oil floating to the top of the mixture. This separation cleans the oil of its waste material, which settles to the bottom of the water level. Exposure to the sun bleaches the oil, making it lighter in color, while exposure to the air prompts the oxidation (drying) process, leaving the oil somewhat heavier and more viscous than pure linseed oil. When the oil is thick enough—and this is a matter of taste—it is siphoned off and stored in small, airtight jars.

Sun-thickened linseed oil is a wonderfully viscous painting medium that tends to leave the trace of brushstrokes and textures behind. It's a good, fast drier because it is already partially oxidized, thanks to its exposure to the sun. This, in turn, helps the oil retain its color in the paint rather than go yellow later. Sun-thickened oil is thought to have been a favorite medium among the Old Master painters, who trusted and liked its fast-drying qualities. Rubens was said to have made his sun-thickened oil in lead vessels to obtain a stronger and even faster-drying oil.

STAND OIL

Stand oil, another bodied medium, is made by heating linseed oil in an airtight, oxygen-free closed container at a steady 550°F for half a day

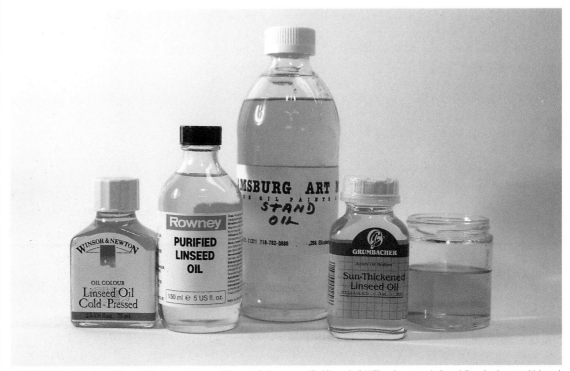

LINSEED OILS. Left to right: Winsor & Newton cold-pressed linseed oil, Rowney purified linseed oil, Williamsburg stand oil, and Grumbacher sun-thickened linseed oil.

or more. This intense heating in a vacuum causes the oil to polymerize without oxidizing, resulting in an extremely viscous, honey-thick oil that is bright and clear.

Because of its high viscosity, stand oil is not a good paint binder but is an excellent painting medium. It is a great "leveler" of paint films; rather than retain brushstrokes or textures, it leaves behind an enameled, syruplike finish. Stand oil is an essential ingredient in almost all glazing medium recipes. Its viscosity easily extends the oil paint, making it more transparent. Although not a particularly fast drier, stand oil produces a paint film that, when dry, is unusually strong and resistant to cracking, particularly when used on panels. It is also the version of linseed oil that darkens and yellows the least.

SAFFLOWER OIL AND POPPYSEED OIL

Linseed oil is not the only drying oil used with oil paints. Certainly it's the best "all around" oil, but because of its defects, mainly its tendency to yellow as it dries, other substitutes have emerged. Currently the two most popular of these are safflower oil and poppyseed oil.

Safflower oil is a very reliable, pale drying oil from India. It has good color retention and does not yellow with age, qualities that have made it the preferred oil to use in making white and other light-colored paints. Such reputable paint manufacturers as Daniel Smith and Winsor & Newton make their whites using only safflower oil.

Poppyseed oil is a pale, almost colorless drying oil that is extracted from the seeds of the opium poppy. Like safflower oil, it is used to make whites and light-colored paints. Poppyseed oil dries slowly and its paint film is not as durable as that of linseed oil. Nevertheless, when used as a painting medium, poppyseed oil gives oil

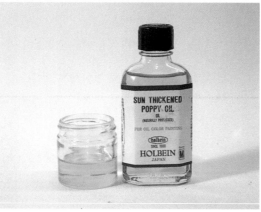

SUN-THICKENED POPPYSEED OIL

paint a beautiful, buttery quality. Sun-thickened poppyseed oil is an especially lovely painting medium; some painters claim it's the best there is.

ALKYD GELS AND MEDIUMS

In spite of their newness, alkyd mediums are quickly becoming very popular with many contemporary oil painters, and to some extent are replacing the traditional painting mediums. Even though at the moment only one manufacturer, Winsor & Newton, offers a complete line of alkyd paints and mediums, other paint makers are hurrying to get onto the alkyd bandwagon with at least their own version of an all-purpose alkyd painting medium. Archival, Daniel Smith, Gamblin, Grumbacher, and Rowney now all have alkyd painting mediums on the market.

Alkyd painting mediums offer the oil painter several distinct advantages. First of all, when mixed with oil paints, they accelerate drying time. They also increase the transparency of oil colors. Both of these attributes, needless to say, have made them excellent oil glazing mediums. But alkyd mediums also offer something more: They give oil paints a more lustrous, jewel-like quality, and a stronger, longer-lasting paint film.

Alkyd painting mediums come in basically two forms: as thick, translucent gels or heavy-bodied painting oils that resemble the "bodied" natural drying oils such stand oil and sun-thickened linseed oil. Alkyd gels are officially described as "thixotropic," a word from the Greek meaning "to change by touch." They are thick, viscous, translucent amber- or golden-colored pastes that come in either jars or tubes. They remain gel-like on the palette but become smooth and transparent when worked (touched) with a brush or knife. Alkyd gels are versatile in that they can be used either in heavy, direct painting techniques or in smooth glazing applications.

LIQUIN

Liquin was developed by Winsor & Newton 40 years ago and seems to be the most prevalent alkyd gel in use today. A mixture of natural oils and alkyd resins, it physically resembles a cloudy, congealed mixture of rabbit skin glue. However, when mixed with oil paints, it becomes perfectly clear and its texture smooth. Liquin makes paint applications smoother, slicker, and more lustrous. Also, like most alkyd gels, it is "nonmigratory"— meaning that you can make very fluid brushstrokes without fear of the paint dripping or flowing into other areas of the picture.

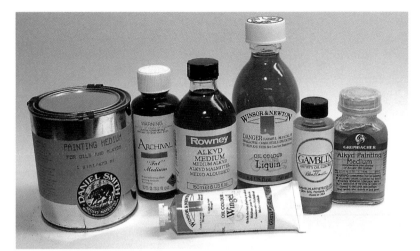

ALKYD MEDIUMS. Foreground: Winsor & Newton Wingel. Left to right: Daniel Smith Painting Medium, Archival "Fat" Medium, Rowney Alkyd Medium, Winsor & Newton Liquin, Gamblin Galkyd, and Grumbacher Alkyd Painting Medium.

Perhaps the best use of Liquin is as a glazing medium, since it accelerates drying as well as makes oil colors more transparent. Moreover, the alkyd resin in Liquin tends to yellow less than natural oils and produces a stronger, more flexible paint film when dry. Glazing is a time-consuming technique because it requires drying time between paint layers. Liquin speeds up this entire process so much that it becomes possible to apply multiple glazes in one sitting.

Daniel Smith, Grumbacher, and Rowney all have their own Liquin-like thixotropic gels. My personal favorite is the one offered by Rowney, primarily because its color is deeper and more golden, and I seem to have less of an allergic reaction to it. Allergies and objections to the odor seem to be the biggest complaints against thixotropic gels. Shop around for the ones you like the best and keep the studio ventilated when working with them.

WINGEL
Winsor & Newton also makes Wingel, a beautiful, amber-colored thixotropic alkyd medium that comes out of the tube as a gel but becomes more like honey in texture when worked a little with a palette knife. Wingel is meant to be thoroughly mixed directly into oil or alkyd paints to give them more body and a glossier luster. It also accelerates drying. Exaggerated brushstrokes and light impastos are safely executed with oils that have been mixed with Wingel.

OLEOPASTO
Winsor & Newton's Oleopasto is similar to Wingel but is much thicker. It is formulated with the same resins as other alkyd mediums, but inert silica is added to make it stiffer and stronger. The primary use of Oleopasto is in heavy impasto paint handling. Traditional heavy oil impasto is slow-drying and susceptible to cracking when dry. Oleopasto counters these defects by accelerating drying and reinforcing the strength of the dried paint film. Archival's Gel Medium and Grumbacher's Zec are very similar to Oleopasto in this respect.

GALKYD
Galkyd, or Painting Medium #1, as it is sometimes called, is an alkyd-based paint medium made by Gamblin that is indistinguishable from linseed oil in appearance. Galkyd dries more slowly than Liquin but faster than linseed oil. It is an excellent, nonyellowing oil that can be used effectively in glazing as well as in direct painting techniques. It dries to a clear, flexible, satiny finish. In addition to being a great painting medium, Galkyd has the advantage of being almost totally odorless.

ARCHIVAL "FAT" MEDIUM
Archival's "Fat" Medium is a very heavy, viscous alkyd painting oil that resembles cane syrup in color and texture and has a very pleasant fragrance. It is meant to be used much like stand oil in that it makes oil paints more level and smooth as well as transparent; the difference is that it dries fast. "Fat" Medium's one defect is that it doesn't have a long shelf life. Once the jar is opened the medium tends to film over. The problem is easily remedied by keeping "Fat" Medium in small jars with glass marbles added for an airtight seal.

Archival also offers "Lean" Medium, which is fast-drying and used in underpainting and glazing; there is also a "Classic" Medium, which dries more slowly, allowing more paint manipulation and greater control of details.

BALSAMS
Balsams are very thick, deep amber-colored liquids that are added to oil paints and painting mediums to lend a tough, jewel-like quality. The most famous is Venice turpentine, which comes from the European larch tree. Although called a turpentine, it is anything but. (Solvent turpentine is the product of distillation.) Having the consistency of thick honey, Venice turpentine sets and dries rapidly, which means it shouldn't be used in great quantity or in alla prima techniques that require oil paints to be workable for an extended period. Used moderately and in small

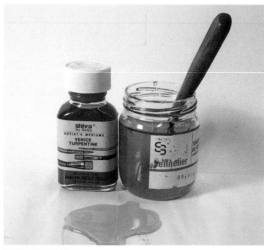

VENICE TURPENTINE

areas, though, Venice turpentine adds a tough yet flexible, enamel-like quality to oils. This toughness makes Venice turpentine a frequent ingredient in glazing mediums, because the balsam reinforces the strength of oil films that have been extended to achieve transparency.

Another balsam oleoresin is Strasbourg turpentine, which is used in exactly the same way as Venice turpentine but comes from a different fir tree in Central Europe. Although now rare, Strasbourg turpentine was, before the 19th century, the balsam oleoresin preferred by most oil painters and was treated as an almost semiprecious substance. (For those who are curious, Kremer, a dealer of rare and exotic pigments, is a reliable source today for Strasbourg turpentine. See List of Suppliers.)

COPAL VARNISH

Copal is the name given to a diverse group of fossilized tree resins found mostly in Africa; the clearest is Congo copal. Copal resin makes an extremely hard varnish second only to amber in toughness. For centuries it was used as the exterior varnish for the decks and wooden spars of sailing ships, a fact that attests to its resistance to moisture.

In the 19th century copal was also used as a painting varnish and medium. It was difficult to make because it involves cooking the resin to make it liquid, but skilled varnish makers of that period had perfected it to a fine art. Today, genuine copal varnish is rare, but two reliable sources are Old-Holland and David Davis. (See List of Suppliers.)

Copal is not recommended today as a final varnish because it is irreversible. Once it's

down, that's it; no solvent can remove it. But this insolubility and toughness are something of an advantage in a painting medium. Adding copal varnish directly to oil paints makes them very fluid, much like syrup, so that they behave like enamels, becoming smooth, fast-drying, and nonbuckling. With copal-thinned oils it is possible to produce effects that range from transparent brushy textures to striking drips and drops.

Copal varnish is not without its detractors, however; paint technicians feel that much of the cracking evident in 19th-century oil paintings was due to the use of copal varnish. But for artists who want a medium that permits flashy, luscious paint handling full of exciting "accidents," copal varnish is just the thing.

WAX MEDIUMS

Wax is one of the world's oldest painting mediums, and for centuries various kinds have been used as stabilizing agents in oil paints. In the days when artists ground their own oil paints, it was found that adding a *2 percent* touch of natural beeswax helped keep the oil and pigment from separating and made a stronger paint film. Wax is naturally compatible with oils. It does not decay or attract parasites or bacteria of any sort, it repels dust, and it is, most importantly, totally resistant to moisture. Its only defects are that it melts if heated and will crack in extremely cold temperatures. Otherwise wax is the most stable material there is.

When wax is combined with oils and resins it becomes a versatile and attractive painting medium. The oldest and most famous commercial brand of wax medium available to the oil painter

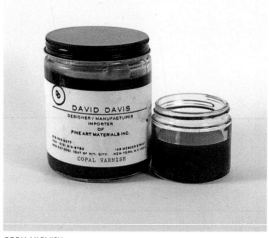

COPAL VARNISH

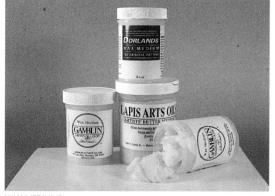

WAX MEDIUMS

is Dorland's Wax Medium, which for years dominated the field. But today there are others as well: Gamblin Cold Wax Medium, Winsor & Newton Opal Painting Medium, and the newest of all, Lapis Arts Artists' Butter #1.

Wax mediums usually contain a combination of natural organic waxes and various oils, resins (varnishes), and solvents. Each brand has a different formulation, but basically all of them perform the same function: They cut the glossy quality of oil paints, giving them a more satiny finish. The addition of wax medium makes oils more transparent as well, but without the gloss of other glazing mediums. Wax mediums also retard drying, keeping oil paints workable longer.

Another use for wax mediums is to thicken oil paints in order to create heavy impasto textures. However, extending oil paints with a wax medium is somewhat risky if carried to excess. Additions of more than 10 percent may result in a weak paint film. If the proportion of wax medium to paint exceeds 10 percent, try adding a bit more stand oil as well to compensate. Any paint mixture containing more than 25 percent wax should be applied only to a rigid panel support rather than canvas to avoid cracking.

THE MAROGER MEDIUM

Looking at great examples of oil painting from the past by such masters as Titian, Rubens, Rembrandt, and Vermeer has often prompted modern artists to wonder if something more than just talent was involved in the production of these spectacular masterpieces. Could there have been some technique or medium, some "secret ingredient" now lost, that would account for the outstanding brilliance of the works by the Old Masters? A reading of Vasari's 16th-century *Lives of the Artists* tells us that such speculations were nothing new even during the golden age of the

Old Masters themselves. Nevertheless, the myth of missing secret formulas persists to this day.

One person who was so obsessed was Jacques Maroger, a curator and head conservator of the Louvre during the 1930s. Maroger was convinced that something was missing from oil paintings done after the late 18th century, and claimed that there truly once had been a great painting "Medium" (capitalization his) common to the Old Masters but now lost to us. His fascinating book *Painting Secrets of the Old Masters* is the account of his search for and attempts to re-create this legendary lost medium. Maroger spelled out in no uncertain terms what he believed the missing medium to be and how it was made. During the 1940s he taught how to make and use his secret medium at the Art Students League in New York and later in Baltimore. His influence was extensive, and after his death there were enough disciples, plus his book, to ensure that the "Medium" would not be lost again.

Essentially the Maroger Medium is made by boiling linseed oil at a high temperature together with a great quantity of powdered lead pigment called litharge. These ingredients are cooked in an open kettle, which allows some oxidation to occur—a dangerous process not only because there is a possibility of fire but also because poisonous lead fumes are given off. The resulting mixture, called black oil, is then combined with other ingredients to produce two varieties of the Maroger Medium. The standard Maroger, used as an all-around painting and glazing medium, is made by cooking black oil with a mastic varnish resin. The second variety, which is used for a heavier, juicier painting style, is the same formulation but with beeswax added, resulting in a neutral-colored thixotropic gel that looks very much like a dark Liquin.

The Maroger Medium owes its popularity and its existence to the artists who like to use it.

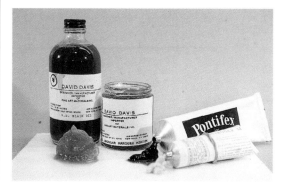

BLACK OIL AND MAROGER MEDIUM

Mixed directly into oil colors or used as a glazing gel, it is a delight to paint with; I myself find it seductive. Colors take on a new life with Maroger added to them. They become richer and feel deeper, including earth colors and blacks, which take on a deep luster that stays even as the paint dries. The paints handle better, too. Because this medium is absolutely nonmigratory, there is no bleeding from one color to the next, and it is easier to render details that retain their individual identity. Paintings done with Maroger Medium do have a unique look to them: rich, warm, with a paint texture that is strangely buttery yet somehow crisp at the same time.

The Maroger Medium has its detractors, however. Leading the charge is the late painter and chemist Ralph Mayer, author of the famous *Artist's Handbook of Materials and Techniques*. Mayer says that Maroger is off base about the historical origins of the Medium, and that the boiled oil-and-mastic formula is nothing more than megilp, a gel used by 18th-century decorative painters that permitted flashy brushwork but produced an unstable paint film that tended to blacken and crack with age. Moreover, the Maroger Medium is dangerous to make, and even using it requires caution because of the dissolved lead it contains. I myself would be too nervous to ever make Maroger on my own, and I'm glad there are reliable commercial sources for the ready-made product (see List of Suppliers). Perhaps in the end much the same results can be obtained with safer alkyd gels like Liquin or Wingel. But on the other hand, in spite of the controversy, Maroger Medium is wonderfully seductive and has many fans who do beautiful work with it. And what if Maroger was right? You just might be working with the very medium Titian himself used.

AMBER VARNISH

Another exotic painting medium that comes with its own built-in mystique is dissolved amber varnish. Copper and gold in color, raw amber is fossilized tree sap left over from the age of the dinosaurs, and is the hardest natural resin known. Since antiquity, attempts have been made to convert amber into a varnish. The problem is that amber is almost impossible to dissolve without heating it in a solvent, and upon melting, it loses its desirable qualities. But when successfully dissolved, liquefied amber is the strongest varnish there is, and as a painting medium it makes oil paint glow and shine as if it were enamel. When

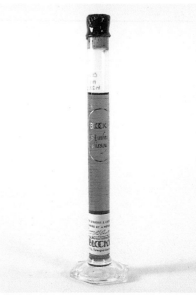

AMBER VARNISH

used for thin oil glazes it creates a beautiful lacquered quality, as exemplified by early Flemish miniatures, whose jewel-like nature is attributed to the use of amber varnish. The Spanish surrealist painter Salvador Dalí (1904–89) once described the process of glazing with amber varnish as a "sublime" experience.

Today the Belgian paint manufacturer Blockx is the only supplier of genuine dissolved amber varnish, which comes royally packaged in a long-stemmed calibrated glass beaker of 25ml capacity. Because amber is scarce and difficult to process, Blockx dissolved amber varnish is very expensive, costing almost $200 a bottle. Fortunately, a little goes a long way. As a painting medium, amber varnish is meant to be used in conjunction with other oils—poppyseed for light colors, linseed for darks. One drop of amber to five drops of oil starts the painting process; the proportion of amber to oil then increases as the painting nears completion. The final coat is done with 100 percent dissolved amber.

The combination of amber and oil produces a paint film that is very, very strong yet also flexible, and that neither yellows nor cracks with age. Amber and oil dry very slowly, so the painting remains "open" for a long time, offering lots of opportunity to make corrections or to produce subtle blendings. Moreover, increasing the level of amber varnish as a work progresses means the completed painting need never be varnished in the traditional sense, since it will already have a highly enameled, resilient finish.

SOLVENTS

Solvents are critically important to the process of oil painting. Perhaps one reason oil techniques did not really emerge before the 15th century was that there was no such thing as turpentine until around 1400, distillation having yet to be invented and operating on a large scale.

All solvents are volatile liquids, which means they have the ability to evaporate and vaporize in the open air, leaving no trace of themselves behind. In this way they are the opposite of drying oils and resins, which oxidize when exposed to the air and eventually become hard, solid substances. In oil painting, solvents function in two ways: as dissolvers and as thinners. For example, most varnishes are made by dissolving a solid natural crystal such as damar or mastic in a solution of gum turpentine. Or, fresh oil paint that is too bulky to be handled smoothly or stand oil that is just a bit too thick can be extended with mineral spirits or turpentine. Because solvents can be used to thin oils, they also serve to accelerate the drying time of paints (although two kinds, oil spike of lavender and Archival's Odorless Slow-Drying Solvent, retard drying time).

Today oil painters can choose from a wide selection of oil solvents, including gum turpentine, organic vegetable solvents, and mineral spirits. And now even water, the universal solvent, can be added to the list, thanks to such innovations as Grumbacher's water-miscible Max oil paints.

GUM TURPENTINE

The most common solvent used in oil painting is 100 percent distilled gum turpentine, whose raw source is the fresh, thick oleoresin collected from living long-needle pine trees. Turpentine is normally distilled two or three times for maximum purity. Gum turpentine is not to be confused with wood turpentine, which is a by-product of the steam distillation of pine tree cuttings that have been boiled to give maximum yield. It is generally impure and not suitable for oil painting purposes.

Fresh gum turpentine is as clear as water and has an agreeable odor. Unfortunately it does not have an infinite shelf life, yellowing as it ages until, after a few years, it darkens to a deep beer color and becomes rancid. Turpentine is best used fresh, of course, but even if it begins to yellow it's still okay to use for a while. When it really starts to go, throw it out. Turpentine that has gone bad will hurt your paintings and may cause allergic reactions.

Because it is the strongest oil painting solvent, gum turpentine is also the best one to use in making paint mediums and varnishes (it can thoroughly dissolve the resin crystals of all varnishes except amber). When used alone, gum turpentine leaves behind a small residue, which is not a problem except where the paint handling is so thin that the color is almost nonexistent. Painting very thin with turpentine must be done cautiously. If the paint film is too extended, it will separate and crack instantly upon drying. Luckily, if this happens early in the painting, the remedy is to wipe the whole thing clean and start over.

The main defect of gum turpentine is its toxicity. Many artists, myself included, experience allergic reactions to it. The fumes can cause lung irritation and headaches; in fact, a friend of mine opened a can of what she thought was fresh turpentine and immediately passed out. I get an itchy rash under my fingers if I've been holding turpentine-soaked rags for too long. Of course, because it is flammable, never smoke when your hands are covered with turpentine. The best approach is to keep turpentine containers closed as much as possible while you work and ensure that your studio is well ventilated.

MINERAL SPIRITS

Mineral spirits is a petroleum by-product and is just about equal to turpentine in status as a solvent in the oil painting studio. A typical brand is Weber's Odorless Turpenoid. Mineral spirits has several advantages over gum turpentine. It is as clear as water and stays that way; it never yellows, nor does it leave any residue behind after it evaporates. It has almost no odor and is also cheaper than gum turpentine, which, depending on the brand, really can get expensive.

Mineral spirits is slightly less powerful a solvent than gum turpentine and as such is perhaps not as satisfactory in mixing paint mediums or varnishes. But it is perfectly fine to thin your paints with and ideal for cleaning your brushes.

CITRUS PEEL SOLVENTS

Because so many people have developed allergic reactions to traditional solvents, several new ones have appeared that are mild to the skin and have a wonderful smell. Two such products are Daniel Smith Citrus Paint Thinner and, from the German maker Livos, a product called Leinos Citrus Thinner Diluant. Both of these solvents are derived from the distillation of raw organic orange and other citrus peelings. They have the fragrant, sweet odor of oranges and seem to cause fewer adverse physical reactions than either gum turpentine or mineral spirits. These citrus peel solvents can be used in all oil painting techniques, from thinning paints to cleaning brushes.

OIL SPIKE OF LAVENDER

Oil spike of lavender, or spike oil, as it is sometimes called, is considered the crème de la crème of oil painting solvents and was the most popular kind in the 16th century, exceeding even gum turpentine in favor. Made by scraping the leaves of the lavender plant, it has an almost intoxicating fragrance.

Oil spike of lavender can dilute oils, but unlike most other solvents, it retards drying. It is recommended for making varnishes, causing them to dry more slowly and evenly and leaving no evidence of brushstrokes behind. One unfortunate drawback of oil spike of lavender is that it is outrageously expensive. Practically speaking, its use can be justified only in the most rarefied of situations.

ARCHIVAL ODORLESS SLOW-DRYING SOLVENT

Made by the Australian paint manufacturer Archival, this new, nonallergenic product is a completely odorless, 100 percent hydrocarbon solvent. It vaporizes very slowly, meaning that, unlike other solvents, it does not permeate the studio with its fumes. Archival Odorless Slow-Drying Solvent's main function is to dilute oil paints, but it also keeps them wet and "open" longer than other solvents do.

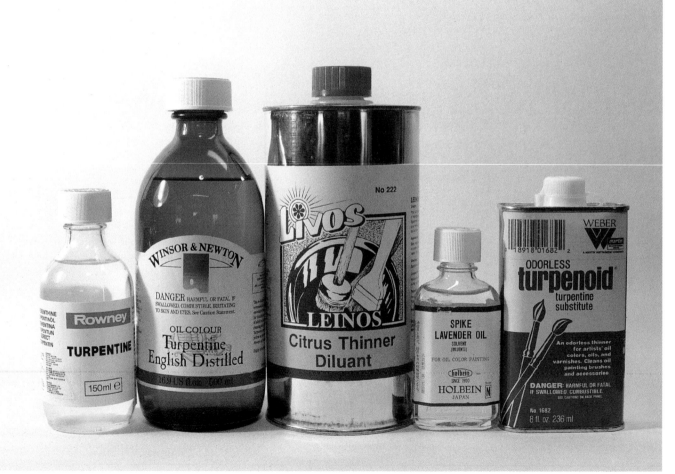

SOLVENTS. Left to right: Rowney and Winsor & Newton gum turpentine, Livos Leinos Citrus Thinner Diluant, Holbein oil spike of lavender, and Weber Odorless Turpenoid mineral spirits.

VARNISHES

From the beginning of oil painting as we know it, applying a protective coat of varnish to finished works became obligatory. In the past, skipping this final step was not considered optional, but today, for any number of reasons, varnishing is very often overlooked. Tradition and custom aside, there are two very good reasons paintings should be varnished: for protection and for aesthetics.

A final varnish is a painting's first line of defense against dirt and atmospheric pollution. Varnish wards off these attackers, keeping at bay the corrosive elements that can eat away at oil paint films and the microscopic particles of dust that would otherwise collect in the crevices between canvas and paint. Dirt lodges instead on the outer covering of varnish, where it can be cleaned off easily. Painting varnishes are meant to be removable; the process of cleaning and restoring aging paintings is often little more than removing the dirt-covered old varnish and replacing it with a fresh coat. If you really care about safeguarding your oils from a corrosive future, you must varnish them.

Varnishing also helps bring a painting together visually, giving it a consistent look. Oil painting techniques are notorious for creating paint surfaces that have an uneven quality about them. Grounds are often variably absorbent, and one pigment may react very differently from another, resulting in a painting surface that is a patchwork of dull and shiny spots. A final varnish can tie these disparate elements together. Moreover, today you can choose the finish you want—high gloss, dull, or satiny.

Oil varnishes fall into either of two major groups: natural, such as damar and mastic varnishes, or synthetic, such as ketone and acrylic varnishes. Regardless of category, all varnishes must be thin, clear, and nonyellowing; they must be flexible, not brittle, and capable of bending with the inevitable expansion and contraction of the painted support; they must not attract moisture; and, finally, they must be removable. Varnishes must be soluble in compounds that do not also dissolve the actual paint film. Ironically, no one varnish today or in the past has ever met all of these requirements perfectly. But they're getting close.

Let's take a look here at a cross-section of contemporary varnishes.

NATURAL VARNISHES

Before the 20th century, all varnishes were made of some type of natural organic resin. Today, even though they share the spotlight with synthetic varnishes, the older, natural resin-based kinds such as damar and mastic are still the most common in the contemporary painter's studio. They are used both as final protective varnishes and as ingredients in certain painting mediums.

DAMAR VARNISH

Damar is the best all-purpose natural resin varnish. It is collected from damar fir trees indigenous to Indonesia and Malaysia. Often named after the port of origin (i.e., Singapore damar), raw damar comes in yellowish crystals the size of small candies. All that is needed to make these crystals into a varnish is to add gum turpentine; a 10 oz. mesh bag of damar crystals soaked in a pint of gum turpentine for a day or two usually does the trick. Ready-made damar varnish is available everywhere, but soaking your own crystals guarantees freshness and saves money.

Damar may look yellow and even a bit cloudy in the bottle, but do not worry about this; the cloudiness is a residue of the natural waxes damar contains, but it all goes down perfectly clear. As with all varnishes, damar is applied in short strokes with a soft two- to three-inch-wide brush that is to be used for no other purpose except varnishing. The brush must be of a high quality, because you don't want loose hairs getting stuck in your wet varnish. Damar dries fast, so the strokes should be made in short, six-inch squares that are perpendicular to one another. Start at the top of the painting and work down, taking care not to touch the varnish once it has started to set. Varnishes should be applied thinly; the texture of the brushstrokes with which you apply them will level out. Wait for the varnish to be completely dry before trying to catch "holidays"—missed spots—with a second light coat.

Damar varnish dries quickly through evaporation. Quick drying is a desirable quality because it prevents the unwanted dust buildup that can otherwise occur on a wet surface. Try to do your varnishing in as dust-free an environment as possible, and to avoid moisture of any sort. Never varnish on damp, humid days, and make sure all jars, brushes, and painting surfaces are totally and thoroughly dry. If moisture becomes trapped under the varnish layer, "blooming" will occur. Blooming looks like an unpleasant blue-white film on the painting. It is definitely something to be avoided.

Though it is the best natural resin varnish around, damar has its faults. Its main defects are that with age it will yellow and its film may turn brittle. The process, however, is not quick and may not even occur during the artist's lifetime. When it does go, it's time to clean off the old varnish and put on a fresh coat.

MASTIC VARNISH

Mastic varnish is very similar to damar but today is less in demand than in the past. Mastic is collected from pistachio trees and, as its name implies, is used as a chewing gum in some parts of North Africa and the Near East, where it is found. Raw mastic comes in small white droplets called "tears." Dissolved in gum turpentine, it makes a beautiful, clear golden-yellow varnish.

Mastic varnish gives a warm, high-gloss, golden finish to oils. This characteristic made it much more popular as a final varnish during the 19th century, when varnishing took on an almost sacramental importance. During our own age mastic is becoming somewhat rare, having been replaced largely by damar varnish. While mastic is beautiful and easy to apply, it has a reputation for going dark and is not as strong as damar.

Nevertheless, mastic is still desirable for its golden quality, an attribute it imparts when used as an additive to paint mediums as well. When mixed directly into oil paints, it gives them a charming "Old Master" patina. Restauro oils, formulated by the Italian paint manufacturer Maimeri specifically for restoration purposes, are made with a mastic varnish to give them a special warm glow suitable for old paintings.

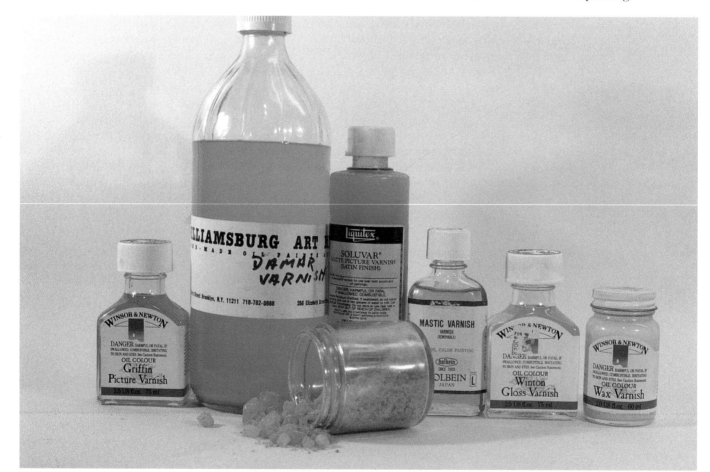

VARNISHES. Foreground: raw damar crystals. Left to right: Winsor & Newton Griffin Picture Varnish, Williamsburg prepared damar varnish, Liquitex Soluvar synthetic varnish, Holbein mastic varnish, and Winsor & Newton Winton Gloss Varnish and Wax Varnish.

NATURAL VARNISHES IN PAINT MEDIUMS

Both damar and mastic varnishes are miscible with oils and can be used to make interesting painting mediums when combined with linseed oil or mixed directly into oil paint, or mixed with both. Either of these resins can be added for the effect it has on colors (mastic in particular), but more typically is used as an indirect siccative, or drier. The varnishes dry through evaporation and the oils through oxidation, and somehow this combination gives more unity to the drying of the oil paint film. One of the most commonly recommended painting mediums is a three-way equal blend of linseed oil, damar varnish, and gum turpentine.

RETOUCH VARNISH

Damar and mastic can be used in highly diluted form as retouch varnish, which is less than half the strength of a final varnish. The main function of retouch varnish is to rejuvenate sunken areas of an oil painting whose colors, for whatever reason (usually the high oil absorption of certain pigments), have gone dull. Retouch varnish is usually sprayed on the dulled area, and because it is miscible in oils and dries instantly, it is useful in all direct painting procedures in which the artist wants to maintain a unified, consistent sheen to his surfaces.

Retouch varnish is also the standard "temporary" varnish used on paintings before they are ready for a final varnish. Oil paintings should be dry for about six months before a final varnish is applied. In the meantime an overall coating of retouch varnish will protect the paint film and provide some degree of unified gloss.

WAX VARNISHES

Perhaps my personal favorite natural painting varnish is the type made with beeswax, such as Winsor & Newton's Wax Varnish. This is nothing more than beeswax mixed with a solvent (usually mineral spirits) to form a milk-white paste. Applying this wax varnish to a painting is as simple as polishing your shoes or waxing your car.

Spread a thin layer of the wax paste over your painting with a bristle brush or a palette knife. Take care not to leave a heavy or uneven buildup. At first the varnish appears dull and lifeless. Let it dry for a few minutes, then begin to buff the surface with a soft rag—better yet, use a piece of lint-free silk. The more you buff, the glossier and more polished the surface texture becomes. It is entirely possible to achieve a high-gloss finish with a wax varnish, but usually the aim is to get a beautifully controlled low-gloss, or satin, finish. Wax varnish is particularly appealing and effective on panel paintings, and applying it to them is not unlike polishing wood furniture. It also has the double advantage of repelling dust. Wax varnishes are reversible with mineral spirits and gum turpentine.

SYNTHETIC VARNISHES

Before the 20th century the only varnishes available to the artist were natural ones like damar, mastic, and waxes. But today these traditional favorites are rapidly being replaced by more effective varnishes made from synthetic resins. Unlike damar and mastic, these synthetic varnishes do not turn yellow with age, nor do they become hard and brittle; instead, they remain clear and flexible. Synthetic varnishes are more permanent than their natural counterparts, but like them are reversible and can be removed with good-quality turpentine or mineral spirits.

A typical synthetic varnish is Winsor & Newton's Winton Gloss Varnish, which is made with a ketone resin and mineral spirits. Winton Matt Varnish contains these ingredients plus a translucent wax solution. The two varieties can be mixed together in any proportion to achieve an in-between satin finish. Similar to these is Liquitex's Soluvar, which also is available in matte and glossy varieties.

In addition to their nonyellowing and more elastic qualities, some of the newer synthetic varnishes now also give protection against harmful ultraviolet light, a major source of color fading in oil painting. Daniel Smith, Golden, and Lapis Arts all offer synthetic picture varnishes containing a UV absorber (such as the compound benzotriazole) that filters out harmful light. Although these varnishes are no guarantee against the eventual fading of fugitive colors, they do give them a much longer life and provide good general protection for all colors against fading.

One thing you cannot do with synthetic varnishes that you can with the traditional resins is combine them directly with oil paints to make painting mediums. Be careful not to mix any synthetic varnish with oil paints; they are not compatible. Synthetic varnishes are made to be used as varnishes only.

SUPPORTS

A support is any physical material or surface that paint is applied to—anything that can "support" layers of paint. Metal, wood, cloth, paper, brick, stone, plastic, vellum, parchment, plaster, glass, even the bathroom door can all serve in this capacity. In practice, however, because of permanence, habit, and convenience, only a few of these materials have emerged as traditional supports for oil paintings, and they fall into two groups: flexible supports, meaning canvas and paper, and rigid supports, meaning wood, fiberboard, canvas boards, and metal.

Canvas is by far the most popular and widely used support for oil painting today. In fact, the word itself is often used interchangeably with "painting" to mean the actual picture, frame and all. But while not new to the history of painting—Pliny, the ancient Roman historian, comments on a full-length portrait of Emperor Nero on a cloth 150 feet high, and Egyptian Coptic paintings on linen have survived even to this day—canvas's status as a standard painting support is relatively modern. The ancients preferred working in wax encaustic on wooden supports, and by the Middle Ages this practice had given way to using egg tempera on panels, the primary form of easel painting at the time. In the early 15th century, in the beginning stages of its evolution, oil painting was simply a method of glazing over the egg tempera; the focus was still on producing small, highly detailed works that were in keeping with the current aesthetic. In executing such paintings, the van Eycks and their Flemish contemporaries preferred to use oil on gessoed wood panels.

In those days by far the most common material for rigid supports was wood—oak and birch in northern Europe and poplar in Italy. Metal, primarily copper, was a distant second. Panel paintings were meant primarily for private collectors and as decoration for church furniture, so most were not big by modern standards. In the 15th and early 16th centuries, large-scale paintings were still executed almost exclusively as wall frescoes. Painting a large composition on wood required gluing several planks together with a mixture of casein and lime, followed by planing, sanding, and priming. If you look closely at larger panel paintings from this period you can see the seams where the panels were glued together.

Today most oil painters work on flexible supports. Nevertheless, panel painting still has its advocates, and choosing a rigid support offers unique aesthetic opportunities.

Canvas didn't make its modern appearance as a support until the early 16th century. The Venetian painters Giovanni Bellini, Giorgone, and Titian were the first to use canvas exclusively and in the contemporary sense—that is, yards of fabric stretched on wooden frames (like the stretchers illustrated below) and painted in a studio. Canvas's light weight relative to panels made it possible to paint large works that were portable. In 16th-century Venice, oil on canvas quickly became the medium of choice for large wall decorations, fresco being difficult because of that city's notorious dampness. From that period in history to the present day, canvas has become almost the universal oil painting support. It is portable, lightweight, beautiful, and, for the most part, strong enough to survive centuries.

The following is a brief survey of the most common flexible and rigid supports used in oil painting today.

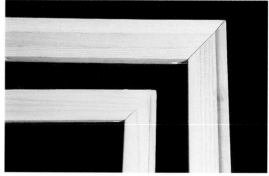

WOODEN CANVAS STRETCHERS. Commercially available types come in a variety of lengths, with ends mitered and grooved for easy assembly.

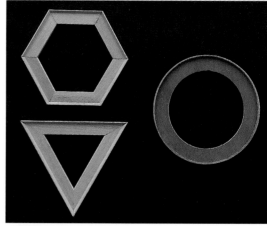

SHAPED CANVAS STRETCHERS. Those shown here were custom-made by Tri-Mar Enterprises.

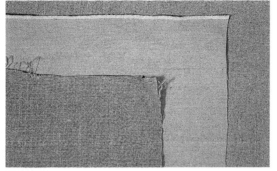

RAW LINEN

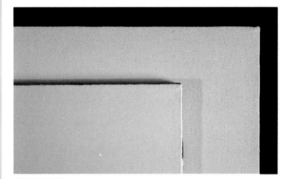

PRIMED LINEN

LINEN

Linen canvas is intimately linked with the chemistry of oil paints. Linen is made from the fibers of the flax plant, specifically *Linum usitatissimum*, the very same species whose seeds give us raw linseed oil. To make linen, the flax plant is harvested whole, roots and all, at the peak of maturity and left to decay for three weeks. The decayed material is processed into a very strong, fibrous yarn that is then woven into canvas for artistic use. The flax plant is common to cool, damp, temperate climates, so it is not surprising that artists' linen canvas comes mostly from Belgium and Ireland.

What makes linen so attractive to painters is its strength and its beauty—primarily the latter. Because of the way linen threads are spun, it never looks as mechanical or as evenly woven as other fabrics. Linen always retains its lively texture through the layers of paint. There's always some play in the weave that seems to invite oil colors to work through the small highs and lows of its surface. This organic beauty is most pronounced in standard and rougher grades of woven linen, but even in the finely woven "portrait" grades such as Fredrix's Rix the fabric displays a subtle unevenness that makes it interact with paint in an interesting way.

It is important to remember that early oil paintings on canvas were executed in relatively thin layers of paint, compared to the thicker applications characteristic of modern works. Impastos were not excessive, and color was applied in multiple thin glazes, so that the overall paint layer was relatively transparent. Therefore the texture of the linen was a critical element in the final look of the painting. The cloth's uneven quality and the occasional nubs added a sparkling light to the glazed and scumbled oil paint. Here, linen has it all over cotton and polyester, whose weaves are smoother and more homogeneous. Ultimately, it "feels right" to paint on linen.

Until the invention of polyesters, linen was the strongest fabric known. It is not easy to tear or puncture, and it can take a lot of scraping and digging with a palette knife. The tremendous weight of drying lead paints and grounds attests to linen's amazing strength. Of course, it isn't eternally permanent; nothing is. When an oil painting undergoes restoration, usually the first step is to reline or replace the linen canvas (often with polyester). Still, linen's main drawback is its expense. It costs at least two or three times more than cotton or polyester—but since it is so much more beautiful, who cares?

Sold by the yard, linen comes in rolls 54" to 120" wide (sometimes even as much as 12' to 14' wide). The various textures of artists' linen are determined by the number of threads per inch. Medium-textured linen has approximately 70 threads per inch; smooth, portrait-grade linen has 90 or more. Linen may be of the single-weave (SW) or double-weave (DW) variety. Double-weave linen is much stronger, heavier, and denser than single-weave, and of course is more expensive. It is more suitable for larger canvases.

Some savings can be had by purchasing linen in large rolls. It's best to buy the fabric raw and stretch and prime it yourself, not only to save money but also for better results. Preprimed linen is convenient, but getting a really tight fit with it is difficult.

COTTON

Cotton is a modern alternative to linen as a canvas support. It was first used for artists' purposes in the 1930s and has grown in popularity ever since, especially in the United States, where most of it is made.

Cotton canvas doesn't occupy the prestigious position among oil painters that linen does, and it has gotten bad press. Some authorities, such as Ralph Mayer, even considered it totally unsuitable as a support for oil paintings. This position seems a little unfair, however, since cotton does have its good points. Cotton is both tough and cheap. It even has as its fundamental component the same cellulose molecule as linen. The cotton weave is tighter and more homogeneous, offering less variety than linen does in the stress between warp and weft, so in comparison cotton is a relatively boring surface. On the other hand, it is more stable than linen, which has a greater tendency to expand and contract with changes in humidity, causing "waves" along the edges of the canvas.

One reason for cotton's bad reputation is that most of what is sold commercially as artists' canvas is really too thin, especially the prestretched kind. Artists' cotton canvas should be heavy (12–15 oz. per square yard). A 15 oz. cotton canvas that is properly sized and primed is an excellent support for serious oil painting. The even texture is not important if paint is going to be applied thickly, so why spend extra for something that's going to be hidden anyway?

Almost all ready-made stretched canvases are cotton coated with acrylic "gesso" sizing. These, as well as canvas panels covered with cotton, are good enough for beginners and students, and for executing studies. Cotton canvas is also recommended for very large, mural-size paintings. But remember, use nothing lighter than the 12- to 15-oz. weight.

If you use cotton for a painting support, get it at an art supply store, not at a fabric store. The cotton sold in fabric shops, which is generally intended for clothing, curtains, and the like, has been treated with commercial resins to reduce wrinkling. The various grades of cotton canvas sold in art supply stores—usually called cotton duck—are meant for artists' use. They are raw and pure, untreated with chemicals that might otherwise conflict with the application of hide glue or acrylic sizing.

POLYESTER

Polyester is a 20th-century synthetic fabric that certainly has no tradition as an oil painting support but is, in many ways, actually superior to both linen and cotton. Polyester is strong and permanent. It is more dimensionally stable than linen and is less susceptible to the acidic effects of oil paint. It will not rot, nor does it expand and contract a lot with changes in humidity. The same grounds and sizes that are used on linen and cotton can be used on polyester. One of polyester's chief characteristics is its complete lack of texture. It is flat, almost like metal.

Advocates of polyester, such as the Australian paint manufacturer Archival, recommend it unconditionally as the flexible support of the future. In this the firm is not alone, but polyester nonetheless doesn't seem to be catching on in any significant way with the majority of oil painters, most of whom are still enamored with the look of linen and the convenience of cotton. In fact, it really isn't yet on the market for artists.

JUTE

Jute is made from hemp, the same material used for rope. Canvas made from this very strong natural fiber has a uniform weave with a heavily pronounced texture characterized by thick individual threads. The texture of jute will go a long way in dominating whatever is painted on it. It is an ideal support for a direct painting style with a lot of heavy paint buildup and impastos. The openings between the threads are very wide, so jute almost has to be double primed to be effective. For paintings with a heavily textured look, a double-weave linen is a better choice because it is much more durable and stable, though costlier than jute.

PAPER

Paper is an interesting flexible support for oil paintings; abundant, convenient, and beautiful, it has an immediacy and intimacy about it that some painters may find lacking in the other, more usual supports such as canvas. Because paper

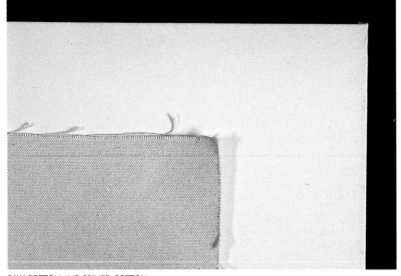

RAW COTTON AND PRIMED COTTON

PRIMED PAPER AND RAG BOARD

WINDBERG ART PANELS. Made by Windberg Enterprises, these are smooth Masonite panels primed with an acrylic ground.

The first of these is obvious: Select only high-quality fine art paper that has a tendency to last anyway. Work only with 100 percent acid-free rag paper, and make sure it's on the heavy side—90 lbs. and up, and the heavier the better. Rag boards are perhaps the best.

Paper and boards must be sized before you can apply oils to them. A rabbit skin glue size painted directly onto raw paper should be enough to protect it against the acidity of the drying paint. Another method is to coat the paper with a thinned acrylic medium or a thinned acrylic gesso. The paper will absorb both of these grounds, and the water they contain will cause it to bend and pucker. To prevent this, you can tape or staple the edges of the paper to a board just as you would when stretching watercolor paper. Or, once the sizing has dried, you can moisten the paper and place it under weighted blotters to flatten it out. A third alternative is to cover the paper with a thin coat of shellac, which is soluble in alcohol and thus won't be affected by paint solvents or oils.

There are also presized and special papers for painting in oil. One is St. Armand Sabretooth, a Canadian paper coated with a clay ground that is impervious to oil solvents. It is available in nine colors in sheets measuring 18 × 24" and 24 × 36". Another is Multimedia Artboard, a 300-lb. rag sheet that has been impregnated with epoxy so that it is both warp proof and immune to oils and paint solvents. Sizing is optional but unnecessary if permanence is a concern, since the epoxy protects the paper from rotting. This board is suitable for just about anything—pastel, encaustic, acrylic, gouache, tempera, and especially oil paint and alkyds. Surfaces available are cold-pressed and plate finish. One disadvantage of Multimedia Artboard is that it can snap in two if something heavy falls or is placed on it. (Well, nothing's perfect.)

HARDWOOD

As mentioned above, the earliest oil paintings were done on wood panels. Think of icons, of the mystical and religious depictions on church altarpieces.

The experience of working on wood is very different from that of painting on canvas. A panel painting is usually smaller and heavier than a work on canvas; it is definitely more of an object, like a piece of furniture. Rigid supports give a sense of solidity and weight.

is absorbent, paint applied to it naturally dries faster and more matte. The variety of textures it comes in makes it all the more tempting a surface to paint on.

But usually paper is not recommended as a support for serious oil painting, because it is not considered permanent. True enough. For important or large-scale works especially, it does not have the strength to make it an alternative to canvas. On a small scale, though, an oil painting done on paper can make a statement that might seem too formal on canvas. Of course, some elementary precautions are necessary when paper is used as a support.

Almost any natural hardwood will do as a painting support—oak, cedar, poplar, birch, walnut, or mahogany, for example. (Soft woods, like pine, are not good because they contain excess resins and offer little resistance to moisture.) It is important that the wood be aged and free of trapped moisture; panels should not be cracked, and should initially lie flat. Thickness can vary from 1" to 1/8", with 1/2" to 1/4" being the norm. If the wood is very thin, over the years the drying oil paint will bend the panel, making it convex like a barrel stave. Wood expands and contracts, especially if it isn't seasoned. Its worst trait is that it warps, and can be really hard to straighten out again. An advantage to working on thinner panels is that warping can more easily be corrected with bracing on the back. But this flaw is in wood's nature, and sometimes a slight unevenness can be part of the charm of panel painting.

Unfortunately, nowadays hardwoods are rare and expensive, but an excellent source is recycled furniture. If the oak in an old school desk or old door is not worm-eaten or rotten, it can be great for panel painting. A little sanding, planing, and cutting the wood down to size and you're ready to go. Many paintings from the late 15th century were done on panels made from recycled timbers of old sailing ships.

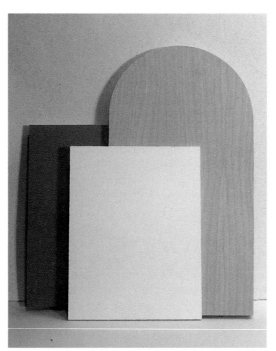

WOOD PANELS

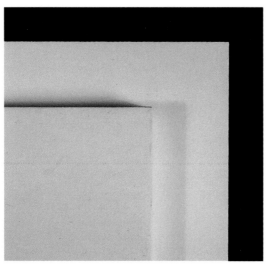

PRIMED WOOD PANELS

PLYWOOD

Because hardwoods are heavy, relatively rare, and costly, today the wood of choice for panel painting is high-quality, furniture-grade plywood. These include birch, mahogany, and poplar, all of which are extremely smooth and strong. One side of a plywood board is rough, while the other has a smooth finish that can be sanded down perfectly for sizing. Plywood panels are usually 1/4" to 1/2" thick. A panel that exceeds 16" in any dimension generally needs to be reinforced with a wooden frame.

MASONITE

Equally popular as a rigid support is Masonite, a synthetic material made of sawdust fibers and glue that is molded into flat boards. Masonite ranges in color from a deep brown to a coffee tan and comes in tempered and untempered finishes. The tempered finish is very hard and may need to be sanded before priming. The untempered finish is looser and more fibrous and is, in fact, the more appropriate of the two surfaces for painting because of its absorbency.

Some Masonite boards have one side that is very flat, with almost a plate finish, while the reverse has a rough, canvaslike surface. The rougher side will convince no one that it is cloth, and its "weave" is much too uniform to imitate real canvas. It's usually better to work on the flatter side. There are also Masonite panels that are flat on both sides. Of course, Masonite lacks the beautiful grain of a hardwood, but this is a feature you lose anyway when you prime a panel. So what's the difference if the wood is beautiful? It's going to be covered with gesso in the end.

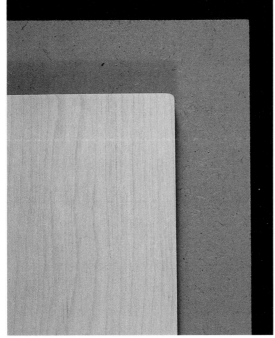

WOOD AND MASONITE PANELS

One problem with Masonite is that it bends very easily, according not to a wood grain configuration but to gravity. This means that if a piece of Masonite is placed against the wall at an angle it will eventually bow inward toward its center of gravity. To prevent this, Masonite panels must sit up perfectly straight in a picture frame or else lie down flat. The other alternative is to reinforce the back with wooden braces—and hope that the wooden braces themselves don't warp on you. A warped wooden frame is difficult to flatten out again, so use very good, aged wood for the backing.

Another problem with Masonite is that in large sizes it gets quite heavy. If you want to work on panel in a fairly big format, it's advisable to use plywood instead, since it is somewhat lighter. Bear in mind, though, that standard-size sheets of Masonite and plywood are no larger than 4 × 8'. If you're working bigger than that, stick to canvas.

Masonite is universally available and cheap. It is also very durable, lasting as long as any hardwood panel. It's very archival. If Masonite serves your purposes, stay with it. It is as good a rigid support as you can get.

METAL

In the Middle Ages it was extremely common to apply a primitive form of oil paint onto armor and shields. Although in later centuries metal was only rarely used as a support, a tradition of painting miniature oil portraits on copper did evolve, most notably in the hands of Pieter Bruegel and other Flemish artists of the 16th and 17th centuries. These small works on metal seem much like jewelry.

The usual metal of choice for oil painting has been copper, but other chemically stable possibilities are iron, stainless steel, tin, and aluminum. Because metal is heavy, paintings done on it traditionally have been on the small side. But today we have a lightweight metallic building material that is perfectly suitable for large-scale works: honeycomb aluminum. It is two thin sheets of aluminum stretched across a core of corrugated aluminum, thus resembling a metallic corrugated cardboard. It comes in large, flat sheets of various thicknesses and is easily cut. The American artist Frank Stella is famous for his shape paintings on honeycomb aluminum.

The important quality of metal is its glasslike smoothness. It is never going to bend or warp with the strain of drying paint or changes in humidity. Before it can be painted on, however, it must be cleaned of any rust with steel wool and coated with a metal primer. (You may also need to bevel the edges of a metal panel.) A metal primer differs from other oil paint primers in that it "etches," or bites into, the smooth metallic surface slightly in order to hold on to it. Without this undercoating of primer, oil paint will not adhere to a metal surface.

Metal supply shops and art stores that sell printmaking supplies including etching and engraving plates are sources for metal supports.

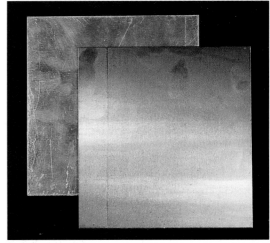

ALUMINUM AND COPPER PLATES

SIZES AND GROUNDS

Besides the support, the additional component in the foundation of an oil painting is the *ground*. Most unprepared supports are too absorbent for proper paint handling and must be primed before paint can be applied to them. The ground is the first (prime) layer of paint, which serves to isolate the support from the actual paint layers and makes it more receptive to paint. The isolation of ground and support is the function of a *size*, which is usually an animal hide glue such as rabbit skin glue or, more typically, an acrylic resin whose dried film matches the flexibility of the dried oil paint. The size isolates the fibers of the support from the acidic action of oxidizing oil paint, which if left unchecked would destroy the support. The size also seals the support and the eventual paint films from the destructive action of moisture seeping in from the rear of the painting.

The second component of a ground is the actual prime coat itself, usually a white paint or white gesso that is applied directly over the sized support. This paint layer serves as a reflector of light; white offers maximum reflection. In an oil painting, light penetrates the paint layers and is reflected back out again from the painting's ground, so in essence, colors are illuminated twice. This white prime layer must have an extremely low oil content, as in lead and titanium oil grounds, or no oil content at all, as in gesso grounds. Only after a support has been sized and primed with a coating of white paint or gesso is it suitable for the controlled artistic application of oil paint.

We don't think too much about priming these days, mainly because we don't absolutely have to. We're not like painters 200 years ago who had no choice but to do their own priming. It's just as easy to buy a roll of preprimed quality canvas as it is to buy it raw—maybe more so (of course, it will also be more expensive!). The general attitude is to just stretch it and be done with it. Why worry about something as tedious and time-consuming as priming your own supports? This position is held by a lot of painters, amateur and professional alike.

But there are rewards for painters who prime their own supports. It's obvious to anyone who's ever done it that there is a qualitative difference between canvases and panels properly primed by the artist from scratch and those bought ready-made in the art supply stores. I'm personally no great craftsman, but even my clumsy attempts at priming my own canvases resulted in the most interesting, reliable, and diversified surfaces I ever painted on. It is definitely worth the effort to do it yourself.

Today there are three distinct types of grounds for oil painting supports: 1) oil-primed grounds, 2) acrylic grounds, and 3) hide glue gesso grounds. Let's take a look at each one.

OIL-PRIMED GROUNDS

An oil-primed ground is the most time-honored—and prevalent—preparation for an oil painting support. Though used mainly for canvases, it can also be applied to wood and Masonite panels. It consists of two parts: the size and the oil ground.

The size, simply put, is a clear, water-soluble, noncorrosive substance that saturates and coats the raw fibers of the support. The traditional material used for size is rabbit skin glue, which is made from rabbit hides and comes in solid sheets or as a fine powder. This strong organic adhesive is a powerful constrictor of canvas. Thus, a linen or cotton support should only be lightly stretched on the frame, because applying the glue size will leave the fabric tight and wrinkle-free.

To make the size, dry rabbit skin glue is dissolved in warm water (the proportions are one part glue to ten parts water). While still warm, the size is applied to canvas or wood in a thin coat. Both sides of the support should be covered; sometimes two coats are necessary. The glue is totally absorbed into the support, sealing its fibers and thus protecting it from moisture and the corrosive action of drying oil paint.

The second part of this traditional oil prime is the oil ground itself. This is actually a solid coat of white oil paint, but one that is specially formulated to act as a ground. This type of paint is made to be as lean as possible—that is, with very little oil. The idea is that the ground should be somewhat "underbitten," meaning that the subsequent layers of oil colors have a leaner foundation that they can "bite" into and adhere to.

Traditionally, oil grounds were made only with lead white pigment, but today they are made with either lead or titanium. Lead white is leaner and faster drying than titanium white, and has a tougher and more flexible film. On the other hand, titanium white is brighter, more opaque, and nontoxic. Zinc white is unsuitable for a foundation ground, its paint film being too unpredictable and too transparent to function well in this role.

These white grounds are much thicker than regular oil paint. They can be applied in their original consistency but rarely are, being much too thick to leave a smooth, even coat. White grounds are usually thinned with mineral spirits or turps to the consistency of heavy shaving cream. The paint must be thin enough to work thoroughly into the weave of the canvas without leaving pronounced brushstrokes. Of course, care must be taken not to thin the oil ground so much that it becomes unstable.

After a canvas has been sized with rabbit skin glue, it is left to dry for 24 hours; then the white oil primer can be applied. One coat is usually enough to do the job, but for a smoother surface or to mask the weave of the canvas almost totally, apply two or three coats, each approximately a day apart. Once the oil prime has been applied, it must cure for at least two weeks before it is ready to receive paint—and the longer the curing time, the better. In the past, six months was standard. When lead white grounds cure in the dark for a long time they become slightly yellowish. Two days of exposure to bright light, however, reverses the process.

Several brands of commercially made oil priming whites are on the market. Fredrix, the large American manufacturer of artists' canvas, makes both a lead white and a titanium white

oil primer. Holbein has four lead grounds to choose from, one white and three slightly tinted ones. Winsor & Newton and David Davis have excellent lead and titanium white grounds as well.

Alkyd-based oil primers have become available recently, with Winsor & Newton, Daniel Smith, and David Davis each offering a titanium white alkyd ground. These alkyd primers are fast drying, nonyellowing, and nontoxic, and, perhaps more importantly, their dried films do not become brittle. As such they are turning out to be more permanent than traditional grounds, and may ultimately prove to be superior to them. An alkyd oil primer can be used as a ground for traditional oil or alkyd paints, but it is not suitable for acrylics.

ACRYLIC GROUNDS

Acrylic emulsion grounds, as they are officially called, are actually the ubiquitous and quite abundant acrylic "gesso." Just about every paint manufacturer offers its own brand, and today it is the most commonly used primer for oil painting supports. Most rolls of preprimed linen or cotton canvas are prepared with acrylic gesso, as are prestretched canvases and canvas boards. Oil-primed rolls of linen are also available but are in a distinct minority, and they are certainly more expensive.

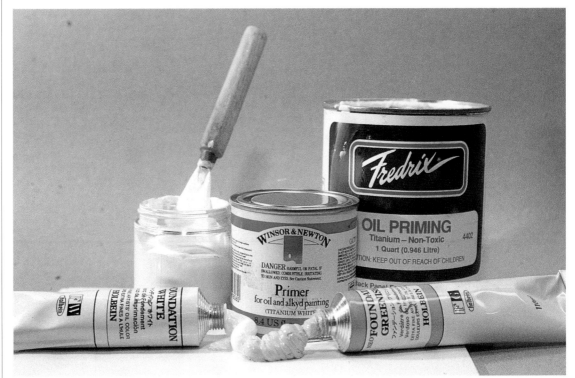

OIL PRIMERS

Acrylic gesso is not at all the real thing; true gesso is a combination of rabbit skin glue, chalk, and pigment. Nevertheless, the misnomer seems to have stuck. Certainly acrylic gesso is the best ground to be used with acrylic paints, but whether the same is true when it is used with oils is a matter of some debate. It is, of course, the most convenient, probably accounting for its current popularity. Traditional oil-based grounds, calling for complicated applications of size and special primers and requiring long drying and curing periods, have been relegated largely to the rarefied world of purists and serious professionals.

Acrylic gesso has a lot going for it. It is a great all-purpose primer that will stick to just about any surface that's free of oil or grease. It dries rapidly, and as it does so, it polymerizes into one solid, very strong molecular substance that never cracks. Once dry, acrylic gesso totally resists water and moisture, meaning that no preliminary sizing is necessary. It also is unaffected by the corrosive action of acids, including that caused by the oxidation of drying linseed oil. It is absolutely nontoxic, safe and clean, easy to use, and inexpensive.

Clearly, the real advantage of acrylic gesso is its strength. As a ground it is harder and tougher than either traditional oil or hide glue primers. In addition, it has the unique ability to remain permanently flexible. Unlike oil grounds, acrylic grounds do not become brittle as they age.

And herein lies what some believe to be the problem with using oil paints on an acrylic ground—a problem that is specific to stretched canvases exceeding three feet in area. Presumably, an acrylic ground will retain the flexibility it had the day it was applied to the canvas, and it will expand and contract naturally with changes in humidity. By contrast, oil paints become harder and less flexible as they dry over the decades. Theoretically, then, applied over an eternally flexible ground, a hardening oil paint layer will eventually lose adhesion and, in time, may fall off its support.

Acrylic gesso, barely 40 years old, is a relatively new invention, and whether disastrous effects will result from using it as a ground on canvas supports for oil paints has yet to be seen. Only time will tell us if oil paints and acrylic grounds are truly incompatible.

Rigid supports pose no such problems. An acrylic ground applied to them doesn't move around or "breathe" the way it does on a stretched canvas, so the problem of bad adhesion between oil and ground does not occur. Acrylic gesso takes perfectly to wood and Masonite panels. Before priming them, it is important to remove all oily and greasy stains, including fingerprints, from the

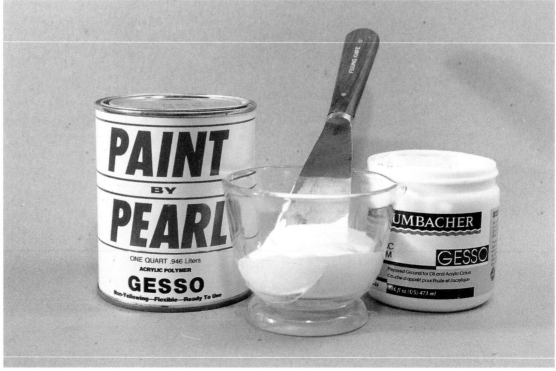

ACRYLIC GESSO

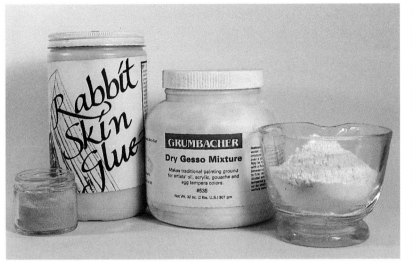

RABBIT SKIN GLUE AND GENUINE DRY GESSO MIXTURE

raw surfaces. You should also know that applying a hide glue size first is both unnecessary and a mistake, because acrylic emulsion grounds do not adhere to rabbit skin glue.

HIDE GLUE GESSO GROUNDS

A hide glue gesso ground is genuine gesso—the real thing, direct from the Middle Ages. Gesso, which means plaster in Italian, is a very simple combination of rabbit skin glue, precipitated (smooth) chalk, and white pigment (titanium or zinc white). It is the best ground to use on rigid supports. Highly absorbent, gesso is compatible with most paint mediums except acrylics, and is especially well suited for oil paints because it is an extremely lean ground.

Toward the end of the Middle Ages, when oil painting first emerged, most easel paintings were done on wood panels, usually in egg tempera on a gesso ground. Oil glazes were subsequently applied over these tempera underpaintings. Such works clearly demonstrate the optical advantages of a brilliant white ground. Egg tempera and oil glazes are both very transparent. Light illuminates paintings executed in these mediums first as it enters the paint film, and then again as it bounces off the brilliant white gesso ground. Because gesso grounds contain no oil, they do not yellow and stay perfectly white. To this day, largely because of their highly reflective grounds, panel paintings from the 14th and 15th centuries still glow with an inner jewel-like brilliance.

Gesso is almost always homemade, but some manufacturers supply it ready-made. Grumbacher makes a genuine white gesso ground that you dissolve in warm to hot (not boiling) water in a double boiler. Perhaps the clearest step-by-step instructions for making gesso can be found in *The Painter's Handbook* by Mark David Gottsegen (Watson-Guptill, 1993). Basically, the glue and the white filler (one part pigment to four parts chalk) are mixed together in equal amounts over low heat. Care is taken to avoid boiling the mixture, as the fresh gesso must be a smooth, warm cream free of bubbles.

The wood or Masonite panel is sanded and sized beforehand with pure rabbit skin glue and left to dry overnight. When the gesso has been prepared, it is brushed onto the support in layers while still warm. It dries almost instantly, so many coats can be applied in a single day. Because rabbit skin glue is such a powerful binder, you must brace panels with a rear frame. Any panel thinner than a half inch is subject to stress and bending from the glue. The front, back, and sides of panels must be equally coated with gesso for at least the first two coats. This will equalize and balance the pull of the glue and prevent the panel from warping.

Each coat of gesso is applied at right angles to the one before it. You may apply as many coats of gesso as you want—eight to ten is not unusual; four is more typical. As the buildup of gesso ground becomes thicker, brushstrokes are bound to leave their mark. These will have to be sanded away when the panel dries. Real gesso is easier to sand than acrylic gesso. Medium to fine sandpaper wrapped around a block of wood is good enough; rough paper is too much. Some artists recommend slightly dampening very fine sandpaper with water to speed the process. This works, but care must be taken to not sand away the whole ground. A wet sanding block works better for the harder acrylic gesso grounds.

Once the gesso has been sanded smooth, it is ready to receive paint. A panel prepared with hide glue gesso may seem a bit too absorbent when the first coat of oil paint is applied. In one sense this is good because it means the oil and the ground are making a true bond. But if less absorption is desired, a highly diluted coating of varnish is first applied on top of the gesso ground. Sometimes this varnish layer is lightly colored to make a toned ground; this is known as an *imprimatura*. The imprimatura can be an initial sketch or underpainting but is not to be confused with a *grisaille*, which is a much more heavily developed opaque monochrome painting executed entirely in grays and used as a foundation for colored oil glazes.

BRUSHES

The paintbrush is a modified extension of the artist's hand and as such serves as the most fundamental of all oil painting tools. At first glance the variety of artists' brushes seems immense, for they come in myriad sizes and shapes styled to perform highly specialized tasks. Often they are made from exotic materials. But apart from size, all oil brushes are categorized by either texture or shape.

Simply put, oil painting brushes come in just two different textures: hard and soft. Hard brushes are called bristle brushes, and they aren't so much hard as they are resilient, flexible, and tough. Made from hog's hair imported from China, bristle brushes are stiff and strong and tend to leave their mark in the paint strokes they make. They hold a lot of paint and release it in a full-bodied textured way. Bristle brushes will do the bulk of the work in almost any oil painting. They are inexpensive.

Soft oil brushes are made from the softer hairs of smaller animals such as squirrel, monkey, and especially sable. Generally smaller than bristle brushes, and shorter and denser, they deposit their paint loads smoothly and evenly, with no trace of brushstroke texture. Soft brushes are almost always used to finish a painting and handle details. Those made of sable are the most expensive; synthetic nylon brushes are often as soft as sable brushes but paint with more resiliency and are, of course, cheaper. They can spread a lot of paint in a big smooth way, as well as handle detail work.

All brushes are identified by the shape of their fibers, regardless of what they are made from—bristle, sable, or synthetic. There are five basic brush shapes, each with its specific function: flats, brights, filberts, rounds, and fan blenders.

Most painters end up with a lot of brushes over the years but find that only a handful are used again and again. Sooner or later, though, they all come into play somehow.

FLATS

Flats are used for making broad, sweeping, painterly strokes. The brush fibers form a flat, wide shape that is perfectly squared at the tip. The flat is meant to have a lot of spring to it. You can render rough lines by painting with the edge of a flat, or easily go into a broad sweep by turning the brush from its edge and working it from side to side. The flat can hold a lot of paint and is often the brush of choice for the early stages of a painting. Its characteristic stroke is hard-edged and rectilinear. It is an ideal choice for a direct painting technique.

BRIGHTS

Brights are modified flats. They have much shorter, stubbier fibers and are used to make a more controlled, dabbing stroke. They hold far less paint than a flat, usually just enough for only two or three strokes. Brights are also very effective in removing small amounts of paint from the canvas, as in a controlled "wipe-out" method.

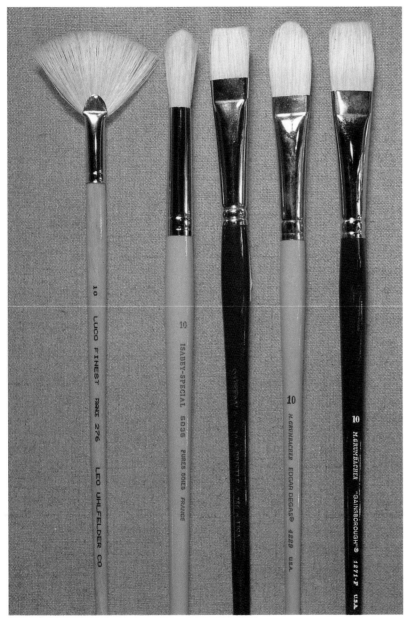

BRISTLE BRUSHES. Left to right: fan blender, round, bright, filbert, flat.

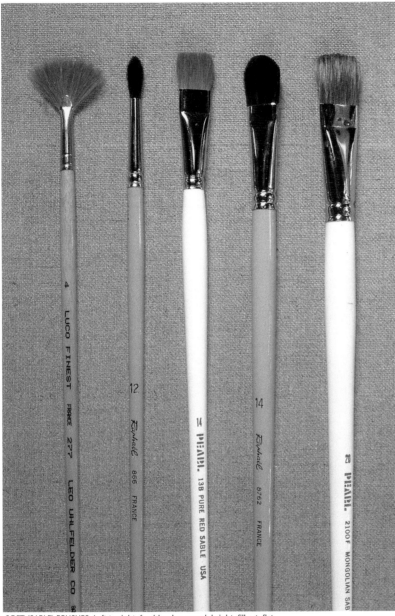

SOFT (SABLE) BRUSHES. Left to right: fan blender, round, bright, filbert, flat.

ROUNDS

A round has fibers gathered into a perfectly round shape, with the tip either pointed or dulled. The round is probably the oldest type of oil painting brush; in the 17th century they were used exclusively, while flats didn't appear until around the 19th century. Rounds are the opposite of flats and are used to make rounder or softer strokes. They hold a lot of paint and are capable of making either thick or thin strokes. This is the brush to use for drawing lines in oil paint. It is also useful for laying in large, indistinct color washes, as well as for dabbing on dots or splotches of color, as in the pointillist technique. In addition, the round is an effective blender. The only thing it's not good for is painting hard, straight edges.

FAN BLENDERS

As its name implies, the fan blender is a flat, fan-shaped brush, the edges of its fibers curving outward from the center. The fibers are usually soft, but not always; some fan blenders are made of bristles. This is one of those specialized brushes that, depending on the artist and the type of work he does, is either totally indispensable or never used at all. It is not meant to hold paint but to be used dry, brushed lightly across roughly applied paint to blend colors together. Fan blenders must always be used clean, so if you do a lot of blending, it doesn't hurt to have a lot of these brushes handy.

HOUSE PAINTING BRUSHES

In addition to the five main brush categories, there are utility brushes such as those used for house painting. Willem de Kooning once said that if you had to spend your money on anything in art supplies, spend it on the best paints you can afford and paint with the cheapest brushes you can find. This advice makes sense if you consider that the paint is what the painting is all about. De Kooning paints with sash brushes that he gets three to a package from the hardware store. House painters are fine to use—why not? Anything that can put down the paint in a way you like is okay.

Today art supply stores carry European house painting brushes for artists' use. These brushes usually give you great quality at a pretty good price. They're especially excellent for painters who like to work large and with a lot of paint. Most such brushes resemble large-scale

FILBERTS

The filbert is a rounded flat. The outer edges of the brush curve slightly inward toward the center of the tip. The tip itself is, however, perfectly straight. This design guides the paint toward the center, giving the stroke a straighter, more concentrated, harder-edged shape. The filbert gives more control than a bright. It is also a more graceful and fluid brush to use on curved strokes, and is probably the ideal shape for any oil painting technique. With a handful of different-size filberts, a skilled painter can do just about anything.

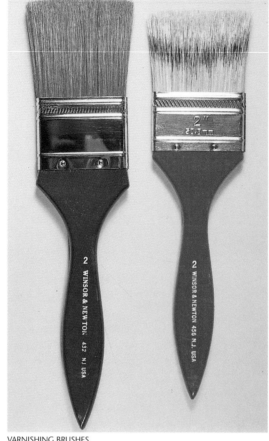

VARNISHING BRUSHES

rounds and are made of bristle, the hairs forming a rough, rounded tip. I find them excellent for applying paint in the early stages of work. I also like to use house painting brushes sort of as "bristle" blenders.

VARNISHING BRUSHES

Varnishing brushes are meant for applying the final varnish to oil paintings that are thoroughly dry. They are very soft and flexible, the idea being that they leave no brushstroke. Coats of final varnish must be applied as smoothly as possible, and for that reason varnishing brushes are flat and thick. This allows the varnish to go down in even blocks, with no "holidays." It is very important that varnishing brushes be well made and of good-quality fibers, since you do not want hairs to shed and become embedded in the varnish coat. If your favorite varnishing brush begins to lose its hairs, get rid of it, or at least use it for some other painting procedure. A brush that no longer can be used for one task might be useful for another before it has to be discarded.

CARE OF BRUSHES

Artists' brushes—even cheap ones—can last a long time if they are properly cared for. Here are some good studio procedures that will help you preserve your brushes.

When not in use, let brushes sit vertically in containers with the working end up and the handle down. This allows solvents and moisture to evaporate thoroughly from the fibers and does not destroy the brush's shape. Once the hairs are bent, they almost never can be straightened out again.

Always have two jars of solvent on hand for cleaning your brushes, one for an initial soaking, the other for a second rinse. To clean a brush, wipe it free of excess paint with a rag or paper towel, then dip it into the first jar of turpentine, swishing it around to get most of the paint off. Wipe the brush off again with a rag. Next, dip the brush into the second jar of turpentine, which should be kept cleaner than the first one. Swish the brush around to get off the remainder of the paint. Wipe the brush a third time. At this point it should be clean enough to resume work with fresh paint— even a different color.

When a painting session is over, thoroughly wash all brushes in turpentine one final time, cleaning off as much paint as possible. *Do not leave the brushes soaking overnight.* Too much solvent will weaken them, and may destroy their shape. Overnight may become a week, by which time the solvent will have evaporated, leaving your brushes stuck to the bottom of the container and ruined.

After washing your brushes in the jar of clean turpentine at the end of a work session, take them to a slop sink and rub them into a damp bar of ordinary soap. Better yet, use a special soap paint cleaner such as Grumbacher's Brush Cleaner. Move each brush about until it lathers. As you do this, you can see the paint coming out of it. This is really cleaning the brush. The final step is to wash out the dirty soap lather with water. Make sure the water does not exceed room temperature, because hot water will weaken the ferrule. After the brush has been washed with soap and water, allow it to dry with the bristles up and open to the air overnight. The brush will be fresh and clean for use the next day. Follow these instructions and your expensive brushes will last you through years of painting.

TOOLS

Beyond brushes, the tools used in the craft of oil painting are almost primitive in their simplicity: a palette to hold colors, knives to mix them with, cups to hold solvents, and rags to keep everything clean. These are the implements every oil painter totally relies on, from the first picture executed in art school to the mature paintings of the professional. Let's take a look at them, and at a few other items that come in handy.

PALETTE KNIVES

Next to the brush, the palette knife is the most frequently used tool in the oil painter's paint box. This implement has a thin, flexible blade that is usually made of steel but is sometimes made of plastic. Unlike a dinner knife, the blade is not sharpened on the edge. Palette knives come in a wide variety of sizes, with blades ranging in length from ½" to 18". Blade shapes are either rounded or pointed, and are sometimes even serrated—that is, milled with grooves. The palette knife is a tool of multiple uses, but its main purpose is to move paint around, both on the canvas and on the palette.

Palette knives fall into two major groups: mixing knives and painting knives. In a pinch they are interchangeable, but the two kinds differ in design according to their intended function.

MIXING KNIVES

The blade of a mixing knife is flat and in straight alignment with the handle. It is much like a putty knife except that the edge of the blade is rounded and more flexible. Mixing knives have very smooth, sometimes highly polished blades, an important feature because they must "wipe clean." That is, after being used to mix paint, ideally the knife will retain little or none of the color on its blade.

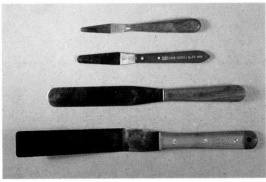

MIXING KNIVES

The rounded tip is another significant design feature; it makes it possible to move color around in a hurry, whereas a square or pointed tip does the job much more slowly. Also, a rounded blade will not gouge the palette, which is especially important if you're working on one made of paper.

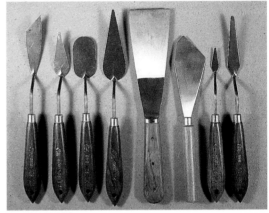

PAINTING KNIVES

PAINTING KNIVES

A painting knife is what most people think of when they use the term "palette knife." Painting knives are used specifically to paint with and come in shapes and sizes that vary far more than those of mixing knives. Blade tips may be rounded, pointed, grooved, or angled, but the feature common to all painting knives is that the blade bends below the handle. This differentiates them from mixing knives. Whereas a brush is held more or less perpendicular to the canvas and paint is applied with the tip, a painting knife is generally held so the blade is parallel to the canvas and paint delivered with the flat part. Thus, the purpose of the bent blade is to keep the handle away from the surface of the painting. This design feature gives the painting knife more flexibility and freedom of handling than the simpler mixing knife.

PALETTES

Simply put, a palette is any flat surface that will hold fresh paint. A plank of wood, a sheet of glass or plastic, even a piece of cardboard can work as a painter's palette. I'll never forget one of my teachers, Paul Georges, painting from a large slab of marble on the floor. Usually, though, a palette is meant to be portable, something you can hold or put on a tabletop to bring paints close to the action of painting.

An artist almost always works not just with one but with an assortment of colors at any given time. So in one sense, a palette is a small, hand-held studio that accommodates everything that is immediately important—paints, brushes, mediums, and rags.

Oil painting palettes are usually made of wood, and are either rectangular or curved. The traditional oil painting palette—the kind we associate with the flamboyant style of, say, the 19th-century American portraitist John White Alexander or John Singer Sargent—is a romantic arabesque shape with a thumb hole and an indentation at one end so it can be gripped by the hand that holds the brushes and rags. This arrangement leaves the painting hand free to handle the brush or palette knife of the moment. The side of the palette that curves inward is meant to be placed against the artist's body for support. The outer, convex edge is the painting "line," where the pure, unmixed colors are placed; mixing space is in the center of the palette, and palette cups that hold the mediums are attached to the rounded outer edge. Rectangular wooden palettes, which are rather small, are meant to rest on the artist's arm instead of against the body, or else simply laid flat on a tabletop or easel tray.

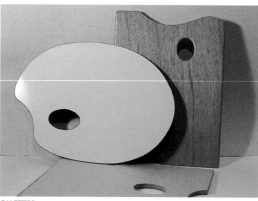

PALETTES

A wooden palette shouldn't be too big if you intend to hold it comfortably in one hand, and for that reason most range in size from 10" to 24". The best ones are stained and varnished to prevent the oil in the paints from soaking into the wood.

These days most people use disposable paper palettes, largely for the convenience of not having to scrape the old paint off after a painting session. Paper palettes come in pads. When you finish using one sheet, you just tear it off and go to the next one. Various sizes are available, including some very small ones. I particularly like these because I can arrange my colors in families on separate sheets instead of putting all of them on a single palette. Disposable palettes come with either coated or uncoated paper; stick with the coated stock.

Palette Cups

Palette cups are small metal containers for mediums and solvents that clip onto the edge of a palette. They come singly or in pairs, and some are chrome-plated with screw-on tops so you can carry them out into the field. These look great, but in actual practice the plain ones are more effective; palette cups usually become dirty and encrusted with dried medium, making screw-on tops useless except for the most fastidious painters.

Generally you need one cup for medium and another for turpentine (or another solvent). Paired palette cups are thus meant as a convenience in this respect. This is fine for some artists, I guess, but I myself prefer having two separate cups. I find that this is a cleaner arrangement—solvents don't get into the medium, for example. Also, my mediums go a lot faster than my turps. (Keep a separate can, jar, or cup for cleaning brushes somewhere off the palette.)

Mahlsticks

Did you ever wonder how artists keep their hands steady enough to paint fine details? They use a mahlstick, which is nothing more than a light, sturdy wood or aluminum rod with heavy padding on one end. The padded end rests directly against the canvas and the artist rests his painting hand on the stick to steady it for detail work.

Paint Rollers

This is an optional tool but one that I find absolutely indispensable. Paint rollers, especially smaller ones, including those made of foam rubber, are very useful for certain oil painting tasks. I use them to disperse paint that has been put down on the canvas by some other means (with a palette knife or brush, for instance). The roller acts as a spreading and texturing device. Sometimes I don't want to see anything that resembles a brushstroke, so I soften the effect by running over the area lightly with a paint roller. What I like best about this tool is that it can be used to spread a light scumble over a painting.

When used for house painting, rollers are great for putting down an initial application of paint, but in oil painting they are not good in this role. Using a roller in this capacity wastes a great

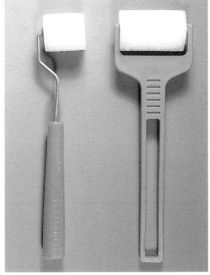

FOAM RUBBER PAINT ROLLERS

deal of paint, is not accurate, and too often results in paint splashing back into your face, especially if you've dipped it into turpentine. Work with the roller only as a modifying tool.

CANVAS PLIERS
Canvas pliers are specially modified gripping tools that are meant to pull fabric taut. The grips are grooved so they will grasp the canvas securely, and a square steel fulcrum increases the pull. Anyone who has stretched canvas with their hands and fingers alone can appreciate what a great invention canvas pliers are. They save your knuckles from the wear and scraping of pulling canvas—especially heavily primed canvas.

CANS AND JARS
Humble as these tools are, cans and jars are indispensable to the oil painter. Giant coffee cans are great for holding wet paintbrushes and solvents for cleaning. The same is true of jars, and so much the better if they have lids. I tend to use two jars for cleaning my brushes, one for clean turpentine and one for dirty turps. As the clean stuff gets dirty, it simply goes into the dirty jar.

RAGS AND PAPER TOWELS
Rags are as necessary to painting as brushes, as wiping things off is a constant activity common to all oil techniques. Old sheets, towels, and shirts make the best rags; avoid heavy fabrics such as canvas, because they are too difficult to control.

Paper towels and napkins are great for cleaning anything. They are especially useful in working with oil sticks. And, of course, they are disposable.

APRONS AND SMOCKS
Painting aprons and smocks protect you and your clothes from paint. Some artists treat them as wearable rags, wiping paint off on them— probably not the healthiest thing to do, but be my guest. Gone are the days when Leonardo would paint while wearing his best velvets just to show everybody that he knew what he was doing in the studio.

BRUSH CLEANERS
Special brush cleaning soaps are available commercially; Grumbacher and The Masters are two common brands on the market. These soaps come in unbreakable containers and are used with water to clean brushes at the end of a painting session. After cleaning, allow brushes to dry overnight before using them again.

ARTGEL AND ARTWIPES
Both of these cleaning products are made by Winsor & Newton. Artgel, which comes in a jar, is a hand cleanser that can also be used to clean brushes and tools. Artwipes are large tissue wipes saturated with a special solvent and skin softeners designed to remove oils and alkyds from your hands. They come in a handy, airtight plastic dispenser and are excellent to have along on outdoor painting excursions as well as in the studio.

ARTGUARD
Artguard, also made by Winsor & Newton, is a protective emulsifying cream that you apply to your skin before a painting session or before you work with raw or toxic pigments. It acts as a barrier to prevent paints from actually touching your skin. Artguard is an excellent safety tool, especially if you suffer from allergic reactions to paints and solvents. It is also recommended for those who work with oil sticks.

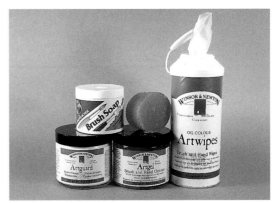

BARRIER CREAM AND HAND AND BRUSH CLEANERS

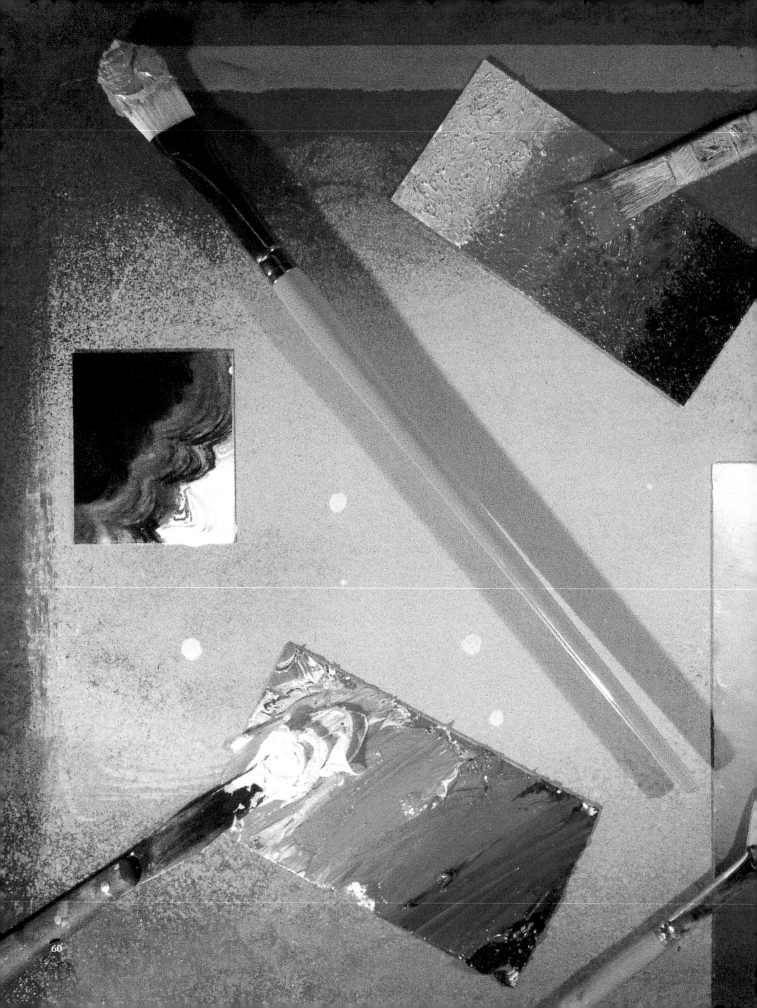

BASIC OIL TECHNIQUES

Oil paint can be applied in thick, opaque impastos just as easily as in thin, transparent glazes. Colors can be blended together softly or left with edges that are in razor-sharp contrast to each other. Since oil paint dries slowly, it can be corrected and changed many times before it sets. Even after a painting has dried, many new layers of fresh oil paint can be applied over it. Yet in spite of the seemingly infinite possibilities, oil painting techniques are classified as being either direct or indirect.

Direct painting is by far the more common of the two approaches, and its techniques are considered the "basics" of working in oil. These simple techniques apply generally to all forms of painting that involve the application of paint right from the tube onto the support. Blending colors, developing textures, working out the composition, and making corrections are all done directly on the canvas, with immediate results.

Indirect painting is a more deliberate process that involves some preliminary planning. Basic oil techniques are executed to perfection, and then many layers of transparent oils are applied to create a jewel-like effect. This method, known as glazing, will be covered in the following chapter.

Here we will look at the basics: wet-on-wet, alla prima, drybrush, and impasto techniques; working with blocks of color; using a palette knife; creating texture; and achieving smooth blending. We will also look at some of the preferred methods of starting a picture.

From Drawing to Painting

Before we get too deep into painting techniques we should pay attention to one very essential but often overlooked fact—namely, the importance of drawing.

Often, painters think of drawing and painting as two very distinct and sometimes incompatible activities. A woman who worked in oils once said to me that she loved to paint but hated to draw. I didn't so much disagree with her as suggest that she redefine what she meant by "drawing." Drawing, to me at least, is nothing more than the simplest form of an idea. Even the Sistine Chapel began as a series of doodles. In my own work I am often amazed to find the genesis of a finished oil to have been nothing more than a small drawing buried somewhere in a sketchbook. For me, and perhaps for other artists as well, it's as if the drawing is the initial idea and the painting is that idea fully developed and ultimately realized. So drawing and painting are not incompatible activities, but analogous steps taken in a process that leads to the same end.

Having said this, I think it is easy to see how naturally a drawing leads into an oil painting. At the earliest stages of work, drawing and painting are one and the same activity. Perhaps this is why starting a painting can be the most enjoyable part of the whole process. It is almost intoxicating to think of your clean, white canvas as a large sheet of drawing paper—a sort of empty stage or arena in which your initial ideas and fantasies can first come to life.

Drawing is by definition a flexible process, one that allows and even encourages changes, corrections, and adjustments, all for the sake of discovering and developing a clear vision. Flexibility is the key ingredient at the beginning of any oil painting, and for that reason alone, it doesn't hurt to spend a great deal of time just drawing—and playing—directly on the canvas as if it were nothing more than a large piece of paper.

Here are a number of drawing mediums and techniques that work great for establishing preliminary guidelines for any style of oil painting. All of these mediums are flexible and easily changeable on the canvas, and when finished or fixed, they combine to work safely with oils.

Charcoal

Charcoal is the almost universal drawing medium to use with oil paints. Both compressed charcoal and vine charcoal are suitable for drawing on canvas or panels. Vine charcoal is preferred because it leaves a lighter mark and is more flexible—that is, it's the easier one to erase. Compressed charcoal pencils, which leave a dense, dark line, are cleaner and more suitable for details.

Drawing with charcoal on a canvas ground is almost like using it on paper, except that the charcoal tends to stick less to the surface. The degree of finish can range anywhere from a few very general strokes to a fully realized value rendering, complete with shadows and highlights. The same tools used in traditional charcoal drawing on paper apply here as well: The soft eraser, the stiff bristle brush, the chamois, and the blending stump all play their part. Corrections can be made easily either by erasing the charcoal or wiping it off completely with a rag soaked in water or turpentine.

Fixing the charcoal drawing is optional, but the more complicated and detailed the drawing becomes, the more likely it will need to be treated with a fixative. Traditional fixative, which is a variation on shellac, will not harm oil paints in any way. When the charcoal drawing is finished and you're ready to put down your first layers of oil paint, spray the surface first with a light coating of retouch varnish. This is especially useful if your charcoal drawing is very detailed and precise and you don't want to lose track of it in the initial painting stages. The retouch varnish will preserve your drawing as you work over it with turpentine oil washes. On the other hand, if you want your drawing to dissolve into the paint, do not spray it with retouch varnish; just let it go. Charcoal rarely affects the final color of oil paints unless it was applied in needlessly heavy amounts.

PASTEL AND CONTÉ CRAYON

Using pastels or Conté crayon is almost identical to using charcoal; the same tools and techniques for blending, smudging, scraping, and erasing apply. The difference, of course, is that color, and maybe lots of it, can be introduced as an element in the drawing stage.

Choose pastels that aren't too soft, such as NuPastel. Pastel pencils are an excellent choice. The idea is to not leave *too* much color on the canvas, which is why hard pastels and Conté are preferable to traditional soft pastels. You do not want too much "powder" on your canvas. Keep the pastel clean, with no buildup. Also avoid using white or light-colored pastels in this approach; instead, let the white of the painting ground work for your light effects. Building up a traditional layer of thick pastel in this situation can be dangerous because it will result in an unstable ground for your oils. So keep the pastels extremely thin—almost like a stain— and you'll be fine. Fix with a spray of retouch varnish if desired.

WATER-SOLUBLE COLORED PENCILS

One very often overlooked way of starting an oil painting is to work up the color and drawing with colored pencils, specifically the water-soluble variety, such as those made by Derwent. This unique medium allows the painter to simultaneously draw in line and paint in washes. When used dry, these pencils work like ordinary colored pencils, but when you put down color with them and spread it around with a damp brush, you can produce transparent washes like those you get with watercolor paints. Light colors and whites are achieved by exposing white canvas. The water-based paint film from these pencils is little more than a stain on the canvas and is not affected by the oil paint overlays. Fixing is not necessary.

This is an ideal medium for the artist who likes the spontaneity of watercolor but wants to push his or her ideas further with oils. As a workable underpainting and drawing medium, water-soluble colored pencils have the same advantage as pastels and charcoal in that they are entirely reversible. That is, if the drawing is not going right and everything's a mess, you can just wipe it off with a wet sponge, leaving the canvas clean so you can start over again.

PEN AND INK

Pen and ink is an interesting way to start an oil painting; van Eyck occasionally did so. India ink and crow-quill pens are best; ballpoints with alcohol-soluble (not turpentine-soluble) ink are okay too. You can also use water-based colored inks. This medium is more effective when used on a rigid support such as wood or Masonite than when used on canvas, whose texture can be a distraction.

Drawing with pen and ink is the slowest of the four methods presented here and tends to work best with a small format. In fact, its main advantage is that it tends to make the oil painter overly aware of details from the very beginning. No wonder it was popular in the detailed-oriented 15th century. There is little risk of becoming too big or "painterly" with a crow-quill pen.

The advantage of a pen and ink drawing is that it stays down exactly where you put it. It will not run or smear when you cover it with oil paint, nor will it come off easily with turpentine. It is also surprisingly easy to make corrections. Because in an oil painting situation this medium is used on supports that are stronger than its traditional paper ground, it is entirely possible to scrape, sand, and erase the ink either to make corrections or highlight details. Steel wool makes a beautifully effective eraser for finely drawn pen and ink cross-hatchings. For painters who have had a grounding in printmaking techniques such as etching, pen and ink is a familiar and natural way to work into oil paintings.

WAYS TO START A DRAWING

A number of drawing mediums can be used to establish the foundation for an oil painting. Illustrated here are several of the drawing techniques that I have found useful because of their flexibility and perfect compatibility with oil paint.

FROM DRAWING TO PAINTING

Preliminary drawing executed in charcoal, along with the various types of charcoal and tools used. Clockwise from left: stump blender, vine charcoal, fixative, compressed charcoal, compressed charcoal pencil, soft eraser, chamois.

Preliminary drawing executed in pastel, with the various types of pastels and tools used. Clockwise from left: Conté pencil, Conté crayon, blending stump, fixative, pastel pencils, hard pastel sticks.

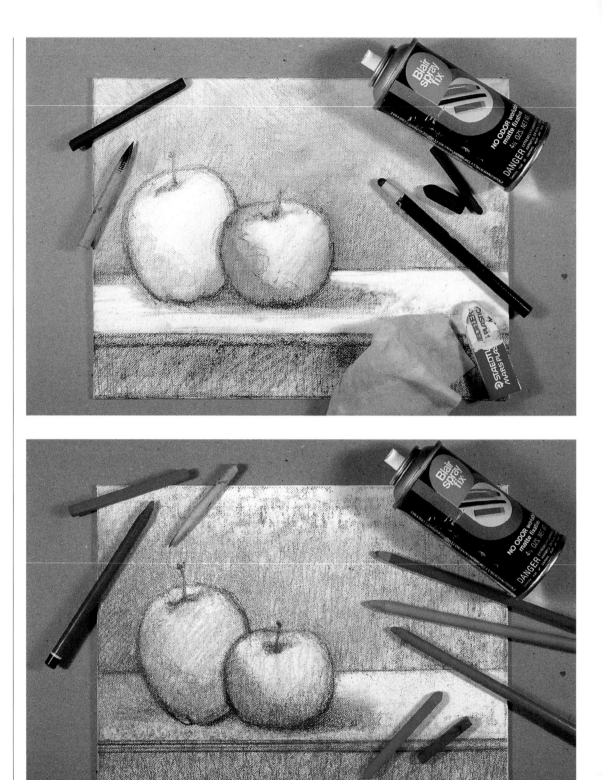

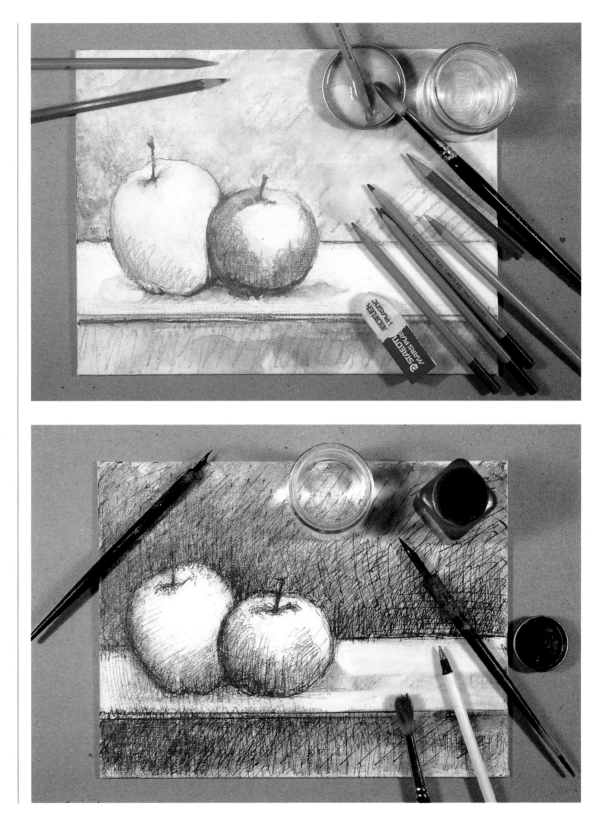

Preliminary drawing executed in colored pencil, with the various types of colored pencils and tools used. Top left: water-soluble colored pencils. Clockwise from top right: water-soluble pencil dissolved in water, jar of water, watercolor brush, standard colored pencils, more water-soluble colored pencils, soft eraser.

Preliminary drawing executed in pen and ink, with the various types of pens and ink used. Left: crow quill pen. Clockwise from top: water, India ink bottle, crow-quill pen, ballpoint pen, soft brush.

WHAT NOT TO USE

Curiously, one of the most common of all drawing mediums—namely, graphite pencil— is not recommended for underdrawings for oils. This is primarily because the graphite has a tendency to rise up through the layers of oil paint and, in time, to show through on the surface of the dried painting. The same thing happens on an even more drastic scale with felt-tip markers. The ink from these pens cannot be covered with oil paints; they come right through even the most opaque colors. For pen and ink drawings it is best to stick to India ink. I've noticed no ill effects from black ballpoint pens, but felt-tip markers are definitely not recommended.

DEMONSTRATION

These two pictures illustrate that a large finished oil painting may have its roots in a small drawing or sketch. A visual idea may have no real final dimensions. What begins as something small, simple, and colorless often can be translated into something else that is quite a bit larger, more detailed, and in full color.

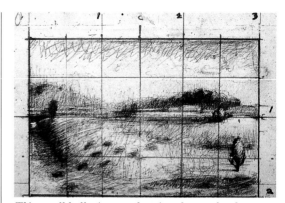

This small ballpoint pen drawing shows a landscape scene that was entirely made up in my head. The beauty and fun of doing small pen and ink drawings like this is that very often simple things become transformed by the imagination into something else. A few ink dots, for example, become a herd of cattle; a few curved lines, a mountaintop. This tiny drawing served to inspire two larger oil paintings: The Herd, *shown here, and* Big Daddy Comes Home, *a more surreal version shown on page 143. I marked off the drawing with a rough grid so I could enlarge and transfer the idea onto canvas.*

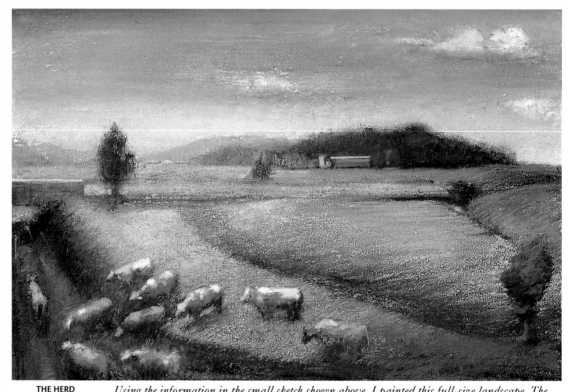

THE HERD
Oil on canvas,
24 × 36"
(61 × 91.4 cm).
Collection of the artist.

Using the information in the small sketch shown above, I painted this full-size landscape. The painting, like the drawing, was done from my imagination, but working it out on the canvas was made simpler by the fact that I had already begun to develop my idea in the sketch. In other words, in some small way the painting had already been made visible. Working in this manner has convinced me that paintings are really "printouts" of ideas we carry around in our heads, and that they can be made as big or as small, or as simple or as complex as we imagine them to be.

THE WIPE-OUT METHOD

While not technically a drawing process, the wipe-out method is yet another way of starting an oil painting. This is a very basic monochromatic approach that exploits the slow-drying quality of oil colors.

The composition is roughly painted in flat tones of a single oil color. Then with either rags or brushes soaked in turpentine, the light tones and whites are created by wiping away portions of the color to expose the white canvas beneath it—a kind of reverse painting. If too much paint is removed, leaving the area too white, or if more detail is needed, then more color can be added. Because oil paint remains wet and "open" for hours, the wipe-out method is particularly suitable for the preliminary stages of an oil painting. The oil color used in this technique should always be one with a low oil-absorption rate, such as iron oxide or terre verte. When the wipe-out layer dries, it works as an underpainting on which to build a more finished painting.

DEMONSTRATION

The wipe-out method is a relatively fast, monochromatic approach that is ideal for anyone who wants an absolutely smooth underpainting. This technique utilizes the white of the ground to lighten color instead of the addition of white paint. When the basic color has been applied and is still wet, brushes and rags are used to wipe out paint to expose the ground where lighter areas are wanted. Corrections are made by adding more of the basic color. The demonstration shown here, a still life of a white eggplant, was done in light red oxide on a very smooth, oil-primed panel.

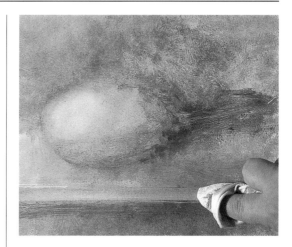

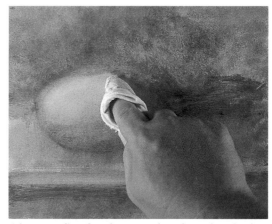

After spreading the color around on the surface, I take a clean rag that has been dipped into a small amount of turpentine and begin wiping away the light-colored areas.

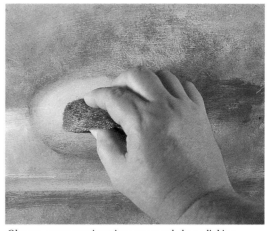

Cleaner, more precise wipes are made by polishing certain areas with fine steel wool.

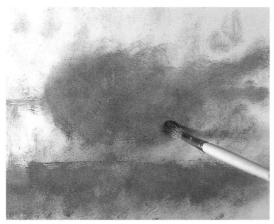

I apply my basic color to the panel.

THE WIPE-OUT METHOD

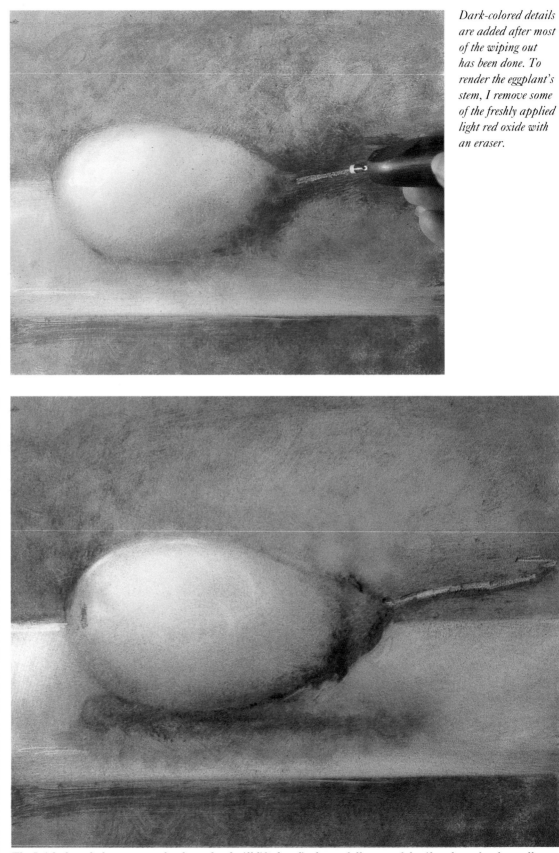

Dark-colored details are added after most of the wiping out has been done. To render the eggplant's stem, I remove some of the freshly applied light red oxide with an eraser.

The finished work shows a very clearly rendered still life that displays a full range of detail and tonal values, all done with one color.

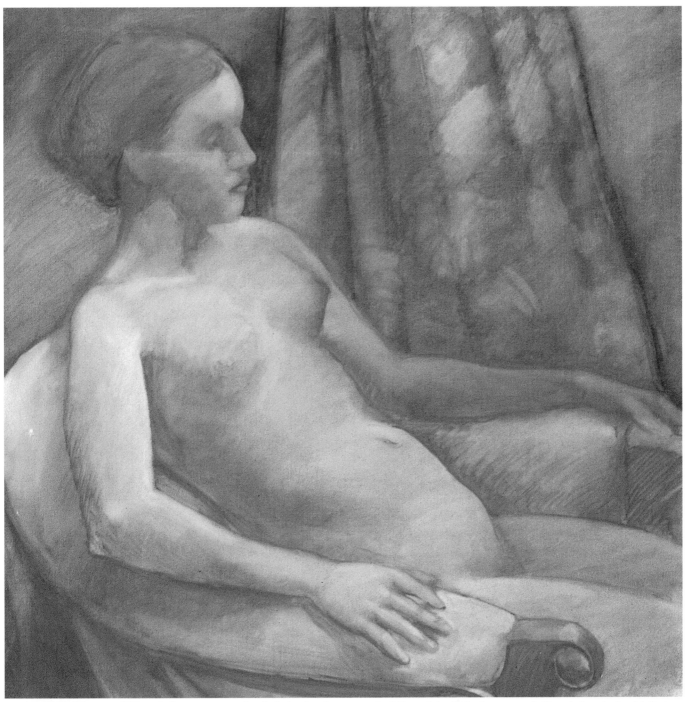

MODEL IN THE WHITE CHAIR
Oil on canvas, 30 × 30"
(76.2 × 76.2 cm).
Collection of the artist.

This painting was executed entirely in the wipe-out method. One of the chief advantages of this technique is that it's fast. Often a composition or a pose can be documented in a single sitting, as was this one. The model was present for a typical three-hour pose; by using the wipe-out method, I was able to compose an entire underpainting in just one session.

PAINTING ALLA PRIMA

Alla prima, roughly translated from the Italian, means "at the first" or "at once." In a general sense all direct painting techniques can be considered alla prima, because they are executed to create a painting in an immediate way, from start to finish, by developing imagery, composition, color, and form more or less as the work progresses.

But more specifically, alla prima usually means completing a painting in just one sitting. It is fast painting—the whole process is finished in one shot, with the success or failure of the results riding on the inspiration of the moment and the skill of the artist. Alla prima painting calls for a totality of vision, a compression of pictorial elements into a simplified scale. It is a disciplined form of painting that demands an economy of technique so as to say more with less.

Oil paint, of course, because of its slow drying time, flexible blending qualities, and textural consistency, is an ideal medium to use alla prima. Medieval painting techniques such as egg tempera and fresco are impossible to do this way. In fact, early practitioners of oil painting, such as Bellini and van Eyck, would never have thought of doing paintings in one sitting. It was only after 17th-century artists like Rembrandt and Rubens began to realize and demonstrate in their work just how flexible and expressive a medium oil paint really was that a new aesthetic came about, one that appreciated the beauties of spontaneous painting.

The late 18th century, with its emphasis on display and performance, became the great age for alla prima painting. Fragonard's portraits, done as much to show the artist's virtuosity as to entertain the sitter, were almost always finished in one session. So, too, were Goya's miniature "Black Paintings," fleeting glimpses in oil paint of a satanic world of nightmares and mythological brutality.

In many ways, then, alla prima painting has played a part in shaping the oil painting aesthetics of our own age. The whole modern concept of spontaneous painting certainly owes much of its existence to the quick and flexible experience of working alla prima. Let's look at some of the variations on this exciting way of painting.

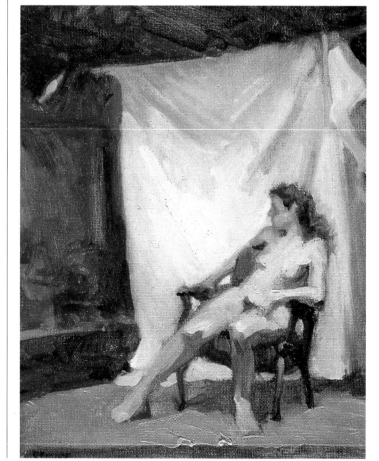

MODEL WITH RED HAIR
Oil on canvas, 12 × 9" (30.5 × 22.9 cm).
Collection of Edward and Gardonna DeSarro.

This small painting contains most of the truly beautiful features of alla prima painting technique: It is spontaneous, simple, direct, natural, unambiguous, clean, and fresh. It was executed in a single sitting, and I feel that it's one of the very best oil paintings I've ever done. The light was right, the pose was great—it was just a good night!

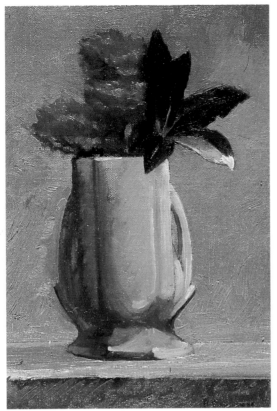

THE BLUE VASE
Oil on canvas, 10 × 8" (25.4 × 20.3 cm).
Collection of Jane Raskin and David Copeland.

Painting fresh flowers is almost inevitably a one-day operation, since they don't last. Here, I used sun-thickened linseed oil as my medium, which accounts for the painting's gentle impasto and deep, rich gloss finish.

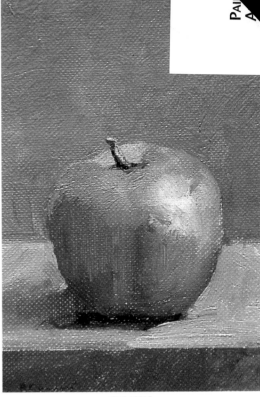

THE APPLE
Oil on canvas, 6 × 4" (15.2 × 10.2 cm).
Collection of Harriet and Milton Rosen.

This is yet another example of using sun-thickened linseed oil as a medium for alla prima paintings. One advantage of this medium is that it is heavy bodied, yet unlike stand oil or even ordinary linseed oil, it dries rapidly.

STILL LIFE ON YELLOW
Oil on canvas, 15 × 30"
(38.1 × 76.2 cm).
Collection of the artist.
Photo by D. James Dee.

This still life is basically an extended alla prima painting. That is, I executed it over the course of several days, yet in my handling of all its individual parts, I employed alla prima techniques—fresh local color, directness, and spontaneous brushwork. This work is like a collection of smaller paintings combined into a single, larger one.

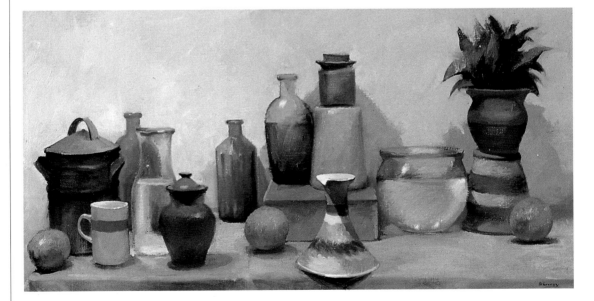

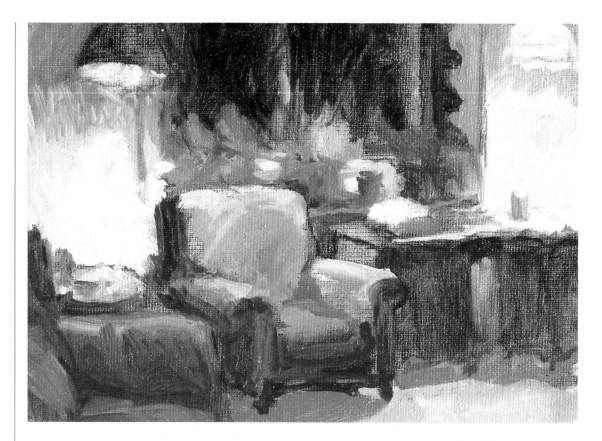

NIGHT INTERIOR
Oil on canvas board,
4 × 6" (10.2 × 15.2 cm).
Private collection.

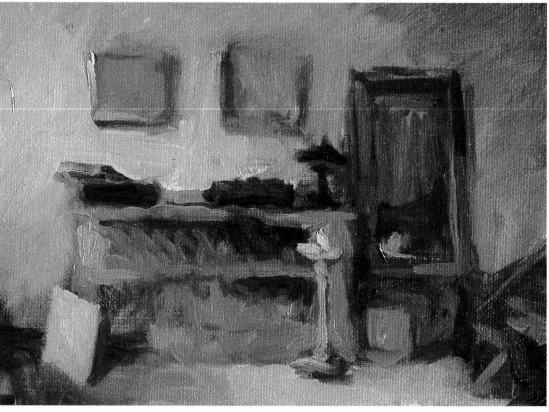

THE ROOM
Oil on canvas board,
4 × 6" (10.2 × 15.2 cm).
Private collection.

*These two small
works show how
close a relationship
there is between alla
prima paintings and
oil sketches. The idea
behind my depictions
of the two interiors
was merely to catch
in each case the
individual quality
of a particular light.
I subordinated
details and specifics
to emphasize the
light's effects on these
settings, and to do
so, I worked as if
I were viewing each
scene through dark
glasses or with my
eyes squinted.*

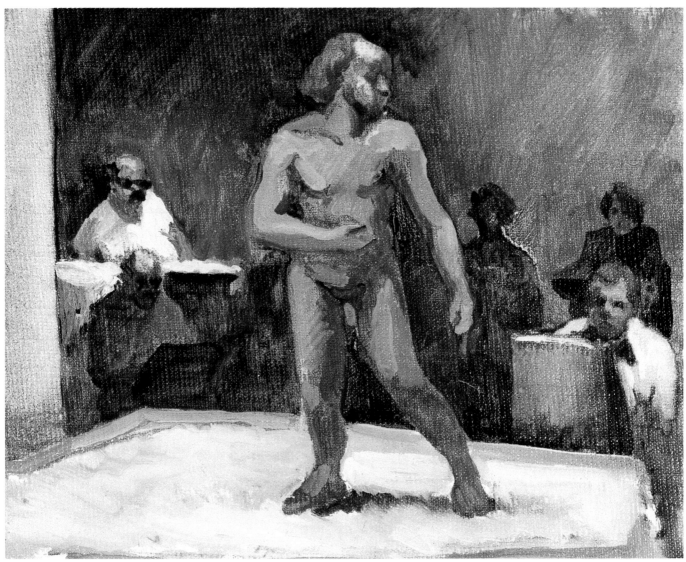

PAINTING SESSION
Oil on canvas board,
8 × 10" (20.3 × 25.4 cm).
Collection of the artist.

As with the interiors shown opposite, my main concern in this painting was the quality of light. Here, much of the illusion of light is achieved by the placement of contrasting values. Notice the effect of the artist's white shirt against the dark shadows on the left, and of the dark figures against the lighted walls to the right.

THE OIL SKETCH

The oil sketch is alla prima painting in its simplest form. Quick painting sessions that are 10 to 20 minutes long are a great way to learn the basics of how to paint fast. Oil sketching is fun and full of surprises. Perhaps because almost nothing is at stake, the oil sketch can be a relaxing and satisfying experience.

Spontaneity and speed are the main ingredients of an oil sketch. The aim is to get down the main "feel" of the subject by working quickly with little more than two or three colors and a few turpentine washes. Just the roughest and sketchiest idea is necessary to get the painting moving and its elements to start working together. Taking this approach on a canvas panel or even on unstretched canvas gives us the opportunity to capture fleeting moments from the posed model or a landscape.

Oil sketches prove in no uncertain terms just how little is needed to make a painting. They sort of break the ice. Working quickly and with an economy of means, we easily come to appreciate how small oil sketches can become extremely beautiful in their own inconspicuous way.

All of the sketches shown on these two pages were done in less than 30 minutes, illustrating just how well oil paint works as a sketching tool.

These quick oil sketches depict trucks in the parking lot across the street from my loft.

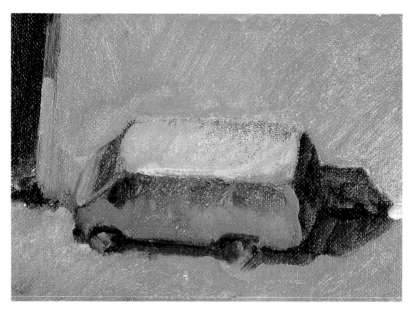

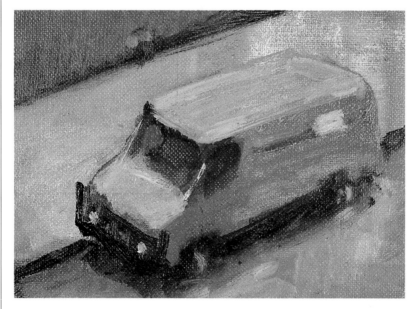

I took out my copy of Eadweard Muybridge's book The Human Figure in Motion *and, using the excess cut ends from a roll of linen, made a set of spontaneous oil sketches based on his photographs. All were done on the same night. Muybridge's photos are, of course, in black and white, so it was fun to just make up the color as I went along. It was also fun to see how fast I could do these sketches; I think the average time was 15 minutes. (My Siamese cat Flatbush made a guest appearance in one of them.)*

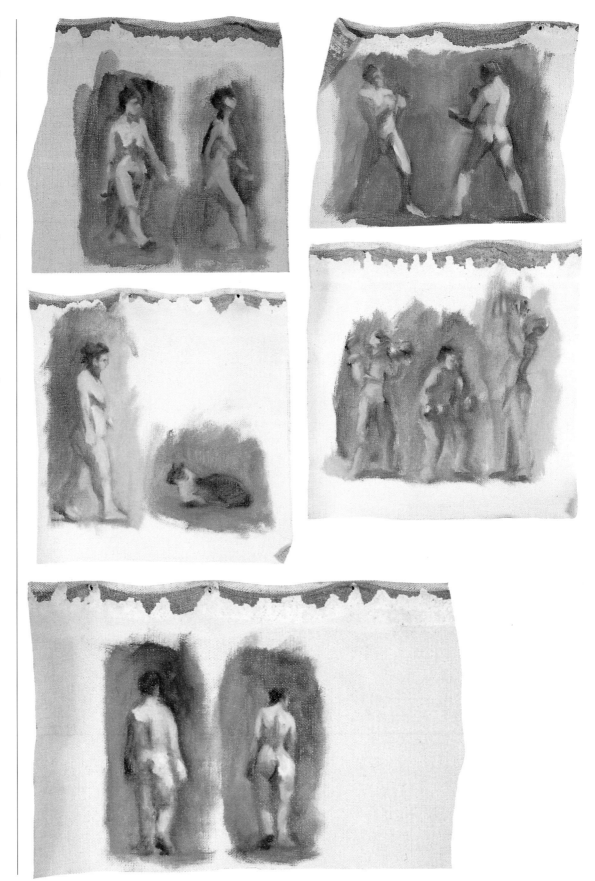

THE EXTENDED ALLA PRIMA

We soon have to go beyond just doing sketches and create more finished pieces. But we keep with us the lessons of simplicity and speed as we go into more extended alla prima paintings. Generally, alla prima paintings follow along the lines described here.

The painting is started by working out the composition with large, diluted turpentine washes. The palette is very limited at first—just two or three colors, or even one is fine. The idea at the early stage is not to worry too much about color intensity or color purity, but rather to think more about the canvas as if it were a large wash drawing. You approach the canvas in its totality. You're building the blocks of your composition. Aim for mass, form, and positioning rather than detail or even color; these will come later.

After the composition is essentially established in this way, details and texture are developed by applying passages of oil paint that are fuller bodied and opaque. Turpentine washes are used in the beginning stages, but as the painting progresses, it is best to introduce "fatter" mediums into the oil paints. "Fat" means additional linseed oil. A great general-purpose oil medium for alla prima painting is the famous "three-in-three" combination of equal parts damar varnish, linseed oil, and gum turpentine. This formula gives the paint some body and also improves its drying qualities.

The alla prima technique can be executed on stretched canvas or on panel. The ground is usually white rather than tinted, since diluted colors seem to be more effective on white grounds. Bristle brushes—especially rounds—are better for this kind of painting than sable or other soft-haired brushes, because most of the color mixing is done directly on the canvas rather than on the palette. This is the best way to achieve spontaneity, but it's really hard on soft brushes, so stick with bristle.

Alla prima paintings finish with more colors than they start out with. As a painting approaches completion, the earlier thin turpentine washes have probably begun to dry and set. This is the ideal time to expand the palette and take more chances with color and details. Alla prima paintings start thin and simple but can end thick and varied.

DEMONSTRATION

Typically, alla prima paintings begin with thin turpentine washes in just a few colors to block in the composition, usually on a white ground. Textures and details are then developed gradually using fuller-bodied, progressively "fatter" paint and a more extensive palette.

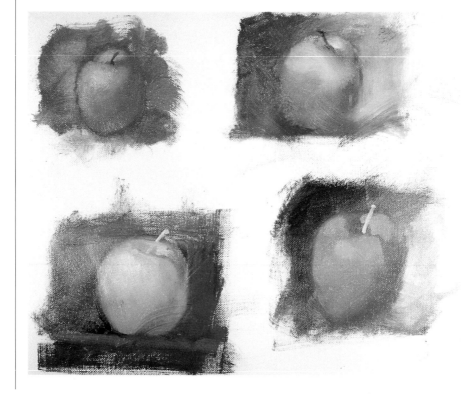

I did this series of small warm-up studies and exercises on canvas panel to work out some color ideas before embarking on a larger painting. Studies like these are basically meant to break the ice and let you have some fun.

To get the preliminary lines of the painting in place, I used burnt sienna and ultramarine blue. The colors have been thinned with turpentine and as such dry quickly.

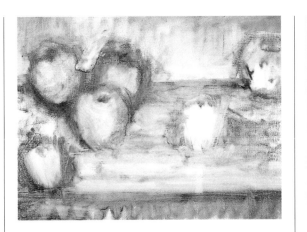

Here I begin to add the first touches of local color. The apples are being painted with a mixture of cadmium yellow light and Naples yellow.

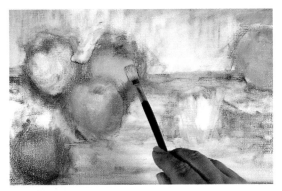

This is a loose application of all the local colors. The oils are still being thinned with turpentine at this point.

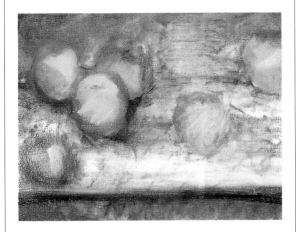

I apply more color and smooth it out with foam rubber rollers.

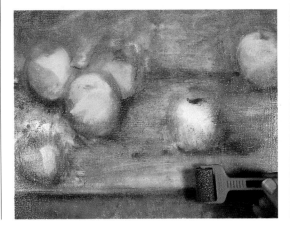

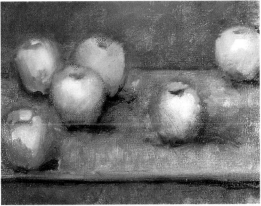

The second layer of local color has been applied and smoothed out even further with foam rubber paint rollers.

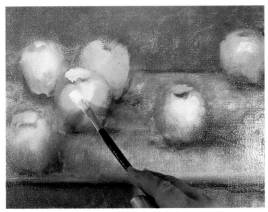

Here I begin to add heavier applications of oil paint. The colors are now no longer thinned with turpentine; instead, I use them just as they come from the tube.

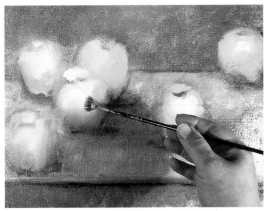

These fresh layers of paint are blended and smoothed out with a fan blending brush.

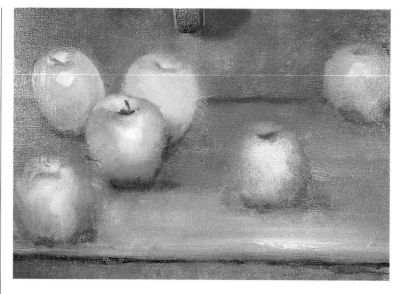

I use a small paint roller to further smooth out the colors.

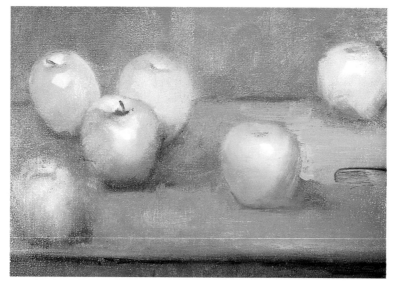

Here I'm applying final opaque colors along the base of the painting.

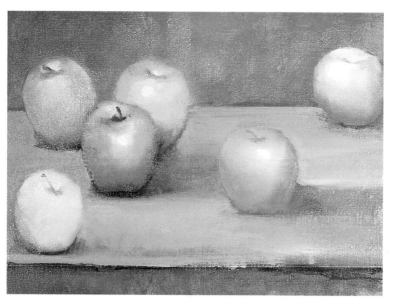

The painting is now almost done. All the apples are finished and have been smoothed out with fan blenders and small foam rollers.

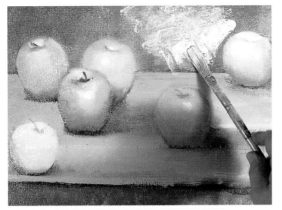

Before I complete this painting I decide to lighten up the background behind the table. I want to exploit that red as an underpainting for a warm white. To do this, I paint over the wall area with a special unbleached, semitransparent zinc white made by Williamsburg.

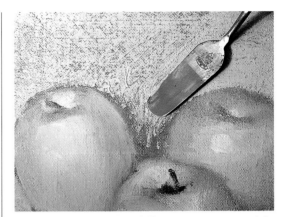

With a palette knife, I carefully scrape away some of the semitransparent white to create a "scumbled" texture.

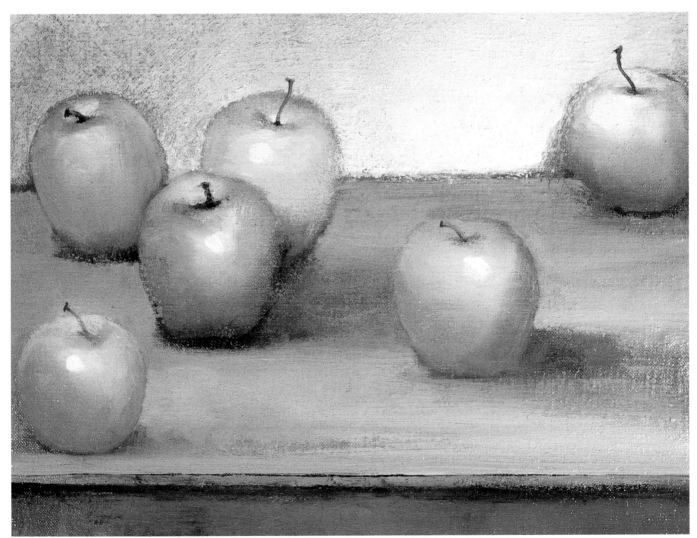

YELLOW APPLES
Oil on canvas, 11 × 14"
(27.9 × 35.6 cm).
Collection of the artist.

This is the completed painting, which I did in one day using the paint in a direct manner with no medium added except for a bit of gum turpentine in the early stages. There is a "blonde" and pearly quality to the work, due primarily to the high-value colors I used and the opalescent white background with a bit of red showing through.

WET-ON-WET

The wet-on-wet method is a variation on the alla prima technique. In this case the painting is developed from start to finish by using large amounts of undiluted oil color and working it together while it is still wet—hence the name "wet-on-wet." With this method it is very easy to blend fresh wet paint into color that is also still wet.

In working wet-on-wet, it is best to stay with long-haired bristle brushes. Keep a palette knife handy, because with a heavy buildup of wet paint, the canvas may become too saturated. If this happens, scrape off the excess with your knife. You can put the leftover paint back on your palette to use in another area. With wet-on-wet, much of the color mixing is done directly on the canvas, where your brush acts as a palette knife.

Remember that it is important that the oil paint not dry too fast when you are using this technique. Most oil colors that come directly from the tube should stay wet and in a workable state for at least 24 hours, though umbers and Prussian and phthalo blue dry to the touch overnight. Other colors will remain workable for days, although they may not be as easy to blend after two days or so. One of the great things about oil paint is that it stays wet for so long that extenders and modifiers to retard drying aren't really necessary. But if for any reason you feel the need to extend the paint's drying time when using the wet-on-wet technique, you can add oil spike of lavender to your colors. Such an extender is best used from the very beginning of the painting through to its completion.

ABOUT COPAL VARNISH

An interesting variation on the wet-on-wet technique involves using copal varnish as a medium. Copal varnish makes oil paint more liquid, giving it the consistency of syrup. It also levels the paint and increases its gloss, making it more like enamel.

Working with copal medium is truly carrying the wet-on-wet painting technique to its ultimate. Pushing the syruplike oil paint around on the canvas can be an exciting experience. Blending becomes a more liquid, flowing process. The paint drips and oozes in beautiful ways, as in the illustration at left below. Jackson Pollock would have loved working with copal varnish medium.

If you can't find genuine copal varnish easily, Grumbacher makes a synthetic one that works the same way. Liquitex's Kopal painting medium is also a great substitute for the original. David Davis (see List of Suppliers) is a reliable source for the real thing.

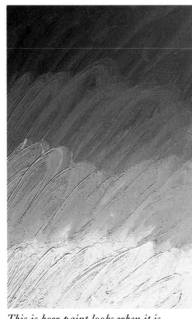

This is how paint looks when it is applied directly and blended while still very fresh and wet. I used copal varnish as a medium for a fluid effect.

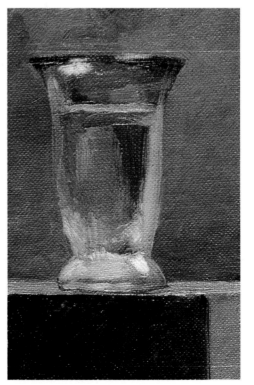

GLASS OF WATER
Oil on canvas, 6 × 4"
(15.2 × 10.2 cm).
Private collection.

Using a very simple wet-on-wet technique, I executed this study of transparency and water basically by working the white and darker outlines of the glass directly into the wet blue background. I used sun-thickened linseed oil as my medium.

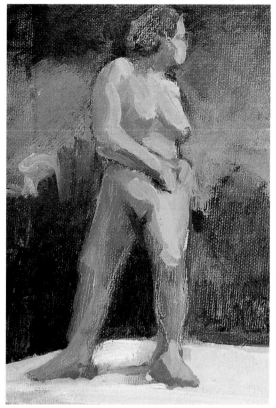

FEMALE NUDE (detail)
Oil on canvas, 8 × 10" (25.4 × 20.3 cm).
Collection of the artist.

This nude, a study done from life, shows the spontaneous and often exaggerated brushstrokes typical of a wet-on-wet painting technique.

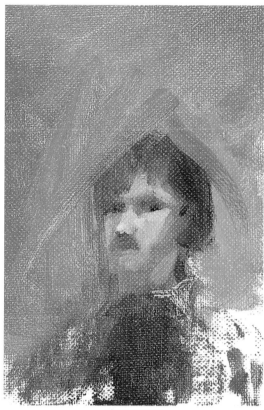

SELF-PORTRAIT
Oil on canvas panel, 7 × 5" (17.8 × 12.7 cm).
Collection of the artist.

Here is an example of how I work lighter colors into a darker base color. I set down my background color first, and while it was still wet, I painted the facial tones and colors directly into it.

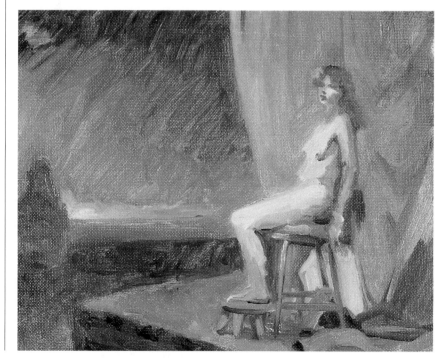

NUDE
Oil on canvas, 9 × 12"
(22.9 × 30.5 cm).
Collection of the artist.

This painting perfectly illustrates the beauty of diffused colors. Throughout most of the composition I worked the colors wet-on-wet. The exaggerated paint strokes created luminous shadows, while the wet-on-wet light areas gave the flesh tones a pearlescent quality.

WET-ON-WET

DUSK
Oil on canvas,
16 × 9" (40.6 × 22.9 cm).
Collection of the artist.

The idea behind this landscape was to keep the details and colors diffused, much as they appear in a real landscape in which the sun has just set. I accomplished this atmospheric effect by painting sky and foliage together wet-on-wet.

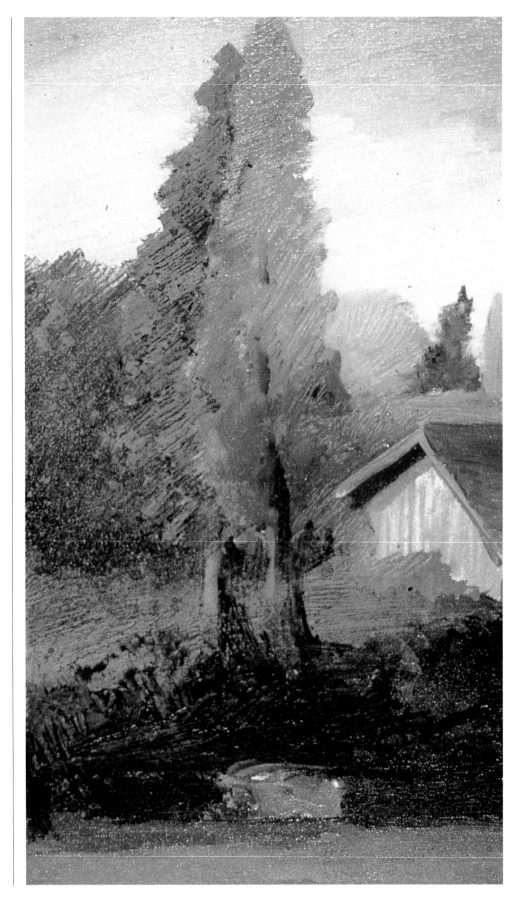

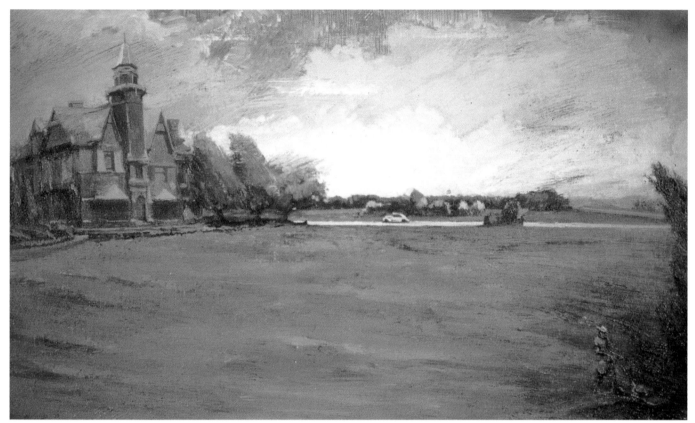

THE SUMMER MANSION
Oil on canvas,
16 × 20"
(40.6 × 50.8 cm).
Collection of Carol Schmidt.

I did this painting from my imagination after looking at a book on old houses. Using a limited, almost monochromatic palette, I worked wet-on-wet to get down the general lights and darks of the composition. The paint quality of the immense front lawn and the surrounding foliage clearly illustrates how the wet-on-wet approach works when color is handled in a thick manner.

BLOCKS OF COLOR

Working with blocks of color is yet another basic direct painting method, one that always makes me think of the 19th-century French painter Paul Cézanne, who took the technique to perfection. In this approach, the artist utilizes large to medium-size strokes of oil paint—"blocks"—to develop his painting. These blocks of paint form a network of color that can be used to build the composition from beginning to end. Cézanne's paintings evolved from just such a network of paint blots and strokes.

In this method, the painting proceeds from broad and simple paint strokes that then become smaller and more complex and detailed as the work progresses. Painting with blocks of color differs from the preceding alla prima approaches in that most of the color mixing is done on the palette rather than directly on the canvas.

Here is how it works. The painter lays out a large palette of colors and, using large flat bristle brushes, begins to block out the composition in a simple format with big, flat strokes, establishing the "feel" of the painting. Here the artist resembles a sculptor modeling forms, but instead of clay the material is oil paint. These first big, simple strokes contain little or no medium. The paint is kept relatively thin in the early stages, and any excess is scraped down with a palette knife.

Once the composition has been established, details and refinements are worked out. Paint applications are still blocklike, except now they are smaller in size and "fatter" with oil and color. As the painting progresses toward completion, the color blocks become thicker and more jewel-like.

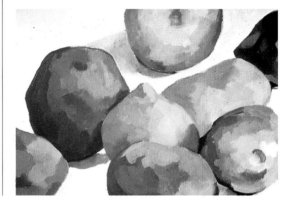

These two still life paintings show in a somewhat exaggerated way the principle of applying oil paint as blocks of color. Color, volume, and plane changes are all indicated by a myriad of color patches. Each color patch, or block, is mixed on the palette first, then is applied to the canvas in a flat manner, with no modeling. The overall effect resembles that of a mosaic.

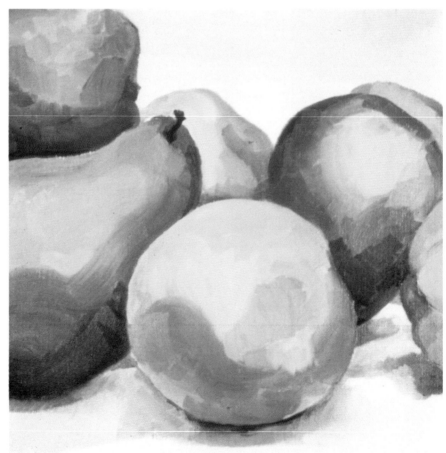

CAMERA
Oil on canvas, 18 × 24"
(45.7 × 61.0 cm).
Private collection.

I made this painting with the idea of just doing an exercise in simple observation. I set up my old 35mm camera on a clean white tabletop with nothing around it and tried to document what I saw. The end result was an image of the camera all right, but a camera that seemed almost as if it were some sort of living creature, tentacles and all. Small blocks of color mark the multitude of plane changes and subtle color variations that I observed in this simple setup.

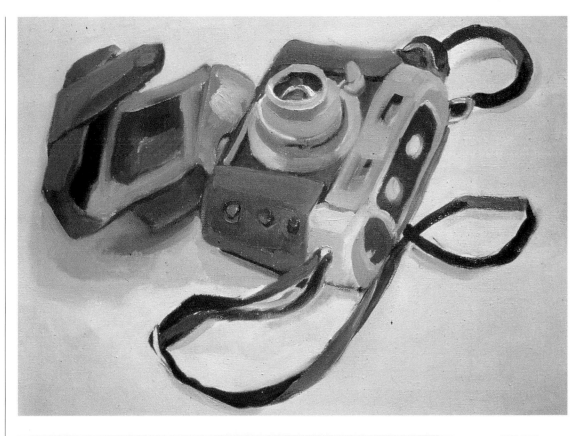

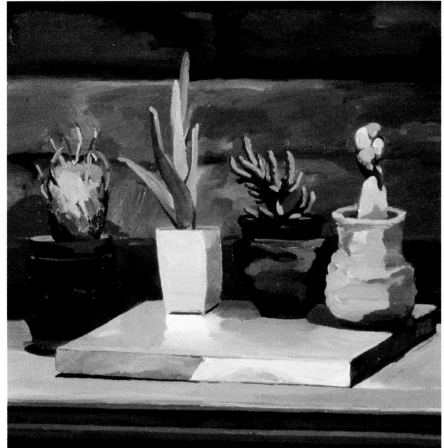

STILL LIFE WITH CACTUS
Oil on canvas, 18 × 18"
(45.7 × 45.7 cm).
Collection of the artist.

I kept the color in this small still life restricted to an earth palette. No cool colors were used. The paint was applied in clearly delineated colored shapes so sharp they could have been cutouts. I used little or no blending, so the color has a sharp, hard-edged quality that gives this painting a crisp, almost "desert" look appropriate to the subject.

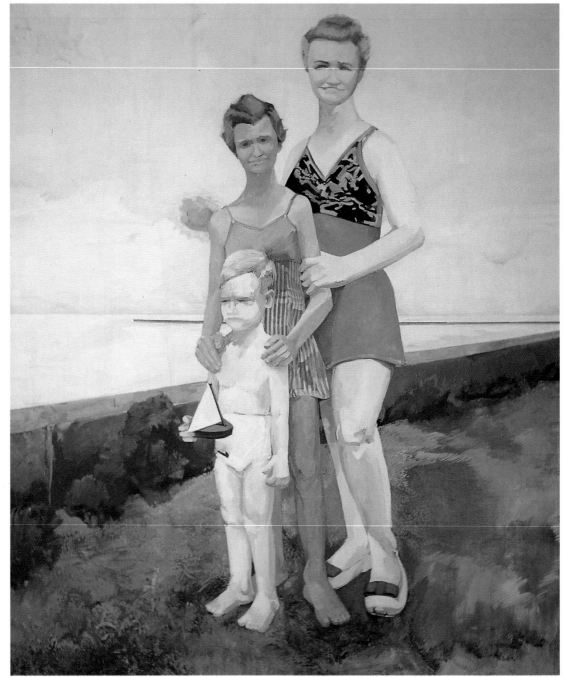

THE MANDEVILLE TRIO
Oil on canvas,
48 × 40"
(121.9 × 101.6 cm).
Collection of
Civia Snow.

In spite of the fact that the light depicted in this painting is hot and hazy, the overall paint quality is one of very clear, crisp color shapes. I used almost no modeling; rather, I achieved tonal variations by breaking color into small but closely related shapes. Because these color shapes are close to one another in value, they indeed appear to model three dimensional form. The three standing figures have an almost architectural quality to them; their presence on this lonely shoreline seems more sculptural than lifelike.

DABBING

Dabbing is a variation of the color block method of direct painting. In this approach the artist uses small strokes—dabs—of oil color to slowly build images into a final picture. In its purest form of execution, dabbing does not involve blending. Paint is applied directly in relatively small shapes to form a mesh of color and light in a sort of large-scale pointillism.

Dabbing calls for strokes that are fairly uniform in size and are sort of like little circles. The oil color is not brushed onto the canvas but rather "poked" onto it. Often, small linear strokes are applied along with the dabs to create textural variety, much like cross-hatching. Yet another variation is to slice into the dab and dot pattern with a palette knife for a slashing effect.

In general, dabbing techniques are best executed with a bright brush—a short, stubby flat. Both bristle and sable brights work well with this method. An effective medium to use in dabbing is stand oil, which allows the paint dabs to puddle and smooth as they settle on the canvas, resulting in a surface that has the look of beautiful appliquéd fabric.

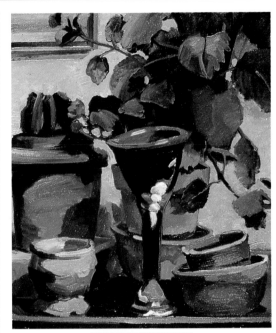

CERAMICS WITH BEGONIA
Oil on canvas, 14 × 12" (35.6 × 30.5 cm).
Private collection.

Dabbing is very much like the color-block technique but employs smaller strokes. In this painting the color shapes and dabs are highly individualized in character. The juxtaposition of light and dark dabs of color are so exaggerated that the painting takes on an overall "camouflage" effect.

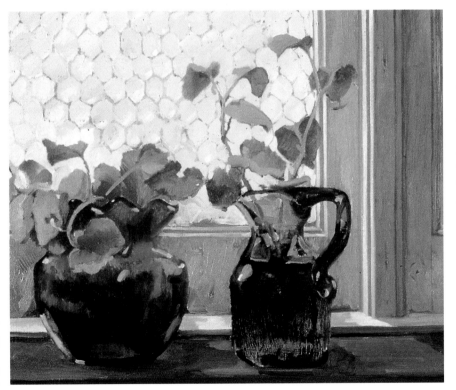

WINDOW CUTTINGS
Oil on canvas, 14 × 18"
(35.6 × 45.7 cm).
Private collection.

This still life depicts the various effects of light on glass. Although its shiny transparencies and polished reflections appear to be smoothly blended, the painting is actually made up of myriad dense, opaque dabs of oil paint. The color has been applied in small "pads" or color mounds; nothing is blended or smoothed together, even though it looks that way.

DABBING

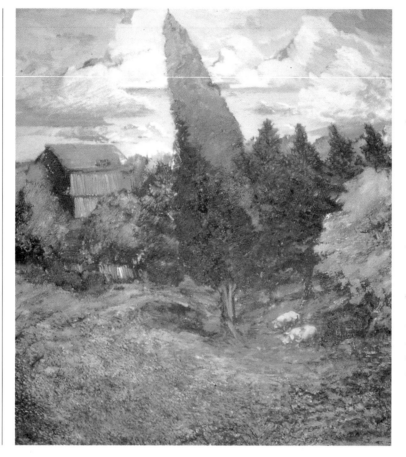

LANDSCAPE WITH PIGS
Oil on canvas, 40 × 30"
(101.6 × 76.2 cm).
Collection of Catherine Grey.

Both of these landscapes were done in a mixed technique of dabbing and palette knife painting. The dense foliage in each was depicted with a monochromatic "carpet" of color dabs. In some areas I indented the dabbing to create a sensual, almost rhythmic feeling that would suggest the living earth itself. This effect is especially apparent in Landscape with Pigs, *where both the sky and, in particular, the richly textured ground seem to swirl with natural energy. This patterned texture is less noticeable in* Jersey Fields; *there, the paint dabs are used to create color and spatial changes.*

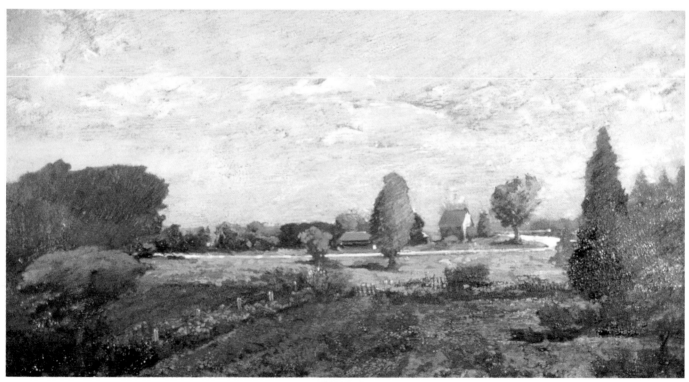

JERSEY FIELDS
Oil on canvas, 24 × 42" (61.0 × 106.7 cm).
Collection of the artist.

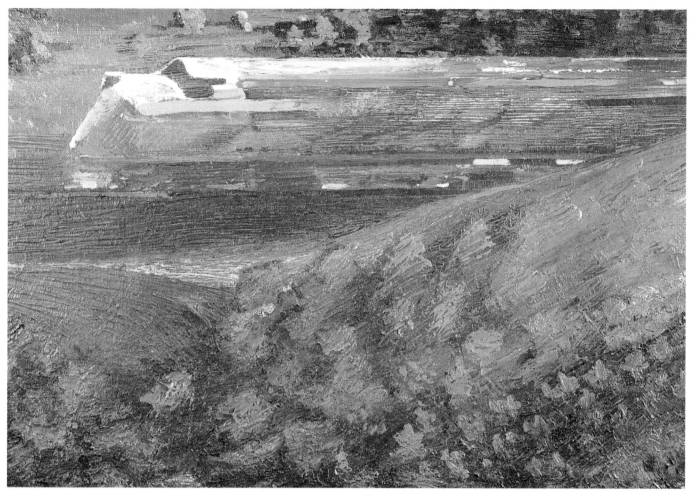

SILVER TRAIN (detail)
Oil on canvas,
18 × 30" (45.7 × 76.2 cm).
Collection of the artist.

This is basically a palette knife painting, but one that employs the dabbing technique. Paint dabs can be made with either a brush or a palette knife, or, as here, with a combination of these tools. The short grass and shrubbery in the foreground hill were made with a palette knife, while the shrubs in the background were executed with a brush. My intent was to create an active, almost "organic" texture for all the foliage in this painting that would make it appear to be in motion.

DRYBRUSH

Drybrush technique, simply put, is a dabbing method that involves using large, stiff bristle brushes to stipple paint onto the support. The paint used in this approach is low in oil and medium—hence the term *dry*brush.

Besides a stiff bristle brush, other tools, such as rags, sponges, and toothbrushes, can be used as stipplers as well; almost anything will do. The tool isn't the important thing, really; what matters is the relatively slow buildup of a broken-color surface. Drybrush leaves a splatter of oil color that is not like a typical brushstroke. Rather than appearing solid, color applied this way is diffused and broken, as if it had been sprayed on thickly.

The quality of drybrush is one of rough edges and glowing, diffused light. Using drybrush to build up color slowly is almost like working with charcoal or pastel instead of oil paint. The advantage of this technique is that only the most general description of what you're after is immediately apparent; the painting idea evolves very slowly, leaving open many possibilities for change.

Drybrush is at its most effective at the beginning of a painting and, perhaps paradoxically, when a painting is nearing completion. In the early stages of work, the diffused brushstrokes keep the composition general, uncluttered, and open to change. Yet when applied at the end of a painting, the same brushstrokes provide a rich and glowing texture.

Drybrush can be done on any support, be it canvas, panel, or paper. I personally like using solid supports such as Masonite panels or paper for my drybrush work. The bounce of a stretched canvas support becomes a little annoying and affects the paint application if you use too much pressure.

In the end, drybrush paintings can stand alone as finished works in and of themselves, but they also can be very useful as textural underpaintings for transparent glazing techniques. The rough, uneven surface produced by drybrush provides a very provocative substrate for glazed oil colors, which catch in its nooks and collect in miniature puddles, attaining a new and vibrant life.

DEMONSTRATION

In the drybrush technique, color is stippled onto the painting surface with a stiff brush or other tool to build layers of diffuse, beautifully textured broken color. To achieve this effect the paint must be somewhat stiff and low in oil and medium.

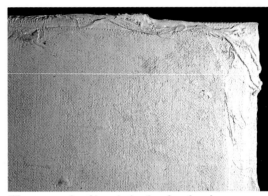

The support for this painting is a handmade canvas panel coated with acrylic modeling paste containing sand. The idea behind drybrush is to create a texture, and a gritty surface offers a head start.

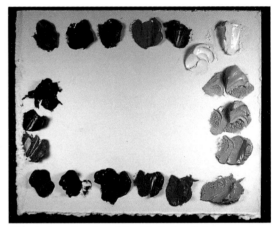

Here is the palette I used for this drybrush demonstration. I laid out the colors 24 hours before I began the painting so that they would stiffen a bit. Drybrush is more effective with non-oily, stiff paints.

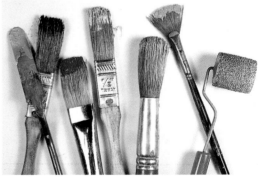

Some of the typical tools used in drybrush are palette knives, bristle brushes (including small house painting brushes) that are loose and flexible but resilient, bristle fan blenders (the tips of the bristles are used to make dots rather than to blend), and small paint rollers.

I draw in the main outline of my landscape—a grassy knoll with rocks overlooking the ocean—with a bristle brush using a simple palette of terre verte and burnt sienna, thinning the color with a small bit of turpentine. This is the only time any solvent or medium will be used in this demonstration. Drybrush means just what its name implies: nothing wet. In other words, no medium.

After drawing the rough outline, I cover the various areas of the landscape with thin washes of the appropriate local colors. I use a long-haired bristle brush and keep the washes active and loose, letting the textured ground show through.

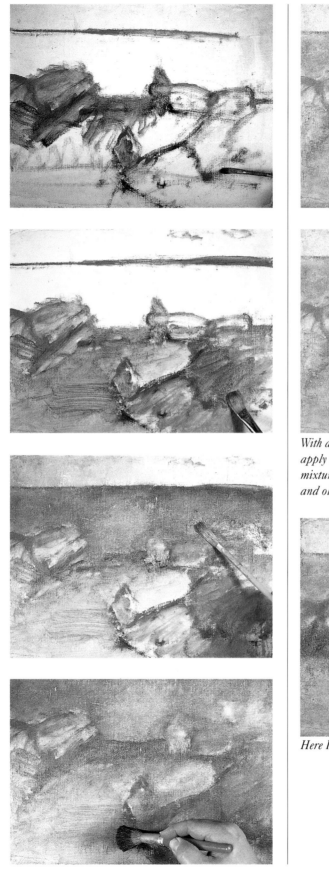

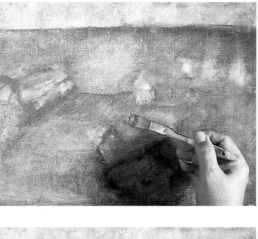

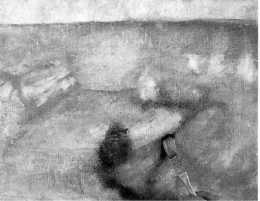

With a short bristle house painting brush, I begin to apply the first layers of pure, "dry" paint, using a mixture of cadmium yellow and viridian for the grass and olive green for the trees.

I use a dry (no paint), short stipple brush to pick up some of the color. This is done to exploit the textured ground even further; it's a kind of reverse drawing. After I get the look I want, I leave the painting to dry for an hour or two.

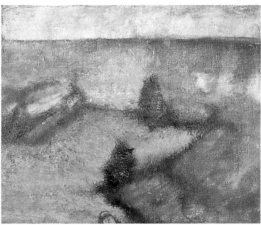

Here I'm spreading the colors across the landscape.

DRYBRUSH

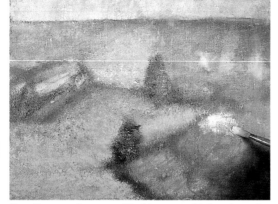

Small areas of opaque off-whites are added to the rocks.

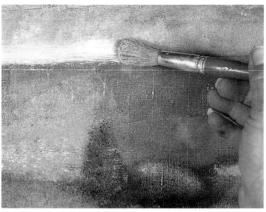

I dab some light tones into the sky along the horizon.

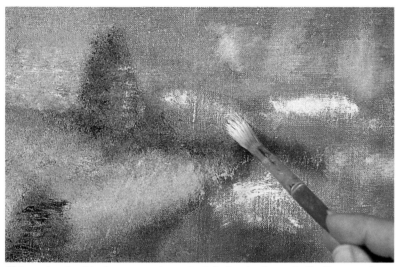

Using a brush with almost no paint on it, I drybrush a haze of off-white onto the dark rocks.

Clouds are drybrushed into the sky.

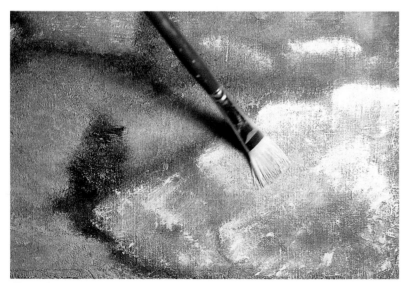

Now using a flat, dry brush, I disperse more white paint, creating a broken texture across the flat rocks.

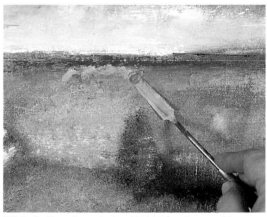

With the flat of a painting knife, I apply more blue mixed with white to the ocean all the way across the horizon. I put the paint down freely and a bit heavily, because in the next step I'm going to spread it with a small paint roller.

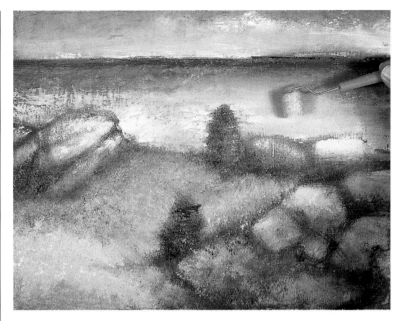

Here I use a small paint roller to spread the blue throughout the entire ocean.

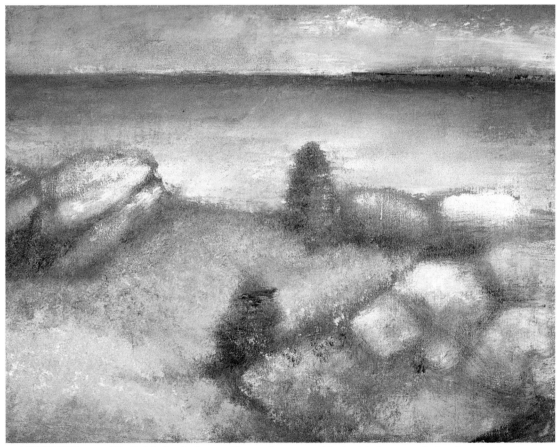

LOBSTER COVE
Oil on canvas panel,
16 × 20"
(40.6 × 50.8 cm).
Collection of the artist.

The finished painting combines a dry, textured look with the naturalistic colors of a landscape. Since no additional oil was used, the overall surface of the painting has a nonreflective matte finish, which in this case enhances the dry, early August feeling of this Maine landscape.

DRYBRUSH

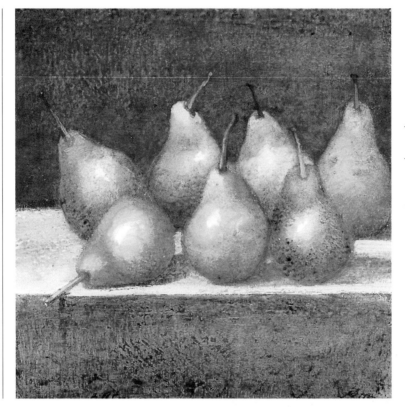

VATICAN ENSEMBLE
Oil on sized paper, 12 × 12"
(30.5 × 30.5 cm). Private collection.

I started this painting using drybrush techniques, especially along the base of the still life. After the drybrush stage had dried for a few days, I used the dabbled textures as an underpainting for several layers of oil glazing. Drybrush paintings often provide interesting underpaintings for glazing techniques.

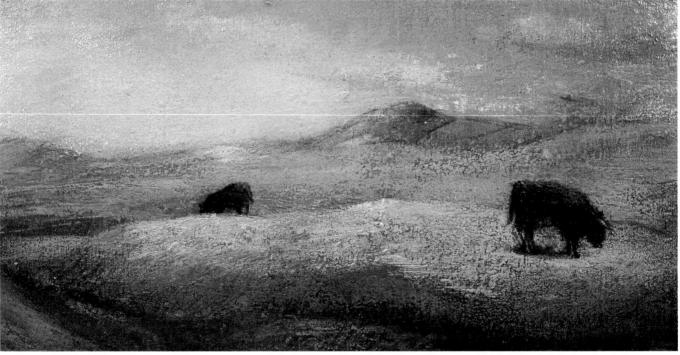

BLACK COWS
Oil on canvas, 10 × 20" (25.4 × 50.8 cm).
Collection of the artist.

The grassy textures of the foreground in this landscape illustrate an effective use of drybrush technique.

PALETTE KNIFE PAINTING

Palette knives are used to create textural effects that cannot be obtained with brushes alone. They come in all sizes and shapes, from sharp and angled to round and flat, so that almost any kind of texture can be achieved with them. Oil paints are a natural for palette knife techniques, their slow drying time working in the artist's favor to produce interesting results. Two of the great advantages of knife painting are that it's fast, and that there are no brushes to clean afterward.

Palette knife painting is about as direct an application method as you can get, short of squirting oil paint onto the canvas right out of the tube. In this approach the white canvas is a little bit like a large palette. Color is applied with the knives and worked all over the surface with them; it can be mixed directly on the canvas or on the palette itself. Changes and corrections are made by scraping off color rather than by painting directly over it. With knife painting it doesn't hurt to use heavy modifiers, such as Grumbacher's Zec, Winsor & Newton's Oleopasto, or Gamblin's Cold Wax Medium. The buildup of paint textures is what's going to happen anyway, so you might as well exaggerate it. Keep a large supply of rags and towels on hand for wiping your knives clean as you work.

Colors applied with palette knives have a unique brightness about them, adding up to an overall quality of paint clarity. Although attaining refined details is not what knife painting is all about, with skill and control, more detail than you might imagine is possible, especially when you use thin, slashing lines and dabs. As such, what's scraped away is as revealing as what is applied; both are telling and beautiful.

DEMONSTRATION

Palette knives come in a variety of shapes and sizes, some of them functioning as drawing tools, others as large flat brushes. In building a composition, they are used both to deliver paint to the canvas and to scrape it away. The result of this kind of loose paint handling is bold texture and fresh, clean-looking color.

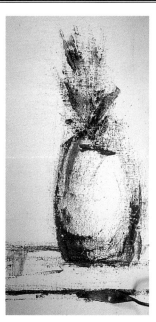

Using just the tip of a thin palette knife, I draw the outline of my subject, a pineapple. I handle the knife as if it were a piece of charcoal.

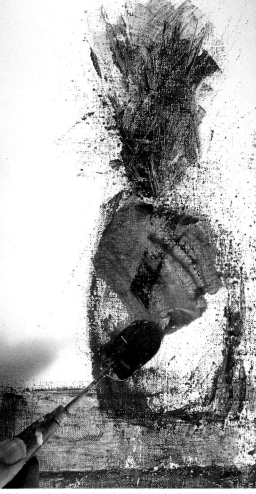

With a wide, flat palette knife I apply the various local colors, handling the knife as if it were a large flat brush to put down the paint.

PALETTE KNIFE PAINTING

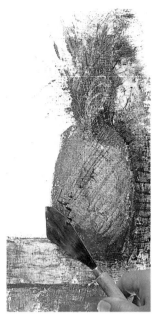

I create a rough texture by scraping down excess paint with a large knife. This scraping down also serves to refine the outlines of the subject.

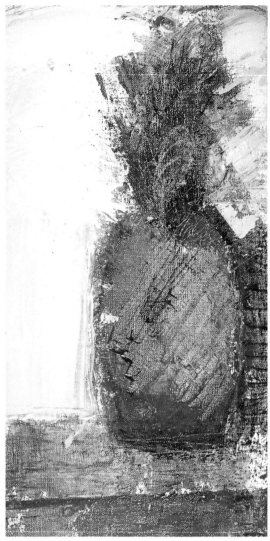

With a multifaceted painting knife I thickly apply white paint to the background.

All of the first coats of paint have been applied. I am now ready to add more color, body, and texture.

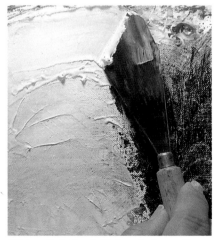

With a thick, flat knife I make large, flat strokes of dark green in the upper part of the pineapple's stem.

I add fuller-bodied color and texture to the pineapple's outer skin, using a flat knife for thick paint applications, a long, thin knife for drawing dark lines, and a sharply angled painting knife for establishing highlights.

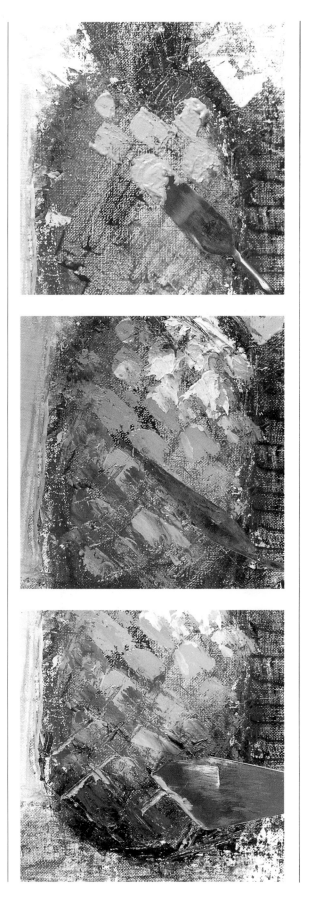

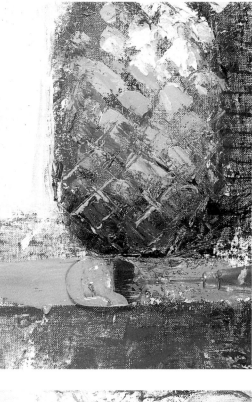

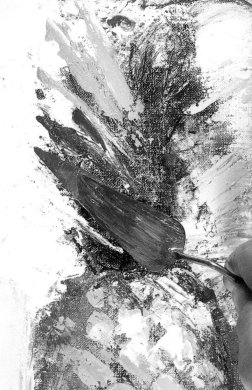

Using assorted large, flat knives I add the final coats of flat color. I've added some oil to the paint for these final coats to create a "juicier" look.

PALETTE KNIFE PAINTING

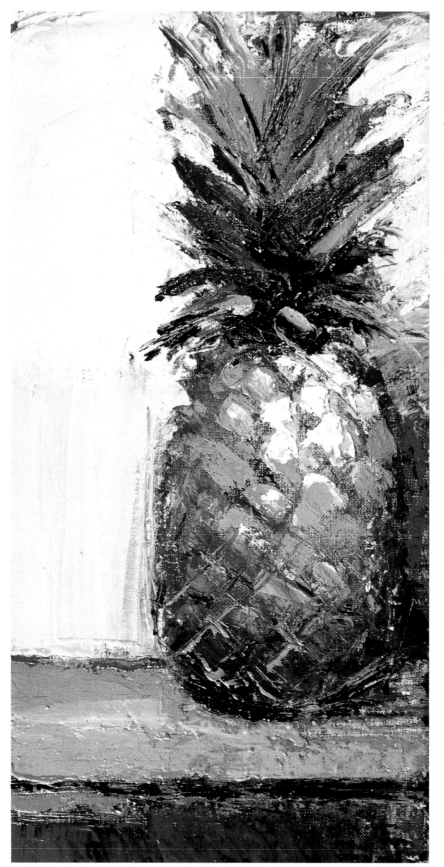

The beauty of palette knife painting is in the looseness of the paint application. It is almost impossible to get tight or smoothly blended passages with the knife. Moreover, there is a clean, fresh look to oil colors that have been manipulated with a palette knife. This technique may not allow for precise paint control, but it does create a situation in which interesting and unexpected pleasant surprises can happen.

REVERSE PALETTE KNIFE TECHNIQUE

One alternative use for the palette knife is as a drawing tool—or, more specifically, as a stylus for doing negative, or reverse, drawings into wet oil paint. Color is applied to the painting surface, and the knife is used to scrape away wet paint to expose the ground underneath. This is a kind of palette knife version of the wipe-out technique, and it is facilitated by oil paint's slow drying time.

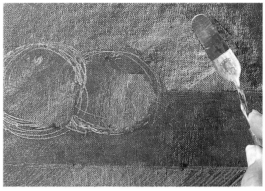

I use the edge of the knife to scrape away larger areas of color.

With a broad knife I totally cover the canvas support with color. I work the knife around in a circular motion in order to get a paint surface that is absolutely flat.

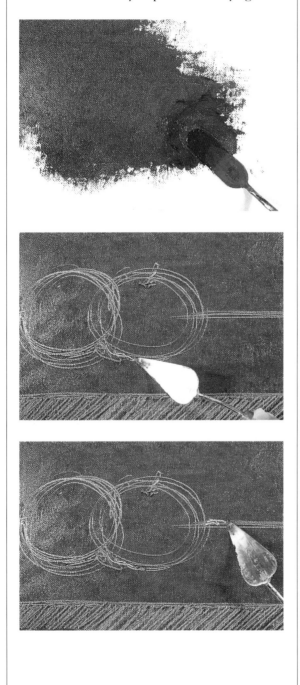

Using the tip of a pointed knife as a stylus, I draw thin lines into my field of wet oil paint. The lines of my drawing expose the white ground.

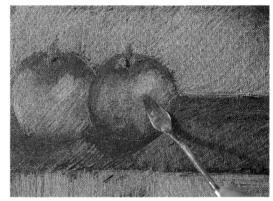

Using the tip and the side of the knife, I refine and finish my drawing.

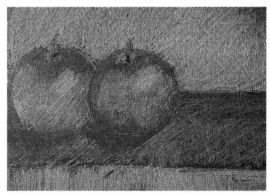

The finished reverse drawing is amazingly subtle and detailed. When it has dried completely, the drawing can be "polished" further by scraping off any excess dried paint with the edge of the knife. A reverse drawing such as this can serve as the first layer of a new painting or as a grisaille for an oil-glazed painting.

SMOOTH BLENDING

Oil paint can be applied to produce a rough-textured surface, as in impasto, or one that is as smooth and seamless as glass.

To make a smooth oil painting, the first thing you must do is pick the right support for the job. Flat hardwood or Masonite panels that have been properly sized and sanded smooth with fine sandpaper are obvious choices; metal is also an option if the painting is going to be small. If your choice is linen, stick with portrait-grade or another very fine weave.

The idea behind doing a smooth-textured oil painting is to have no impastos whatsoever throughout any stage of work. For that reason, it is important to avoid mediums that cause oil paint to dry in ridges. Obviously this includes wax mediums, such as Dorland's, as well as impasto-producing modifiers such as Oleopasto or Zec. However, it is also important to keep linseed oil down to a minimum; use the paint pretty much as it comes from the tube, thinning it only with very, very small amounts of gum turpentine.

Make a careful drawing of your composition on a smooth support. To do this preliminary drawing, you can use either charcoal or pastels. In smooth blending techniques, a good clear drawing is essential. Any searching and developing with paint runs the risk of its building up to form ridges—which are to be avoided if eggshell smoothness is the goal. The first coat of oil paint is applied in clean, even strokes. Either bristle or soft brushes are okay, as long as they do not produce ridges.

From the very beginning of the painting, colors are blended together and smoothed using fan blenders. The fan blender is the most important brush in any smooth blending technique. Both bristle and sable are employed, sable, of course, yielding the most seamless blends. Keep several of these brushes on hand as you work and clean them often.

Remember, the idea is to keep everything smooth and avoid ridges. If unwanted ridges do occur along your paint strokes, there are several things you can do to eliminate them. If the paint has dried, scrape the edges with a palette knife, and if it's really dry, sand it with fine sandpaper (oil paint sands beautifully). If the paint is still wet, dab any ridges with a soft, dry brush, or with some sort of soft rag, like cotton. Alternatively, use foam-rubber brushes to flatten out the unwanted paint edges; small paint rollers will do the same trick.

To achieve a smooth surface, you may find it necessary to apply several layers of paint before the work is finished. Multiple layers and several sittings are okay, but be careful not build up too much paint. It is useful to keep in mind that smooth blending is a technique that works best when it is only part of the picture. Too much smooth blending is not a good thing. In its overall look, a painting should have a variety of textures—smooth blending in some areas, impasto and drybrush in others. Too much smooth blending results in a painting that seems weak and out of focus.

SMOOTH BLENDING SCHEMATIC

This sequence of illustrations shows how blending and manipulating wet oil paint can change the whole quality of an image. Here, the subject is a sphere on a tabletop. The basic composition is established with flat, hard-edged color shapes, which are then blended with soft brushes. The result is an atmospheric effect and a sphere that gives the illusion of being three-dimensional.

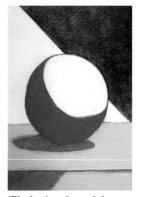

The basic colors of the composition are painted in a flat, hard-edged manner.

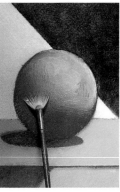

With a fan blender brush I blend the colors of the sphere.

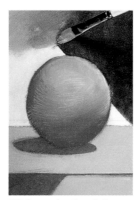

With another brush I blend the colors of the background shadows.

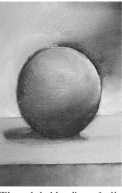

The subtle blending of all the flat colors gives an illusionistic effect.

DEMONSTRATION

To execute a painting in the smooth blending technique, you must start with a smooth support, such as a panel that has been sanded to a fine finish or finely woven, portrait-grade canvas. The idea is to keep everything eggshell-smooth and avoid having paint build up to form ridges. As work progresses, colors are blended together and smoothed with fan blenders.

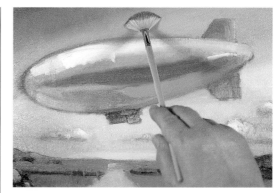

I sketch in my subject using pastel pencils and charcoal, then fix the finished drawing with a coat of retouch varnish.

Using oils thinned with turpentine and Liquin, I cover the main areas of the painting with a transparent glaze in preparation for the more opaque coats of paint to come later. The painting is left to dry for a few hours.

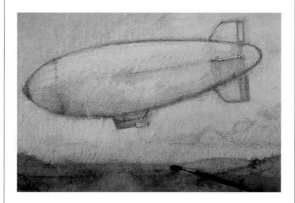

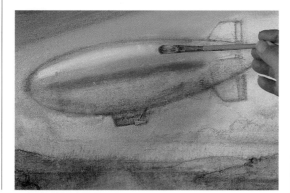

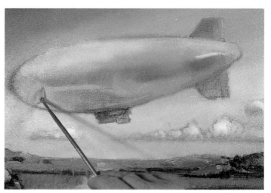

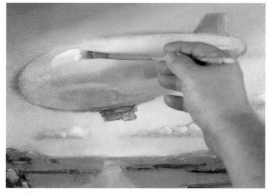

While the paint is still wet, I start to blend together all the hard-edged bands of color. I use several bristle fan blending brushes to do this, employing large brushes for the big areas and smaller ones for sections that call for more precision.

I add more white to intensify the highlight created by the sunlight reflecting off the nose of the blimp.

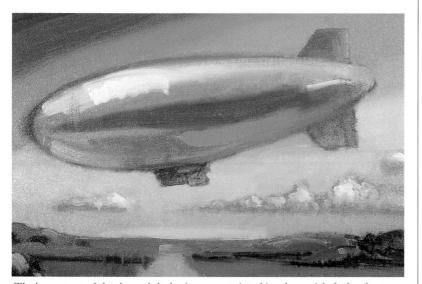

The lower part of the sky and the horizon are painted in along with the landscape underneath the blimp.

Smooth Blending

I deepen the color of the sky by adding French ultramarine blue at the top left corner of the painting, then use a soft sable fan blending brush to smooth out the deep blue sky even further.

I heighten the light along the horizon by adding a coat of a warm, off-white color between the land and the low clouds in the sky.

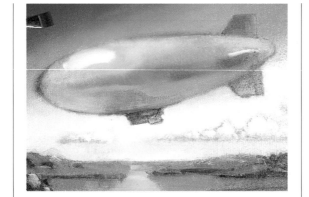

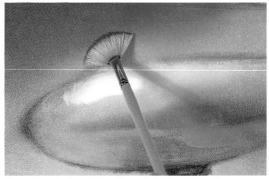

I work at the final blending of the deep blue sky.

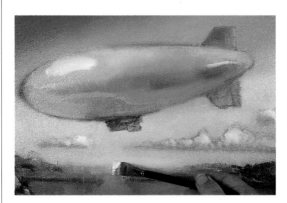

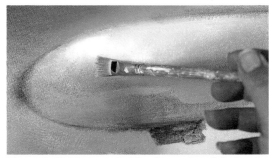

The main highlight on the blimp's nose is polished and refined with a soft-haired brush.

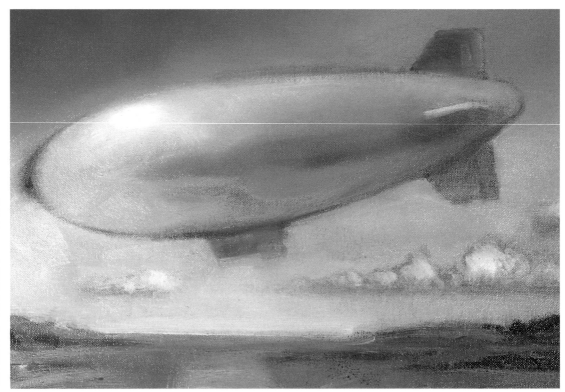

BLIMP
Oil on canvas board,
11 × 16"
(27.9 × 40.6 cm).
Collection of the artist.

My intent in this almost surrealistic painting was to depict a highly polished, silver-coated blimp in a clear sky. Because the blimp has a reflective surface, its colors are determined by the colors of the sky and surrounding landscape. Smooth blending techniques help create the illusion of a metallic surface as well as a clear blue sky.

IMPASTO

Impasto (meaning "dough" in Italian) is the opposite of smooth. This is paint that is mountainous, thick, and juicy. One of oil paint's unique and attractive qualities is that it really can be built up into high ridges. Thanks to oil's long open time, impastos can be scraped, manipulated, and reconstructed many times before the paint finally sets.

Impasto is a deliberately heavy buildup of paint, done to create emphasis and texture. It transforms an oil painting from being a two-dimensional illusion into becoming a three-dimensional object. Impastos give oil paintings their "meaty" look.

Here are some things to bear in mind as you incorporate impasto into your repertoire of painting techniques. To begin with, work on supports that are heavily textured. For canvas, select rough linen or jute; heavy #12 cotton is also great. For panels, rather than sand the ground smooth, you might juice up its texture with modeling paste, adding sand or carborundum to the surface. In addition to the usual oil painting brushes and palette knives, many other tools can be employed to make impasto paintings, from house painting brushes to spatulas—anything that creates a surface. Forget your sable and badger brushes for this technique.

The important thing is to select the right kind of paints and painting mediums. Impasto paintings are best achieved by using full-bodied oil paints that tend to be stiff and that dry relatively quickly, such as Winsor & Newton's Quick Drying White, and heavy-bodied textural mediums like Oleopasto and Zec.

Another great impasto builder is wax in the form of an oil painting medium, such as Gamblin's Cold Wax Medium or Dorland's Wax Medium. The exotic Maroger Medium, which contains wax along with mastic and black oil, is another fine producer of impasto, and it enriches color at the same time it builds texture.

DEMONSTRATION

Impasto is an application of very thick paint so that it has an almost sculptural quality. Its texture is usually enriched by the marks of the brush, palette knife, or other painting tool. Impasto techniques call for stiff, heavy-bodied paints and textural mediums, and are best when executed on a heavily textured surface.

The support for the painting in this demonstration has a very rough surface. I glued several layers of canvas together and attached them to a Masonite panel and, to make the edges particularly rough, stuck down the loose ends with modeling paste.

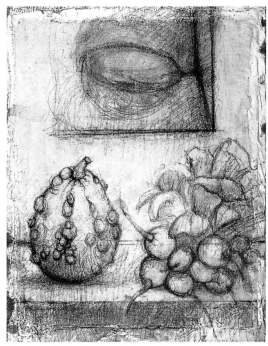

A pen and ink drawing with touches of charcoal serves as a foundation.

IMPASTO

The first coat of paint is a transparent mixture of oil color with Winsor & Newton's Oleopasto and Grumbacher's Zec, both fast-drying mediums noted for creating heavy impasto surfaces.

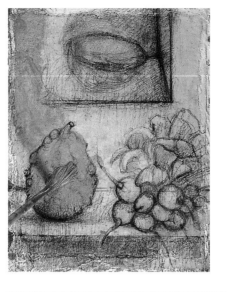

Here you can see the basic buildup of local color. All the colors have been mixed with a combination of Oleopasto and Zec. I apply off-white to the background of the still life, then the various green local colors, and then brown and yellow in the small niche area.

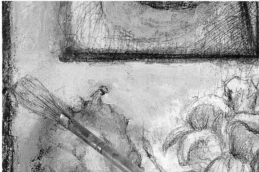

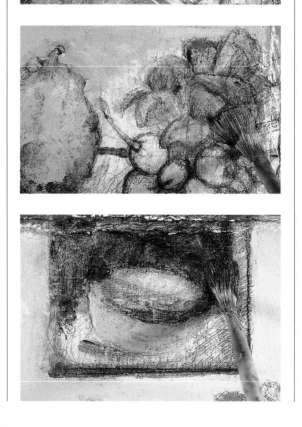

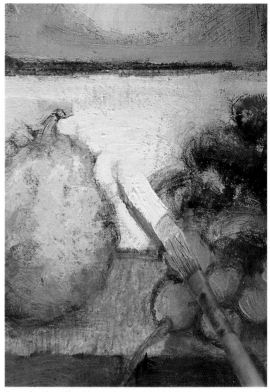

I make the off-white color particularly heavy and thick.

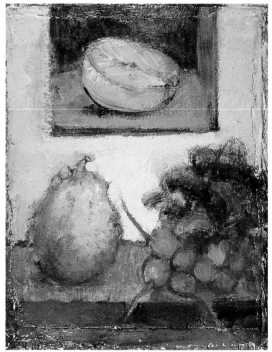

The painting has been totally covered with its first heavy coat of local color. At this point it is allowed to dry for a while, but since the paint has been mixed with Zec, this doesn't take too long. In about three hours I am ready to come in with the second layer of paint. Without the Zec or the Oleopasto, the drying would take days.

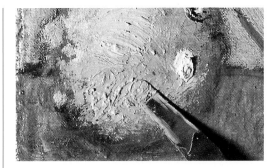

I use a palette knife to build up a rough texture at the base of the gourd. In the finished painting you can see the extremely heavy final color applications. They, too, are mixed with Zec, but this time I used less than in the first coats. However, I did add large amounts of the alkyd medium Wingel, which makes the colors both thicker and more fluid, as well as adds a gloss. Note the mounds of very fluid white and cadmium yellow in the grapefruit slice. The extra gloss in the radishes is the result of adding Wingel to my oil colors.

STILL LIFE WITH GRAPEFRUIT, GOURD, AND RADISHES
Oil on handmade canvas panel, 14 × 11" (35.6 × 27.9 cm). Collection of the artist.

The thickly encrusted, heavily painted passages in this still life mimic the textures of the surfaces they are intended to depict. The final layers of paint were applied almost directly from the tube in order to achieve a maximum richness of color and impasto texture.

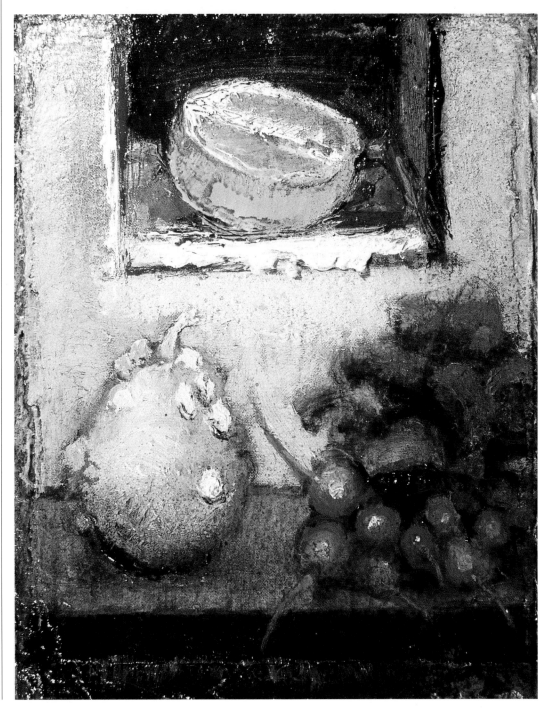

SHADOW

One of the most unifying elements in any oil painting is the successful use of light and shadow. It is the distribution of light tones and dark tones that gives a painting a sense of reality. Even more than color, tonal value is what endows a painting with solidity. The proper control of tonal value is essential to any oil painter who wishes to create a sense of realism in his or her work.

Lights and darks work in several ways in basic oil painting, one of which is to establish form. The manner in which light and dark colors are placed in a painting creates a "lighted direction." And when light comes from a clear direction, the objects depicted display a believable quality of illumination—convincing highlights and shadows. Depicting light as illumination is totally a function of tonal value, and mastering tonal control is crucial to developing an effective oil painting technique.

Lights and darks can also create an overall mood. A painting can exist completely within the world of one major tonal value. In other words, the colors in a given composition can favor a palette that is predominantly dark, or one that is predominantly light. Oil paints work equally well in either case, since they easily can span the entire range of tonal values. This quality has enabled artists to use oils to depict perfect "emotional atmospheres"—moods and feelings expressed solely in terms of lightness or darkness.

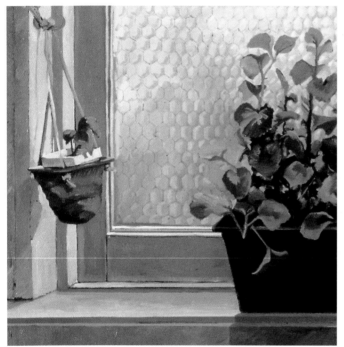

WINDOW BOX
Oil on canvas,
18 × 18" (45.7 × 45.7 cm).
Private collection.

An important factor in creating a successful illusion of three-dimensional form is to have a clear light source. If nothing else, this still life certainly has that. The basic light comes in through the frosted window, putting the window box in silhouette and creating the cast shadow of the hanging plant. Reflected light throws more illumination on the objects as well.

QUARTET
Oil on canvas,
36 × 36" (91.4 × 91.4 cm).
Collection of the artist.

Four plants in ceramic pots are rendered simply, modeled by light that appears to enter the scene from the painting's upper right-hand corner. By juxtaposing the light-colored pot and plant against the dark background at left and the dark pot and plant against the light background at right, I reinforce the illusion of real space. The central white flower acts as an anchoring compass point.

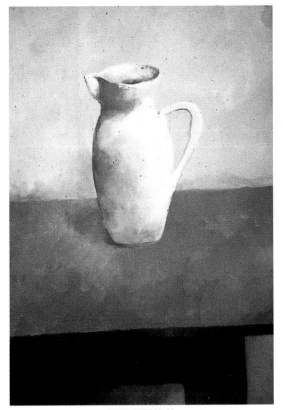

THE WHITE VASE
Oil on canvas, 24 × 18" (61.0 × 45.7 cm).
Collection of the artist.

Here the depiction of form is very subdued. There are hardly any cast shadows, and the rendering of volume is kept to a minimum. The point is that modeling does not always have to be excessive to be effective.

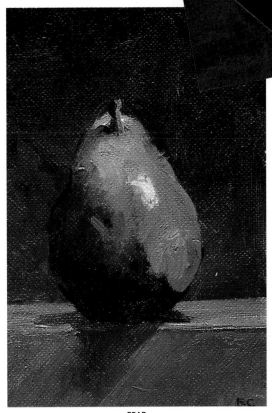

PEAR
Oil on canvas, 6 × 4" (15.2 × 10.2 cm).
Private collection.

Dark colors and dramatic lighting can always be relied upon to create a strong sense of realism and volume. Vincent van Gogh once said that darker colors always created a stronger sense of reality. In this painting, the medium I used was sun-thickened linseed oil, which deepens colors and creates a gently textured impasto.

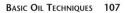

CITY VIEW
Oil on paper, 12 × 16"
(30.5 × 40.6 cm).
Private collection.

This landscape was done in a high-value mode to capture the light of high noon on a hazy day. The high-key color and overhead lighting destroy any illusion of form; individual items appear flat. Still, the painting retains a feeling of deep space, achieved through atmospheric effects rather than linear perspective.

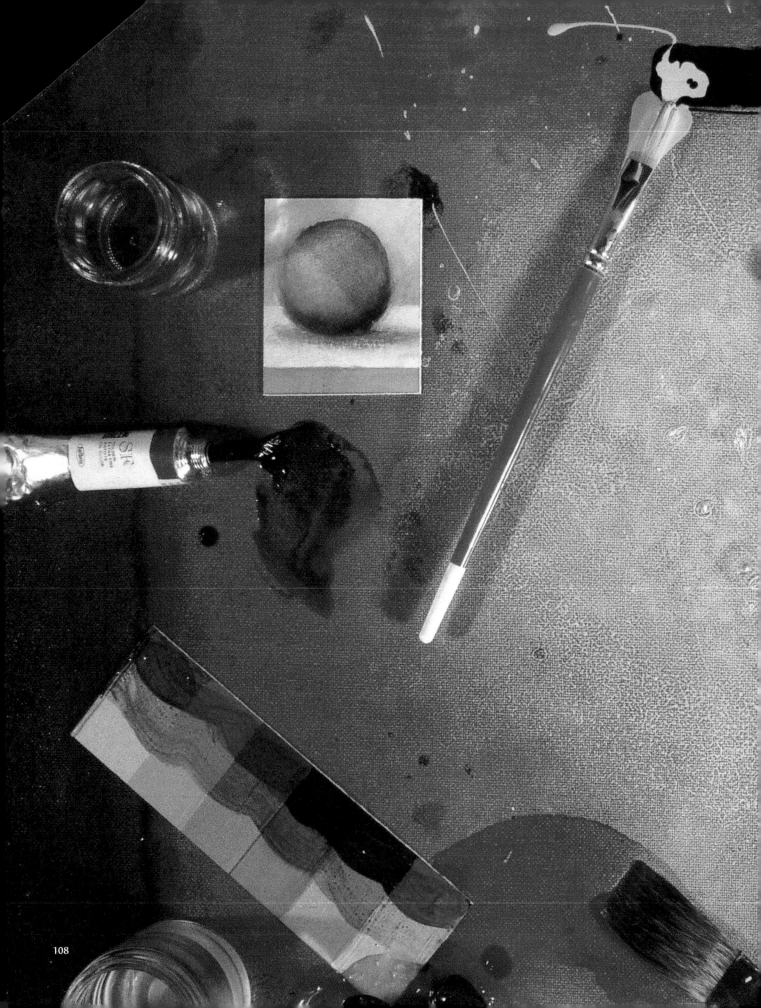

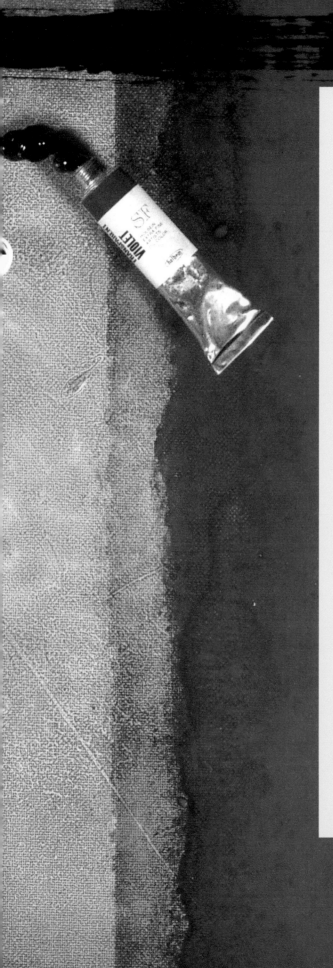

GLAZING AND SCUMBLING

The glaze is the oldest known form of oil paint used in easel painting, its inception dating back to at least the early 15th century. At the time, oil paint was used only in its transparent mode, acting as a sort of colored varnish to unify the cross-hatching of the more opaque egg tempera underpainting. But this additional step changed the look of painting forever. The optical interactions produced by applying a deeply colored, transparent glaze over an opaque base resulted in an array of jewel-like effects never before seen in painting. It was this technical relationship between opaque and transparent painting that gave us the beautiful masterpieces of the next 400 years.

Glazing isn't particularly popular these days, having died out around the same time as the Beaux-Arts academic traditions. Nevertheless, it is a perfectly natural way to work with oils. As a technique it is fairly easy to do, and today there are many new developments that make it even more flexible and easier to master.

Here we will look at various ways to handle transparent and opaque color, examining different kinds of grisaille, or tonal underpaintings, and addressing which actual colors work best for glazing. Both classic and offbeat approaches are covered. We will also see how to incorporate texture and direct painting techniques into the glazing process.

THE CONCEPT OF OIL GLAZING

Glazing with oils is a very simple idea. Basically it means that instead of mixing two colors together directly to create a third, you instead layer one over the other separately, treating each like a piece of colored glass. The third color that results is the product of an optical combination rather than a direct physical mixture. In each case, the resulting third colors have the same final hue identity, but not the same visual effect. The glazed one will appear to have more depth, more of a glow than the mixed one. The glazed color seems to reflect light, while the mixed one appears to absorb it.

When we look at a jar of linseed oil we can see right through it. Obviously it's not as clear as water; it's a little golden-yellow, but very transparent nonetheless. This quality of transparency often carries over to oil paint made with linseed oil, depending upon the individual pigment involved. Every oil color that exists is considered either transparent or opaque, with more than half the available palette naturally transparent to begin with. They and many semitransparent colors can be made even more transparent with the addition of extra oil or a glaze medium. So potentially, the majority of our oil colors can be converted into glazes so that they perform, as mentioned above, like sheets of colored or stained glass.

Some colors are truly opaque and cannot be made transparent. These include the cadmiums, Naples yellow, and cerulean blue, just to name a few. The most opaque oil color of all is white, especially lead and titanium white. Nothing can make white transparent, and any color (transparent or otherwise) added to it becomes opaque as well. Thus, all the colors in the oil palette have the potential for opacity with the simple addition of titanium or lead white.

The almost equal balance between transparent and opaque colors in the oil palette gives this medium an advantage over other painting mediums. It also makes glazing in oils a fairly easy and natural process, one that yields astoundingly beautiful results.

Here is how it works in actual practice. Any paint passage that has adequately dried can serve as an underpainting, or ground, for a layer of color to be glazed over it. Light-value underpaintings give the best results; in fact, the closer to white they are, the better, because each glaze applied will darken the overall tonal values. Dark underpaintings can work too, but not as effectively.

The theory behind the practice of glazing is that color and form are kept separate. That is to say, the design and composition that give a painting its essential form are planned and executed without the use of color. This is done through a device called the *grisaille*, a preliminary layer of paint traditionally executed in monochrome, usually a gray (*gris* in French, hence the term), that describes in a very complete way what the painting will look like. It is the absolute foundation of the painting. In addition to being done in monochrome, the grisaille is also rendered in as high a value—as "blonde" a finish—as possible. This is important because, as noted above, the subsequent glaze layers will darken the overall tones of the painting.

Once the grisaille has dried, colors are applied to it in the form of transparent, oil-extended glazes. These colored glazes can be modified in myriad ways while still wet, but once dry, they stay put. Multiple glaze layers are possible, even as many as 20 or more. Opaque textures can be added and corrections made in any number and at any point along the way; such additions are called *scumbles*. Scumbles put additional "meat" into the overall look and feel of the painting.

For all the variables involved in the glazing and scumbling stages, the constant that remains is the solid foundation of the grisaille on which these multiple layers of paint are built. The grisaille is the "security blanket" of the entire painting; it is more or less absolute. Because of this, most glazed paintings require a fair amount of advance planning, unlike alla prima paintings, in which color and form are worked out spontaneously and simultaneously on the canvas.

This doesn't mean that in-progress changes are completely out of the question with glazing, though most of the pictorial searching is done at the drawing level long before paint even touches the canvas. The preliminary drawing may be as loose and flexible as any action painting, but the point is to establish the framework for a very clear underpainting. If the grisaille more or less expresses everything you want to say, then all else, especially the color, will automatically fall into place. With that in mind, it's easy to see why in the past so much emphasis was placed on solid drawing techniques. In one very real sense, glazed paintings can be considered colored drawings.

DEMONSTRATION

This sequence of illustrations demonstrates, in a simplified, schematic manner, how oil glazing works. The basic idea behind this technique is that color and form are kept separate. Composition and volumetric form are established in a monochromatic underpainting, or grisaille, and color is added in transparent washes, or glazes. Here I use the primary colors yellow, blue, and red.

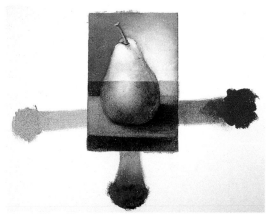

Here I apply a red glaze over the yellow and blue.

A simple grisaille underpainting of a pear.

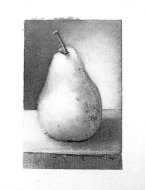

I apply a yellow glaze to the lower half of the grisaille, leaving the top half gray for comparison. Note how the color affects the painting.

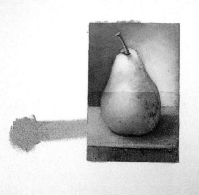

Over the yellow I glaze a blue.

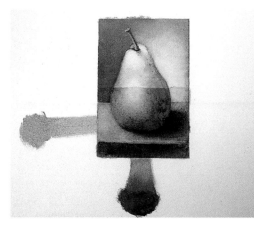

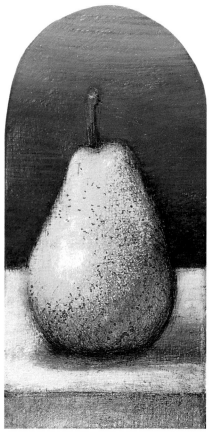

VENETIAN PEAR
Oil on wood panel, 8 × 4¹/₂" (20.3 × 11.4 cm).
Collection of the artist.

This is not the same pear depicted in the demonstration, but its development was similar. The painting started off as a pen and ink grisaille, on which I built numerous layers of colored glazes. In the title, "Venetian" alludes to the predominance of rich, glazed color characteristic of early Venetian painting, and to the deep blue background reminiscent of works by Giovanni Bellini.

Color and Oil Glazing

When glazing with oils, it helps to know which colors are transparent and which are opaque. It also helps to know a bit about color mixtures, even on the most fundamental level, such as that black and white make gray and yellow and red make orange. There is absolutely no mystery to any of this; it just takes a little experience and some basic information to get started.

Whether a particular oil color is transparent or opaque has to do simply with its inherent chemical makeup. An opaque color will offer more coverage than a transparent one; that much is obvious. But it is important to remember that opacity and transparency have nothing to do with color strength or color permanence. Both groups contain their share of fugitive colors as well as permanent ones, and weak tinters as well as powerful ones. Phthalo blue, for example, is a transparent color that is both very permanent and has powerful tinting strength. Chrome yellow, on the other hand, an opaque color, has weak tinting strength and borders on being fugitive.

Today many manufacturers, such as Rembrandt and Blockx, indicate whether a color is opaque or transparent right on the tube, and it's a big help. To make things even easier for you, here is a somewhat extended list of basic opaque and transparent colors. Use the opaque ones for your underpaintings, base colors, and scumbles, and use the transparent ones for your glazes.

Opaque Colors	Transparent Colors
Whites	
lead white	zinc white (semitransparent)
titanium white	
Yellows	
cadmium yellow (all tones)	aureolin (cobalt yellow)
Naples yellow	Indian yellow (all tones)
yellow ochre	transparent gold ochre
jaune brillant	transparent oxide yellow
nickel titanate yellow	stil de grain jaune
Reds and Oranges	
cadmium red (light & dark)	alizarin crimson
cadmium orange	rose madder (light & dark)
English red	ultramarine red
Mars red	quinacridone red
Venetian red	quinacridone burnt orange
terra rosa	transparent red oxide
vermilion	naphthol scarlet
	anthraquinoid red
	perinone orange

Opaque Colors	Transparent Colors
Greens	
chromium green oxide	viridian
permanent green	phthalo green
cadmium green	phthalo turquoise
	green gold
	terre verte
Browns	
burnt umber	burnt sienna
raw umber	raw sienna
Pozzuoli earth	brown madder alizarin
	transparent brown
	stil de grain brun
Blues	
cerulean blue	ultramarine blue
	cobalt blue
	phthalo blue
	manganese blue
	Prussian blue
	indanthrone blue
	indigo
Violets	
cadmium purple	cobalt violet
Mars violet	manganese violet
caput mortuum violet	carbazole violet
	quinacridone violet
	rose doré
	dioxazine purple
Blacks & Neutrals	
lamp black	ivory black
peach black	Davy's gray
Mars black	Payne's gray

It is interesting to note that all the basic hues are represented with both opaque and transparent versions—even white (though zinc white is only semitransparent). None of the opaque colors can be used as glazes; the cadmiums, for example, are just too dense and powerful ever to be extended into a glaze. The transparent colors, on the other hand, can be extended with oil-based mediums almost to the point of invisibility.

The list of transparent colors is longer than the opaque list, and some of them may seem unfamiliar, bearing such names as quinacridone, perinone, indanthrone, carbazole, anthraquinoid, and the like. These relatively new colors, including the phthalos, are synthetically made from organic compounds derived from coal tar. They are strong tinters and very lightfast, and some are good substitutes for more fugitive colors. Anthraquinoid red, for example, works well as a stand-in for the less reliable alizarin crimson. They can also substitute for more opaque colors—quinacridone red being a great transparent equivalent of cadmium red, for instance. The new synthetic colors have revolutionized oil glazing and expanded its possibilities.

It is obvious from this list that the blues comprise the largest number of transparent colors (cerulean being the only genuinely opaque blue), followed by the violets. But all of these transparent colors can be made opaque simply by adding white to them. And to make the transparent colors truly work as glazes, they must be extended with glaze mediums, which we'll talk about a little later on.

All the colors in this list are standard in the modern oil painter's palette. But today there are specially made transparent colors that are put out specifically for glazing. Three manufacturers offer different versions of these very useful colors. Holbein has a range of 10 transparent colors, as does Lefranc & Bourgeois, while Shiva offers 20 colors in its Permasol line—including a genuinely transparent white. Made of aluminosilicate and just enough titanium and zinc to make it white, Permasol white is almost a contradiction in terms, but produces a milky, opalescent texture that is occasionally useful. All of these special colors are made from lightfast pigments and are so transparent that they can be used for glazing straight from the tube without the addition of a glaze medium. They are a terrific modern asset to an ancient technique.

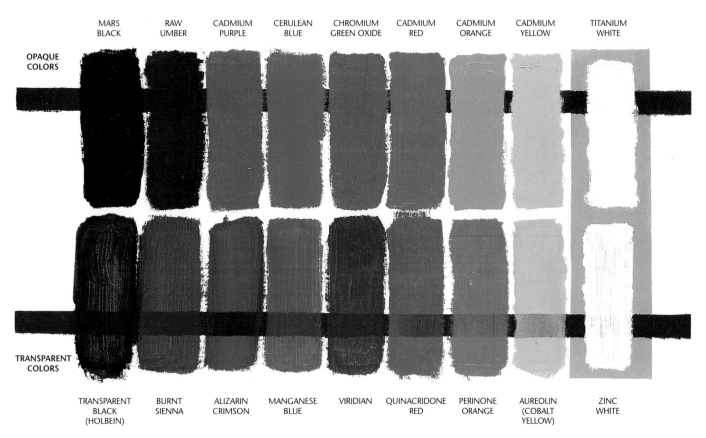

All oil colors fall into one of two distinct categories: opaque colors and transparent colors. Knowing which colors are which is essential for the obvious reason that some can be used as glazes, while others are best employed as opaque undercoats. It's important to know that cadmium yellow, for example, is very opaque and almost impossible to glaze with, but aureolin yellow is very transparent and glazes beautifully.

This chart organizes the major oil colors according to transparency and opacity. To make it, I first painted two thick black horizontal lines. When they were dry, I painted the transparent colors over the bottom line and the opaque colors over the top one, using my paints full strength and with no medium or solvent.

The results are very clear. In the opaque row the black line is completely covered by the color swatches. In the transparent row the black line clearly shows through all the colors except for zinc white, which, although the most transparent of the whites, is still little better than semitransparent when used full strength. (Photo by D. James Dee.)

Color and Oil Glazing

PERUGIAN QUARTET
Oil and alkyd on wood,
12 × 8" (30.5 × 20.3 cm).
Collection of the artist.

This painting and the one opposite perfectly illustrate the characteristic color and beauty of the oil glazing technique, demonstrating as well that myriad color effects can be created with a minimal palette. The still life of four pumpkins was based on a light blue grisaille, which gives the painting an overall blue light. I chose an orange and blue complementary scheme to create a color vibrancy in an essentially monochrome setting.

I used a very light Naples yellow to establish the whitish yellow undercolor of the pumpkins, over which I then layered glazes of yellow and orange. The lighter-colored pumpkins were the result of lightly removing the orange glaze while still wet to allow the underpainting to show through. Shadows and darks were created with complementary glazes of blue and orange.

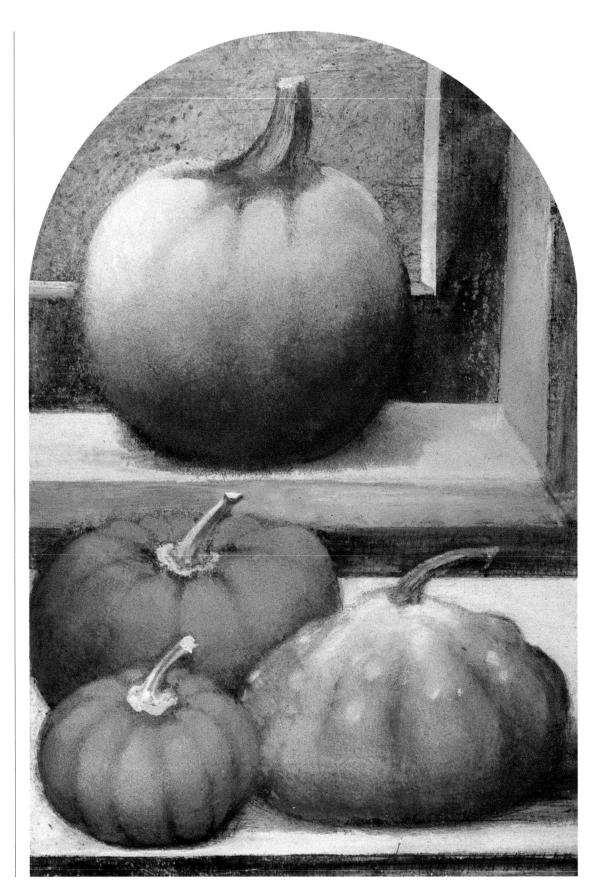

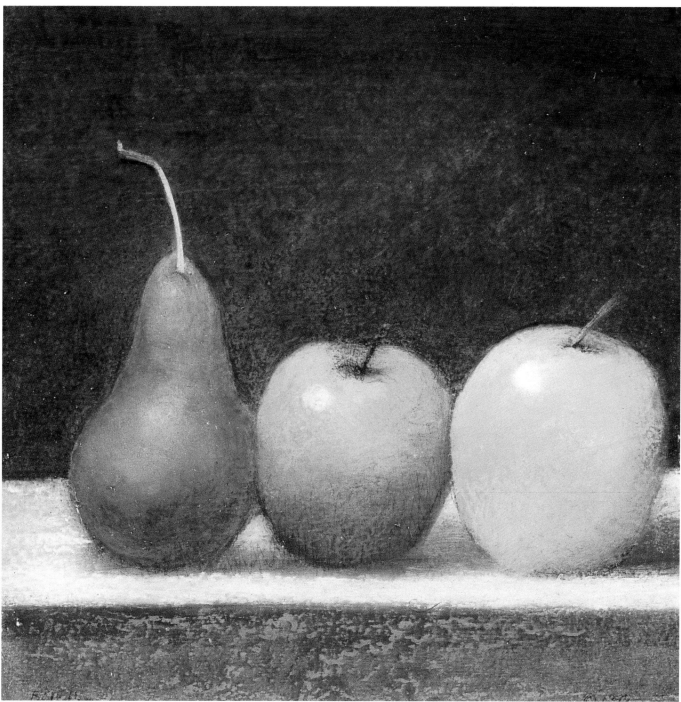

TRIO
Oil on sized paper,
10 × 10" (25.4 × 25.4 cm).
Collection of the artist.

In this painting, all the subtle warm tones of the fruits were the result of glazing with a harmony of different reds and yellows. The red of the pear was eventually neutralized by a thin glaze of ultramarine blue. The rich, dark brown background was created not with any brown pigments but with a mixed, neutralized glaze of reds and blues. The Old Masters of oil painting were fond of creating their darks in just such a transparent glazed manner. The effect is much subtler and more luminous than what a direct mixture of the two colors could ever produce.

GLAZED COLOR MIXING

Part of the fun of oil glazing is the pleasure of seeing what actually happens when one or two colors are glazed over another. The result is almost always a surprise. As I've said earlier, there is a difference between the results you get from mixing two colors together directly and what you get when you glaze one of those same two colors over the other. The glazed colors seem somehow deeper, more lustrous, and more reflective. Additionally, the subtlety of brushwork used in glaze applications plays a factor in the glazed color's final look. Glazes, as we will see later, are rarely mechanically applied.

Knowing how oil glaze colors will look in combination is not an exact science—not that you'd necessarily want it to be. However, with experience, you will be able to remember which combinations give certain effects that you would like to repeat. One of my favorites is the rich, naturalistic deep orange I get by glazing cobalt violet over cadmium yellow. Another is the warm blue-gray that results from glazing ultramarine blue over burnt sienna tinted with white.

If you're just starting out and have yet to discover your favorite glazing combinations, here's a visual aid: a chart that shows 110 glazed color combinations created from an equal balance of warm and cool colors as well as a handful of neutrals.

To make this chart, I picked 11 very basic colors that are commonly used in any standard oil palette: underpainting white, cadmium yellow, cadmium red, alizarin crimson, viridian, terre verte, phthalo blue, ultramarine blue, cobalt violet, burnt sienna, and ivory black. The idea was to use each color opaquely (that is, mixed with white) as well as transparently in a glaze to see how they would look in combination.

The horizontal rows consist of the opaque colors, leading off with underpainting white as my pure white, which I painted with a lot of texture so it would show up photographically. Each of the others, from cadmium yellow down to ivory black, was mixed with an equal amount of titanium white (50 percent) to make them opaque. I left the white and pure color unmixed at the left so you can see the individual "ingredients."

The vertical rows consist of the same colors used in the horizontal rows, but this time in the form of transparent glazes. The paints are used pure—with no white added—and are extended with an oil glazing medium, in this case Gamblin's Galkyd. Each color is glazed downward in a transparent stripe over the opaque horizontal stripes. This way we get to see how each color looks when glazed over the 10 others plus itself. The result is a handy reference that is helpful in making initial decisions about what colors will look like before and after they're glazed.

I should point out that in making this chart I had to make two exceptions to the pattern. In the vertical glazing column I substituted aureolin (cobalt yellow) for cadmium yellow and quinacridone red for cadmium red, since the cadmium colors are too dense to work effectively in glazes; aureolin and quinacridone red are their closest transparent equivalents.

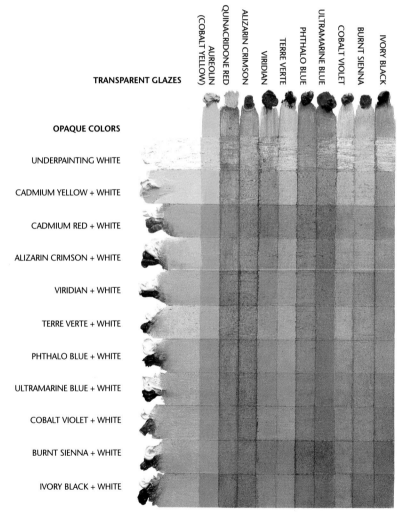

In this chart, the horizontal bands show colors mixed with titanium white in proportions of 50-50. The vertical bands show the same colors as transparent glazes. (There are two exceptions: I substituted the transparent colors aureolin and quinacridone red for the very opaque cadmium yellow and red, which don't work as glazes.) Note how each vertical stripe reacts with the opaque, blended colors. (Photo by D. James Dee.)

DEMONSTRATION

This demonstration shows how just a few colors go a long way in the oil glazing technique. Only four colors were used in this still life: ultramarine blue, raw sienna, burnt sienna, and viridian. The effect of the final piece is a simple distribution of warm and cool colors, but somehow the entire painting resonates with an inner color unity.

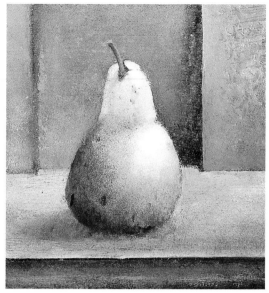

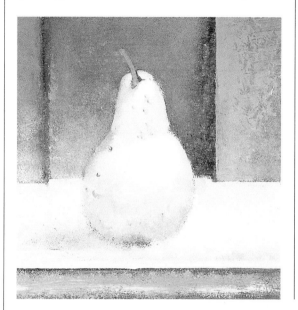

As you can see at left, the still life starts off as a simple grisaille: ultramarine blue for the background, raw sienna mixed with titanium white for the pear, and raw and burnt sienna in the foreground.

Burnt sienna is then glazed over the foreground and the pear. The idea is to create a reddish yellow pear and establish the illusion of a strong light source to the right of the picture.

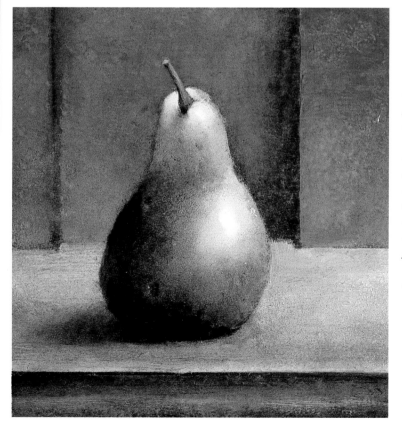

THE FLORENTINE PEAR
Oil on wood,
6 × 6" (15.2 × 15.2 cm).
Collection of Darlene and
Robert MacNamara.

I add viridian to the pear alone, making it more solid in form. Viridian and burnt sienna combine to make a beautiful, organically earthy green. Then I glaze ultramarine blue over the entire composition, applying it particularly heavily in the background and more lightly on the pear itself. I add just a breath of blue glaze to the burnt sienna foreground, neutralizing its effect. Ultramarine blue is definitely the dominant color in this painting.

Classic Oil Glazing Technique

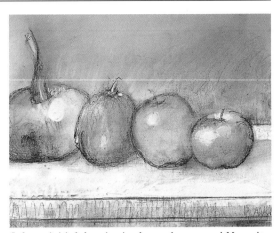

I do my initial drawing in charcoal on gessoed Masonite. Charcoal is the most flexible drawing medium for this, because it allows for maximum manipulation and corrections.

Now that we've talked a little bit about how glazing works and have a handy color chart that shows how our colors will look, let's walk through the stages of a typical oil glazed painting from start to finish.

The following demonstration shows the "classic" approach to glazing—classic in the sense that it employs most of the standard techniques typically used in producing an oil-glazed painting. Bear in mind, though, that there are as many variations on oil glazing as there are artists who do it. We'll take a look at some of these later on. If you start to do glazed paintings yourself you will surely develop a technique and style all your own.

This step-by-step sequence is presented in four installments that represent the major stages in executing an oil-glazed painting: making a preliminary drawing, establishing the grisaille underpainting, applying colored glazes, and scumbling for details.

Preliminary Drawing

The first step is to execute on the support the most accurate drawing you can of what eventually will be the finished painting. Glazed pictures depend more on clear, successful underdrawings than do direct, alla prima paintings, which can stand on just a vague charcoal sketch outlining your main ideas. Not so with indirect paintings; they require that your idea be fully realized in the drawing before any paint is applied.

Nobody says that you have to do this initial drawing in a hurry. This stage of work can be a long, drawn-out, "searching" affair with lots of starts and stops and a lot of corrections along the way. In a sense you're working alla prima with your drawing, and here flexibility is okay. Use any drawing medium you feel comfortable with—charcoal, pastel, pen and ink, watercolor—anything that you feel you have complete command over. The goal of the drawing stage is to establish form, design, and composition. Color is of no importance whatsoever at this early point. The thing you're after is a clear picture of your idea. You're building a framework upon which you will paint your underpainting.

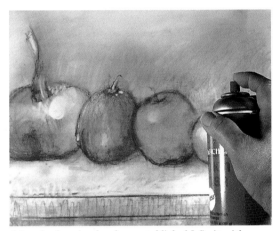

After the drawing has been established I fix it with a spray retouch varnish. This is an important step because it totally preserves the drawing and keeps it from smearing—which is essential if there are fine details. Moreover, the retouch acts as an isolating varnish for the first layers of paint, an especially useful function if the ground happens to be too absorbent.

THE GRISAILLE

The traditional term for the type of underpainting used in the glazing technique is grisaille, or "gray picture," from the French *gris*, meaning gray. The grisaille is the true foundation of your picture. As its name implies, it can be executed entirely in grays mixed from black and white, although as you'll see, the grisaille can be in any color you want it to be. Rubens, for example, did most of his underpaintings in ochre and white. Polychrome grisailles are also possible; in one traditional technique for painting a nude figure group, the female figures and foreground are underpainted in a cool, greenish monochrome, while the male figures and background are defined with a warm, earthy red underpainting.

Whether done in the traditional gray or in a color, the grisaille has a monochrome clarity to it and is always dominated by white. It is absolutely essential that the grisaille be in the high-value range, rendered in the lightest tones possible, because with the application of each colored glaze the painting will become darker. Another reason for the high-value tonality is that the grisaille must also be "lean"—in other words, it must be executed in paint that contains a minimum of oil. ("Fat" paint is one with a lot of oil in it.) White oil paints are very lean in their makeup, lead white being the leanest of all oil colors. The foundation for an oil painting should be a very stable paint film, and thus as lean as possible—much like the actual ground itself. Most dark colors, especially lamp black and ivory black, are extremely fat, so their presence in the grisaille must be kept to a minimum. The idea is to do the grisaille as a sort of "white on white" painting, using just enough black or other dark color to define the forms and shapes. I have to admit that keeping the value high in a grisaille is not all that easy. There is a temptation to do the rendering in its full value range, which, of course, means a tendency to go dark. I know that my own grisaille handling needs improvement in this area. So keep it light. Your darkest tone should be way above middle gray.

By tradition a grisaille should have an ultra-smooth finish. The important thing is to keep down the paint buildup along the edges of forms. Buried impastos and meaningless paint ridges will later show when glazes are applied, so if you don't want them to appear in your finished painting, make sure they are not present in the grisaille.

When I do a grisaille I keep my fan blenders close at hand and smooth the paint down a lot. I put my heavy paint strokes (scumbles) only where I know I really want them and then leave the rest of the grisaille smooth. If I notice unwanted ridges after the paint is dry, I smooth things down with my palette knife, or even resort to sanding it down with very fine steel wool.

So clearly, in oil glazing the grisaille is an important—if not the most important—step. Design, composition, and form are all well defined in the finished grisaille; color is the only thing missing. This separation of color and form works in many ways to the benefit of the colorist. The struggles with design and composition are over once the grisaille is completed; they've been resolved already, "engraved in stone," as it were, so that all attention can then be turned to color and texture. Color interaction can now become the total focus of the painting.

I know that this absolute separation of color and form is alien to almost all other contemporary painting techniques, where the search for color balance and design are dealt with as simultaneous activities. But the indirect method offers the security of knowing you have something to hold on to: the composition, in the form of the grisaille. The application of color then becomes something like a dance performed according to a well-thought-out choreography. There's a lot of room for improvisation and modification along the way, but the basic moves are always there to fall back on. While oil glazing is a disciplined approach, it also provides an undeniable sense of freedom.

Before color is applied there is an optional procedure that many painters, myself included, find useful. When the grisaille has been completed, let it dry for at least a couple of days (though the longer the drying period, the better), then isolate this paint layer with a coat of retouch varnish. If the grisaille is really dry and a stronger coating is desired, use a thin (but undiluted) coat of Liquin alkyd medium as an isolating varnish. Coating the underpainting with a varnish facilitates the application of the oil glazes. Glazes are fat with oil but vary in how much they contain, meaning that their absorption into the lean grisaille can be uneven. An isolating varnish helps prevent this, and also provides a slick surface that is similar in look to the glazes themselves and makes wiping and manipulating the glazes easier.

Classic Oil Glazing Technique

With my preliminary drawing in place, I make the first applications of paint to the grisaille using titanium white and Mars black. Mars black is the black of choice for underpaintings because it has a very low oil-absorption rate of 15 percent—the same as a white. This is in contrast to ivory black and lamp black, which are extremely high in oil content and therefore not recommended for use in underpaintings, which should be as lean as possible.

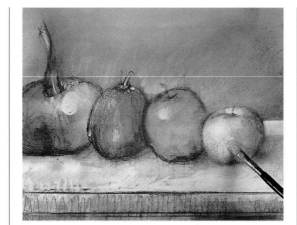

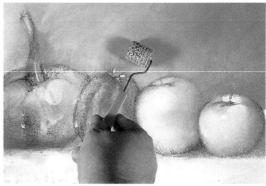

I use a small paint roller to keep the underpainting smooth and even; I want no brushstrokes at this stage.

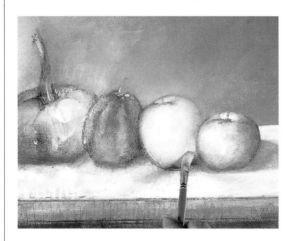

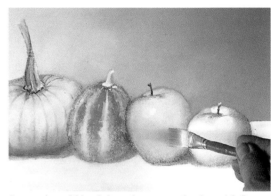

I smooth and blend the paint texture further with fine, soft-haired brushes.

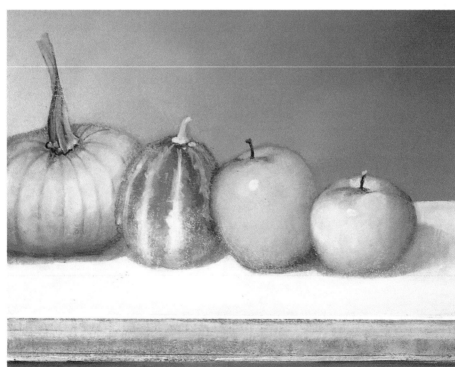

Here is the finished grisaille underpainting. The tonal values are on the high side; there are no real darks. The composition, drawing, and design are firmly established. This is the foundation upon which I will build my painting from now on.

COLOR

The next step is to introduce color, the first layer of which serves to set up the painting's overall temperature. While the initial colors are almost always applied as glazes, it is possible to begin instead with opaque applications of local colors that further enhance the underpainting.

These early color layers are very general; they are applied in broad washes to cover large sections of the painting. In the still life painting that serves as our demonstration, for example, the whole row of fruits becomes a cool yellow-green, while the foreground and background environment becomes a warm earth red. These big, simple glaze washes start the color process.

Each glaze must dry before the next one can be put on top of it. The waiting time involved is perhaps the most frustrating aspect of the oil glazing process, since it takes at least a day for a single glaze layer to dry sufficiently, and even that might not be long enough—often two days or more are needed. Wet-on-wet applications sometimes work, but not necessarily as glazes. You might be able to place a wet glaze on top of another wet one in a single shot, but certainly little or no manipulation of color is possible. If wet glazes begin to mix, they simply become a transparent form of wet-on-wet painting— which you may find occasionally has a place in your technical repertoire. But to follow the traditional approach, you must allow one glaze to dry thoroughly before applying another over it. In practice, this means that you can put down no more than one or two glazes per painting per day. For this reason many artists have several paintings going on simultaneously.

Further applications of color give objects their individual identity and create a sense of space. Small, isolated glazes are used to define the local colors of the various compositional elements. In our still life demonstration, for example, all the fruits are initially the same yellow-green color, but are subsequently differentiated by various applications of red, green, and yellow glazes. Likewise, ultramarine blue is added to the background to distinguish it from the earth-red tabletop in the foreground.

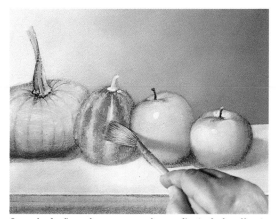

I apply the first glaze, a coat of aureolin (cobalt yellow), to all of the fruits. No modeling or wiping out is attempted at this stage, just a smooth wash. Here and throughout I use Gamblin's alkyd-based medium Galkyd to create my glazes.

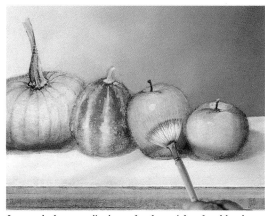

I smooth the aureolin layer further with a fan blender.

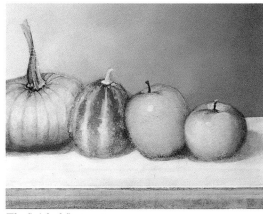

The finished first coat.

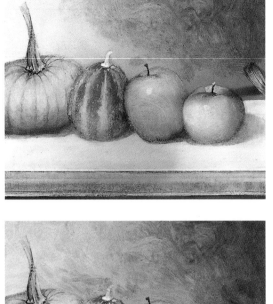

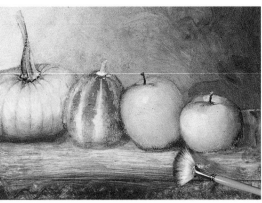

With a fan blender I smooth out the color.

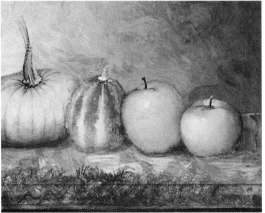

The background and foreground are painted in with a rough glaze of burnt sienna.

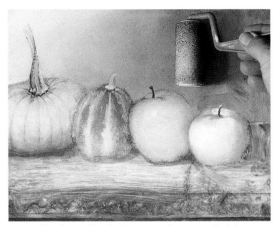

A small paint roller further smooths out and picks up some of the burnt sienna layer.

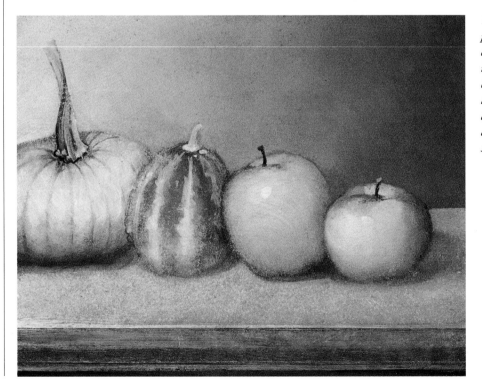

The entire painting is now covered with its first glaze—burnt sienna in the background and foreground, aureolin on the still life objects.

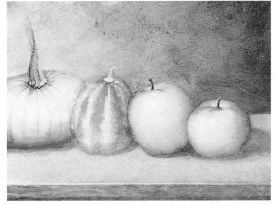

A layer of ultramarine blue is added to the background as well as very faintly in the shadows under the fruit.

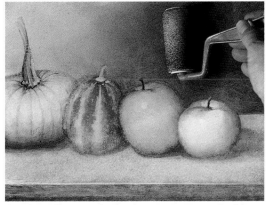

A paint roller smooths the glaze even more and adds a "dabbled" texture to the background.

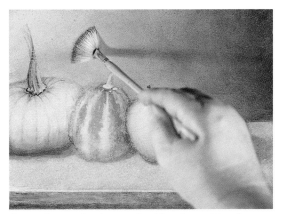

I smooth over the ultramarine blue glaze with a fan blender.

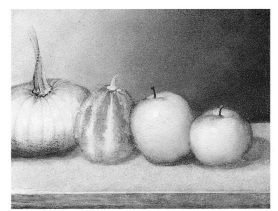

The first level of glazing is finished, and I leave the painting to dry for a few days.

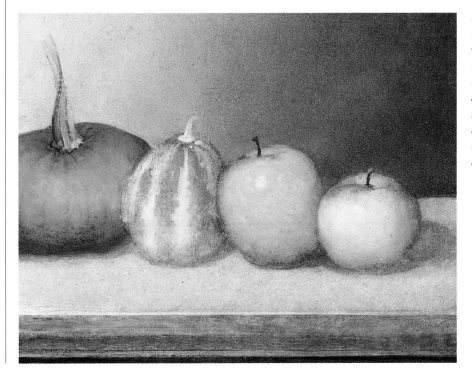

I apply a glaze of Indian yellow—a very transparent orange-yellow— over the pumpkin, and a glaze of Lefranc & Bourgeois transparent yellow over the larger of the two apples.

CLASSIC OIL GLAZING TECHNIQUE

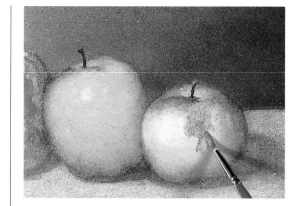

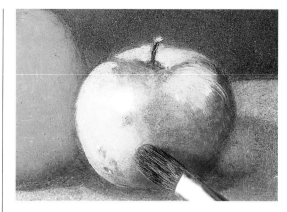

With a sable brush I glaze quinacridone rose over the Macintosh apple. I use a bristle brush to stipple the surface of the quinacridone rose glaze, and then a soft imitation-sable brush to smooth the color.

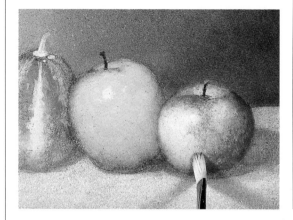

At this stage all the pieces of fruit except the gourd have received their second glaze coating. The painting is left to dry for a day or two, and then the gourd and the pumpkin receive another glaze of Indian yellow. This time I use an Indian yellow made by Old-Holland, which has a more orange cast to it than the one I used earlier.

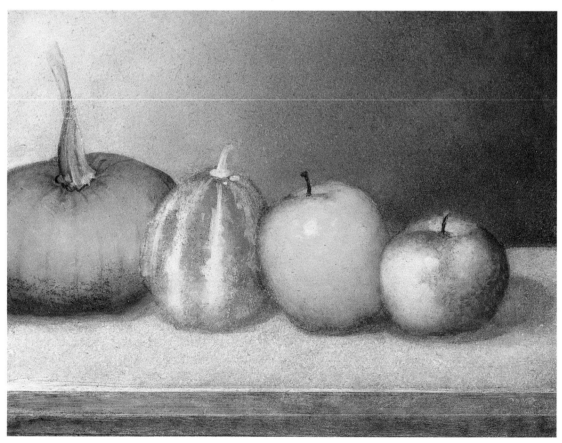

SCUMBLING

As refinements of detail and color become more apparent with each glaze layer, scumbles may be introduced—applications of opaque paint to add body, texture, highlights, and details to a glazed painting. Scumbles can be painted over glazes that have dried or worked into them wet-on-wet. They can be left as they were applied or, in turn, covered with glaze layers, depending on the situation. The critical point to remember is that most scumbles contain a lot of white, and as we've said, whites are lean. Therefore, in keeping with the "fat over lean" principle, extra oil must be added to scumbles that are applied over a glaze. If you violate this principle, the risk down the road a few decades or centuries later is that this lean scumble may crack. It's a good rule of thumb when doing glazed oil painting (or any oil painting, for that matter) to make sure you add oil to all your colors beyond the first one or two levels, and that you do not thin any of your colors with turpentine alone at any point in a work except at the very beginning. Thinning paint with straight turpentine makes that paint film lean, and if you place such a film over a juicy, fat one, it's probably going to crack. In oil glazing techniques you must stick with the glaze medium all the way to the end of the painting and never thin your paints with just turpentine. In fact, after the grisaille, forget that turpentine even exists except for wiping off mistakes and cleaning your brushes. Paint only with oily mediums.

A glazed painting can continue to be developed with layer upon layer of glazes and scumbles until it is finished. Only the painter knows when to stop. When asked how many glazes were required to finish a painting, Titian, the great master of the technique, suggested "30 or 40." There is no magic number. Two might be enough; and 40 may not yet be enough.

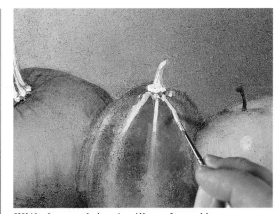

While the second glaze is still wet, I scumble very opaque off-white details onto the appropriate areas of the gourd.

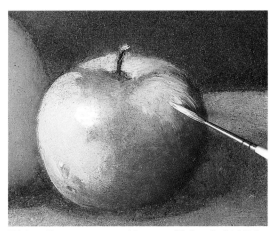

Light yellow opaque scumbles are added to the highlights of the Macintosh apple.

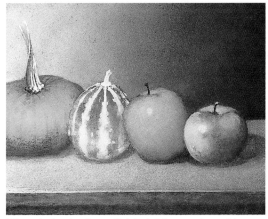

The painting is almost finished; I just need to add yet more glazes to enrich the color further.

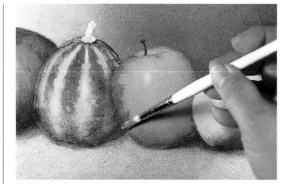

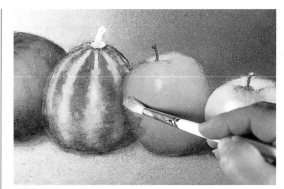

A deep red oxide glaze has been added to the pumpkin, giving it a rich, golden brown-orange glow. The same red oxide is also glazed onto the gourd, but here it gives a different effect—namely, that of a shadow.

While the red oxide is still wet I add yet another glaze of Lefranc & Bourgeois transparent yellow to the yellow apple. As you can see in the illustration, my brush is loaded with oil and is being used to create a hard edge against the yellow apple and the gourd.

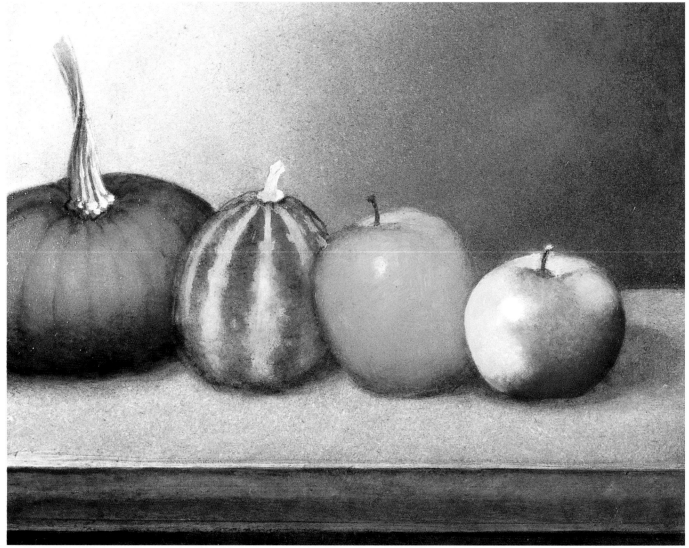

APPLES AND PUMPKINS
Oil on Masonite,
12 × 16" (30.5 × 40.6 cm).
Collection of the artist.

I leave the completed painting to sit for a few months, after which I will varnish it with a beeswax varnish. I prefer wax varnishes because they are not as glossy as other kinds and repel dust during application.

Underpainting Variations

As we said above, probably the most important step in the technique of oil glazing is the execution of the underpainting, or grisaille. We also described the classic grisaille as a gray monochrome done in a high value range. But other possibilities exist. Let's take a quick look at some underpainting variations.

The first thing we should note is that not all underpaintings are done in black and white. Any color will do—green, blue, even yellow is fine—as long as it is light in value. There is nothing sacred about gray. In fact, sometimes the color interactions that result from glazing over a purely gray underpainting can be problematic. That is to say, the gray may cool down some of your early yellow glazes, which is not desirable if you want your yellow to be hotter. An ochre or sienna underpainting in that case might be more appropriate.

In fact, perhaps the ideal underpainting may be one that is polychrome instead of just monochrome. Baroque painters often worked this way, laying down polychrome imprimaturas (glazes used to create colored grounds) of terre verte for figures and terra rosa for backgrounds. Since the whole idea of rendering a grisaille is to build a foundation, it makes sense for early color considerations to factor into the plan as well. The important thing is to keep the design and form in focus, and to maintain a high value range.

Just as the color (or colors) you use for a grisaille can vary, so, too, can the medium; it doesn't have to be oil paint at all. In the late Middle Ages all underpaintings were done in egg tempera, which was slow to paint in but dried instantly and was absolutely lean. Today we have other options. Acrylics, for example, are a great choice for underpaintings because they are fast-drying, completely lean, and nonabsorbent. If you're good at handling the speed of acrylics, you can create an underpainting in no time at all that will dry and be ready for glazing in minutes.

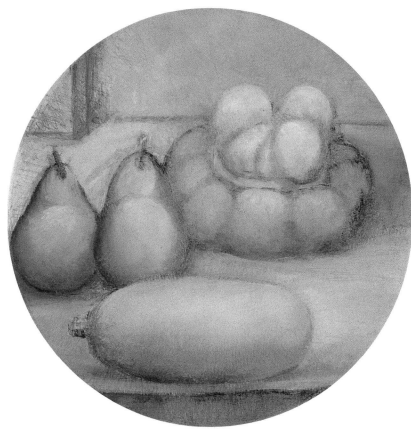

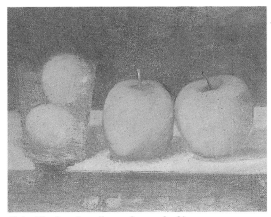

Grisaille done in yellow ochre and white.

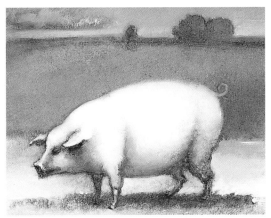

I executed this polychrome grisaille using blue and white for the background, terre verte and white for the pears, Naples yellow and white for the foreground gourd, and light red oxide and white for the turban squash.

Grisaille done in Maimeri's ultramarine green and white.

UNDERPAINTING VARIATIONS

Another excellent underpainting medium is alkyd. Alkyds feel and paint like oils (and are oils in a sense) but have the advantage of drying completely in less than 24 hours. They are not as fast as acrylics but are easier to blend and mix, and it's simpler to get a smooth finish with them than with acrylics. Alkyds form a flexible paint film that is ready to receive oil glazes within as little as 18 hours' drying time.

An underpainting doesn't even have to be a painting; a finely rendered pen and ink drawing can serve as a starting point for your oil glazes. Unfinished panels by Jan van Eyck reveal that this 15th-century master of exquisitely detailed paintings was fond of doing just that. The oil glazes do not affect the pen and ink in any way. They can be applied directly over the ink drawing to begin the painting process, and opaque scumbles are added somewhere along the way. A pen and ink underpainting is a unique foundation for an oil-glazed painting, especially if you're after fine detail.

Finally, the underpainting doesn't have to be a grisaille in the traditional sense. In fact, excellent results can be obtained by using an old, perhaps failed oil painting that is completely dry as a starting point for your glazes. Boring, lifeless, sunken-in passages may suddenly spring to life with the application of a fresh glaze, giving the picture a new existence.

DEMONSTRATION

The painting in this demonstration is based on a childhood photo of my older sister and myself in our suburban New Orleans neighborhood. When you're working small, as I am here, and want a lot of detail, pen and ink is a practical choice for the underpainting. India ink is the best, but alcohol-soluble ballpoint ink and water-based liquid inks are okay, too; the oil paint is not affected by these choices. Do, however, avoid graphite pencil and felt-tip markers. Graphite will eventually seep through the paint layers to the surface, as will the ink from markers, which even the most opaque paint won't cover.

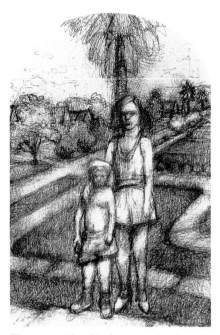

The support for this demonstration is an acrylic-primed wood panel. With pen and ink I drew directly on the panel, aiming for as much detail as possible and making all major design and compositional decisions at the drawing stage. Corrections and alterations were done by sanding and scraping with steel wool and electric erasers.

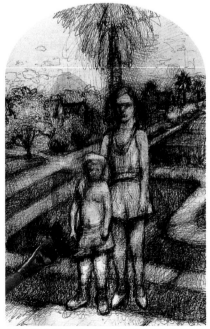

After finishing the drawing I spread a faint overall glaze, or imprimatura, of transparent light red oxide over it. This seals the ink and unifies the picture with a warm, earthy tone.

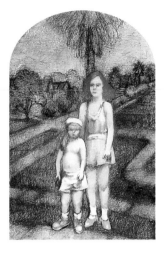

Here, opaque and transparent colors work together. The landscape behind the figures is glazed with transparent viridian, while the figures are painted with opaque local colors. The value of these local flesh colors is kept very high and modeling is kept to a minimum.

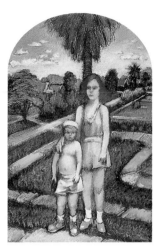

Now the landscape is painted with opaque colors, and these, too, are kept flat and relatively neutral. At this point the painting is largely covered with opaque color, but from here on, all else will be accomplished with transparent glazes.

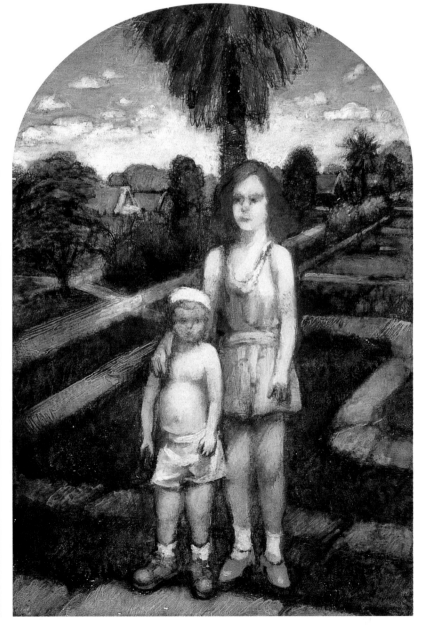

BIG SISTER/LITTLE BROTHER
Oil on wood panel,
12 × 8" (30.5 × 20.3 cm).
Collection of the artist.

The finished painting has multiple layers of transparent oil glazes, yet only four colors were used to create them: ultramarine blue, cobalt blue, viridian, and transparent light red oxide.

UNDERPAINTING VARIATIONS

This panel painting of a goat is about a year old and I want to bring more contrast to the composition. Since the goat is basically white, I'm going to accomplish my goal by darkening the sky. I don't want to change the animal in any way, but neither do I want to apply dark blue opaque paint to the sky in such a way that the goat becomes a hard-edged silhouette. Not only would I deaden the sky, but also I might lose my painting of the goat. The solution is to glaze in a new sky.

I paint in a dark, flat tone of cobalt blue mixed with a slow-drying glaze medium of stand oil and Venice turpentine.

DEMONSTRATION

Paintings that never quite worked out can serve beautifully as underpaintings. Often the application of oil glazes can revitalize the look of an older painting, or can help unify color that is somehow disjointed. Finished paintings are ideal starting points for glazing, since their paint films have had sufficient time to dry.

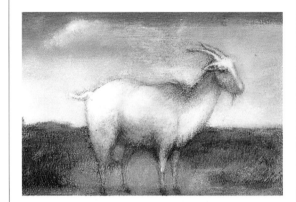

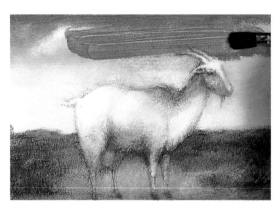

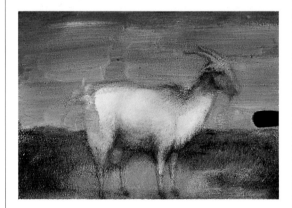

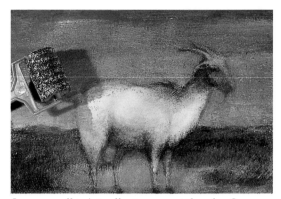

I use a small paint roller to even out the color. Some of the goat's form and details are covered in the process, but this is okay, because the glaze can be easily wiped off where I don't want it.

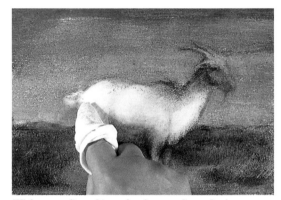

With a rag dipped into the glaze medium, I wipe away color from parts of the animal that were accidentally covered in blue.

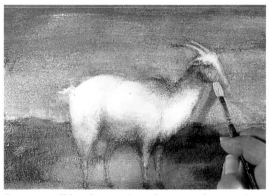

I use a small brush to continue the removal process in a detailed area.

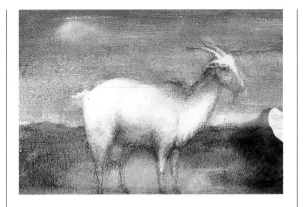

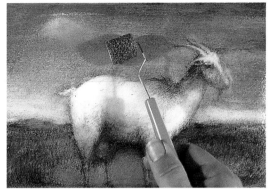

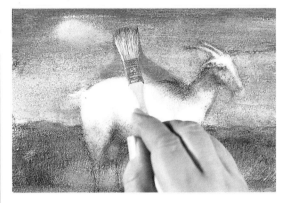

With another oil-soaked rag I begin to lighten the blue along the horizon, creating a more atmospheric space. I then slowly remove some blue glaze from the sky with a clean bristle brush dipped in glazing medium, creating a more exaggerated cloud. More areas of blue are removed along the horizon and in the clouds. Tiny foam paint rollers are used to even out the texture and smooth the paint.

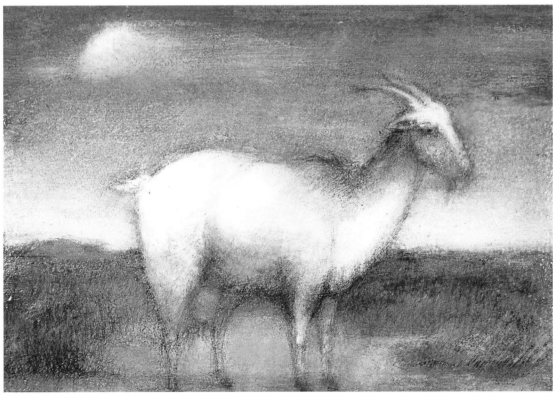

THE GOAT
Oil on panel,
8 × 10" (20.3 × 25.4).
Collection of the artist.

What I wanted to do with this painting has been achieved, and it took almost no time at all—about half an hour. Glazing and subsequent wiping out is a fast and absolutely painless way to modify older works, giving them new life.

Glaze Mediums

Colors like viridian, ultramarine blue, and Indian yellow are naturally transparent to begin with, and a few of them are so transparent that they can work somewhat effectively as glazes right out of the tube. But while the natural transparency of a particular color makes for a good start, true glazing technique requires that all colors be extended for use as glazes with the addition of a clear glaze medium.

The idea of a glaze medium is very simple. To become truly transparent for glazing purposes, a color must be "stretched," or extended, beyond its usual consistency. The function of the glaze medium is to hold the extended paint film together physically and to simultaneously provide enough flexibility to let the artist manipulate it to get the desired effects. A glaze medium must also allow the glaze to dry properly and ensure that, once dry, it won't be disturbed by the further application of varnishes and solvents. To achieve these ends, almost all glaze mediums depend upon the interaction of two basic ingredients:

a heavy oil and a resin (or varnish). The oil gives strength and weight to the stretched paint while the resin helps control its behavior, primarily by affecting its flow and facilitating its drying.

In light of how much a glaze medium does, it's suprising to find out how simple its ingredients really are. The oil is almost always either stand oil or sun-thickened linseed oil, and the usual resin is damar varnish, or sometimes mastic varnish. Both stand oil and sun-thickened linseed oil, as we learned earlier, are called "bodied" oils because they are more viscous than cold-pressed or refined linseed oil. Stand oil dries more slowly than sun-thickened oil, but both are good, solid extenders of color. Refined gum turpentine is added to thin the oils a bit, and occasionally a small amount of a balsam oleoresin such as Venice turpentine or a variant, Canadian balsam, is used as an ingredient. The balsam adds gloss, retards drying, and adds even more strength to the paint film. A drop or two of cobalt drier, the standard mineral-based siccative, is another optional ingredient. That's about it; everything mentioned here is fairly ordinary and universally available.

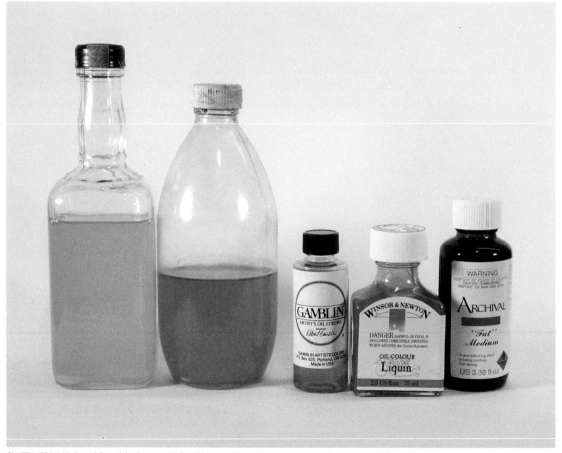

GLAZE MEDIUMS. From left to right: homemade fast-drying medium, homemade slow-drying medium, Galkyd, Liquin, and Archival "Fat" Medium.

There are lots of ready-made oil glaze mediums available in the art supply stores, but most of them are made from the ingredients listed above. It's easy—and cheaper—to make your own. Here are a few easy recipes for standard glaze mediums. The first one comes from *The Artist's Handbook of Materials and Techniques* by Ralph Mayer. It is a good all-purpose, relatively fast drying medium that's excellent for glazes worked in one sitting and dry to the touch the next day.

FAST-DRYING OIL GLAZE

1 oz. stand oil
1 oz. damar varnish
1 oz. gum turpentine
15 drops cobalt drier (optional)

Pour all ingredients into a clean jar or bottle and shake until thoroughly mixed. The medium is then ready to use.

Complementing each other in this recipe, the oil provides elasticity to offset the possible brittling of the varnish, while the varnish allows the oil to dry quickly and evenly. Stand oil, the great leveler of paint, makes this a very smooth glaze, but because it is notoriously dense and viscous, it needs gum turpentine to help make it more liquid. The cobalt drier is optional but its presence in the formula guarantees quick drying—though in excess it darkens colors.

These next two formulas yield slower-drying glaze mediums and come from Robert Massey's splendid little book *Formulas for Painters* (Watson-Guptill Publications). Either one can be mixed directly with tube colors on the palette, or with raw pigments. Both glazes will stay open for a day or two to allow for refined blending or corrections.

SLOW-DRYING OIL GLAZE

4 parts damar varnish
2 parts sun-thickened linseed oil
1 part Venice turpentine

Mix all ingredients in a clean bottle and shake until thoroughly blended. Make sure the Venice turpentine dissolves thoroughly, as it is often very thick.

Venice turpentine adds gloss and works well as a retarder, making this glaze formula ideal for situations that call for a long open time or involve very large areas to be smoothly glazed and blended, such as a vast expanse of sky in a landscape. Stand oil can be substituted for sun-thickened linseed oil, in which case drying will be even slower. If this formulation is too heavy and viscous for your personal taste, carefully thin it with pure gum turpentine. Drying time may vary from two to three days.

HIGH-GLOSS SLOW-DRYING OIL GLAZE

1 part sun-thickened linseed oil
1 part Venice turpentine

The Venice turpentine adds a high gloss to the linseed oil as well as retards its drying. This heavy-bodied glaze is almost like a gel. Thin with turpentine if desired. You can substitute stand oil for sun-thickened linseed oil in this formulation.

The glaze mediums described here all contain the very same materials that have been used for centuries. But in addition to those made of traditional ingredients, oil painters now have at their disposal several new and very useful modern substitutes.

All of these new painting mediums have one thing in common: Instead of a traditional fossil resin such as damar or mastic, they contain a synthetic alkyd resin that functions as the varnish stabilizer of the oil film. Three of the more successful and interesting examples are Winsor & Newton's Liquin, Gamblin's Galkyd Painting Medium #1, and Archival's "Fat" Medium.

These alkyd-based mediums are all fast-drying, especially the thixotropic Liquin, which dries to the touch in a few hours or less and leaves a high-gloss finish. "Fat" Medium and Galkyd, on the other hand, are heavy-bodied liquid mediums that dry completely overnight and are not excessively glossy, yielding more of a satin finish. Besides functioning as glaze mediums, all three can be used as "straight" painting mediums for opaque passages as well. This means that you can use a single medium consistently throughout an entire painting.

Another positive attribute of alkyd-based resins is that they do not yellow as the traditional damar does. Moreover, they display the combination of strength and flexibility that characterizes alkyd paint films. These three alkyd mediums—and there are more brands out there, including Rowney, Daniel Smith, and Grumbacher, to name a few— are ideal for the painter who must work fast and wants his glazes to dry in a hurry.

GLAZE MEDIUMS

NEAPOLITAN PEARS
Oil on canvas,
8 × 10" (20.3 × 25.4 cm).
Collection of the artist.

I executed this still life of two pears in oils and alkyds using large amounts of Galkyd medium in proportion to small amounts of paint to create an almost watercolorlike effect.

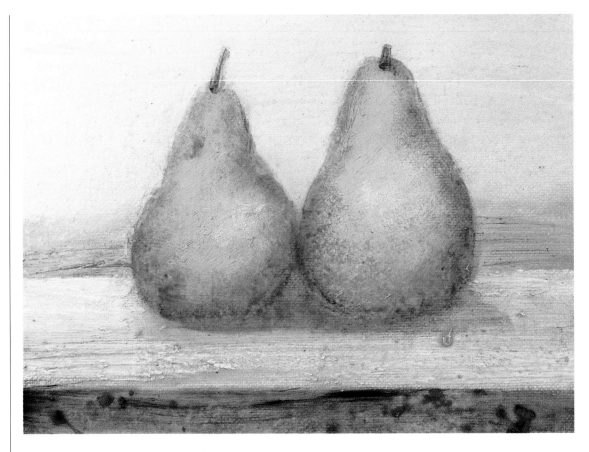

WHITE EGGPLANT
Oil on wood panel,
6" (15.2 cm) diameter.
Collection of Ellen Rudley.

Here I used Archival's "Fat" Medium as a glaze and painting medium.

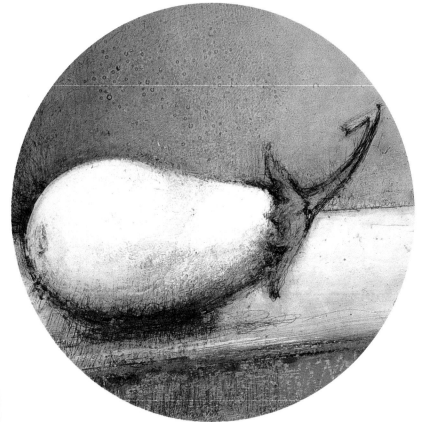

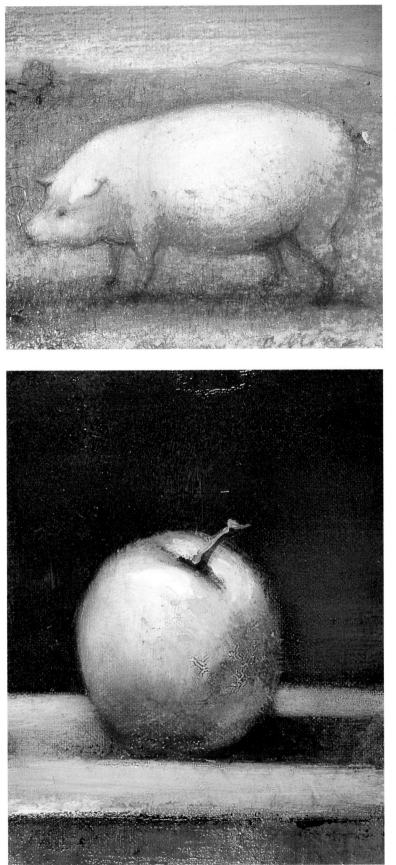

PIG
Oil on wood,
3 × 4" (7.6 × 10.2 cm).
Private collection.

This tiny painting was made using oils diluted with a slow-drying glaze medium of 4 parts damar varnish, 2 parts sun-thickened linseed oil, and 1 part Venice turpentine.

APPLE
Oil on canvas,
10 × 8" (25.4 × 20.3 cm).
Collection of the artist.

I built up this painting using a combination of fast-drying glaze medium and Maroger medium. The Maroger medium seemed to operate on two levels. It thickened the texture of opaque colors, making them seem more "meaty," yet made transparent colors and glaze medium flow very easily.

Manipulating Oil Glazes

The way an artist applies oil glazes and manipulates the wet colors is integral with his or her individual style. The techniques used to move glazes around can define the "touch" of a particular artist very much the way virtuoso brushstrokes in an alla prima painting can reveal the identity of the painter who put them there.

Applying oil paint transparently is anything but routine. You can stroke glazes on slowly for a smooth, even covering or in a brushy manner for dynamic effects. Glazed oil colors can display brushstrokes just as clearly as any opaque paint can, and can be just as expressive. The difference is that their texture is apparent not in high profile, as with opaque paint, but in the way they interact optically with the colors and images beneath them. Any number of techniques can be employed to adjust the look and texture of a wet glazed color. Above all, it requires a willingness to take a few chances. With that, plus a little imagination and experience, many wonderful things can happen.

There are no hard-and-fast rules. Any tool that puts paint down on a surface (or removes it, for that matter) can be used to manipulate a wet glaze. Obviously brushes are the main tools—smooth, soft-haired rounds to make the initial gestural strokes and stiff bristle brushes to remove paint, exposing the undercolors in a dramatic way. Fan blenders are also indispensable. With their wide sweep, they can remove large areas of color smoothly, or, lightly dipped into fresh paint and used tips first, they can create beautiful drybrush textures.

Besides brushes, a clean, soft cotton rag wrapped around your finger is one of the best tools for manipulating a glaze. One swipe with your forefinger and you have an instant highlight. Used as a dabber, a rag is also a convenient way to blend and soften fresh glazed color. A few dabs sometimes is all that's necessary to get a smoothly blended passage. Sponges and sponge brushes (the kind used for painting windowsills) are great for picking up wet colors in a smooth way, and are a delight because they are inexpensive and disposable. Sponge paint rollers are ideal for smooth blending, leaving an even, almost mechanical-looking surface in seconds. For glaze manipulations I personally find the sponge roller an indispensable tool, second only to the fan blender. Beyond these implements, I have found palette knives, toothbrushes, sticks, crumpled paper towels, and masking tape all occasionally playing a part in the manipulation of glazed colors.

One technical detail that I'd like to point out is this: Whenever you want to make a clear, hard edge by wiping away a wet glazed color with some sort of solvent, never use standard solvents like turpentine or mineral spirits. Instead, use the glaze medium straight from the jar and undiluted. Turpentine and the like will go beyond the edge you want to sharpen and really soften its effect. Solvent freshly applied to a glazed color will have the same effect that additional water does on watercolors: It creates a wet-looking soft texture. Needless to say, while this may be undesirable in some cases, such as when a hard edge is wanted, it may be just the thing in other situations. So remember to be flexible.

Demonstration

This demonstration shows how different tools perform different functions in the application and manipulation of oil glazes, and what a broad variety of effects you can achieve.

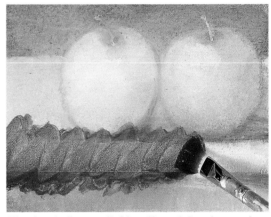

The glaze is first applied heavily and directly over the painting with a soft-haired brush.

The same brush is used to spread and thin the applied glaze.

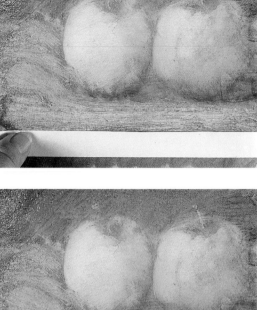

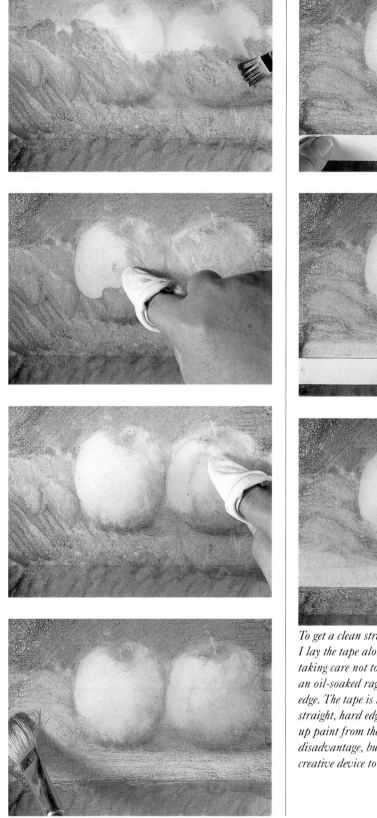

I dip a clean rag in glazing medium and use it to wipe away the glazed color from areas where I don't want it.

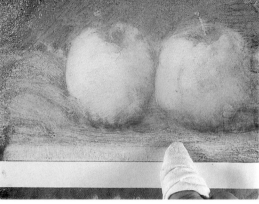

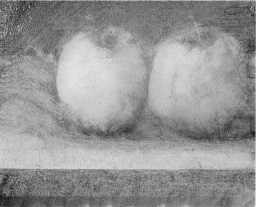

With a dry (no oil added) bristle brush, I remove more of the glaze color. This is a more sensitive technique than just wiping out with a rag. It can be used to create a delicate stippled texture as it removes color.

To get a clean straight edge, I use artist's drafting tape. I lay the tape along the base of the plane to be wiped, taking care not to apply too much pressure. Then I use an oil-soaked rag to wipe away paint along the taped edge. The tape is then removed, leaving a perfectly straight, hard edge. It should be noted that the tape picks up paint from the areas underneath it. This can be a disadvantage, but it can also be turned into yet another creative device to achieve an interesting texture.

Manipulating Oil Glazes

A flat foam rubber paintbrush is used to pick up and smooth the glaze.

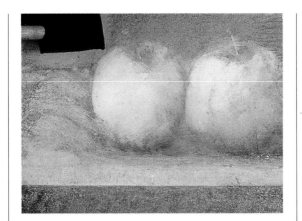

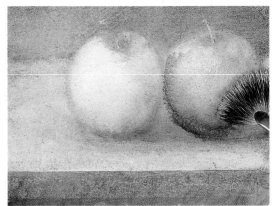

I use a second fan blender, this time a dry one, to make final refinements. The brush used for this task should be large and extremely soft.

A foam rubber roller is another tool for picking up glazed color. It also spreads small amounts of the glaze, leaving a "frottage" texture behind.

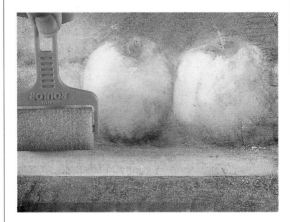

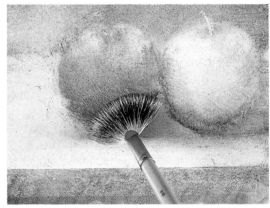

At this point the painting has been allowed to dry for a day. With a small fan blender, I sensitively apply a second glaze color (viridian).

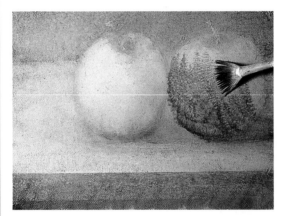

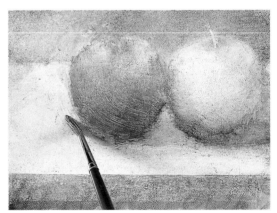

I repeat the glaze application process with a third color.

The same brush is wiped clean of paint and is used to blend and pick up the wet glazed color.

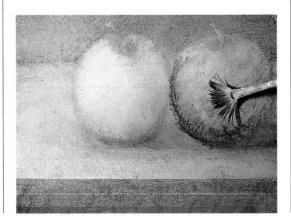

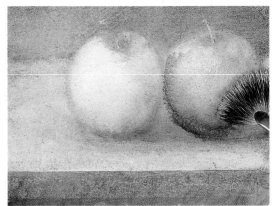

Fan blending can make the edges of objects a bit fuzzy. To get a hard, clean line, I use a soft sable brush to polish off the edge. The use of oil here is optional; it depends on how easily the paint is picked up.

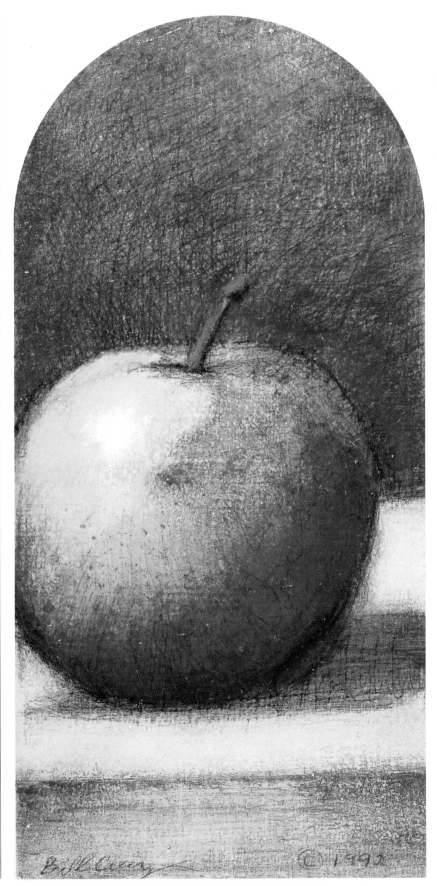

THE RED APPLE
Oil on wood panel,
8 × 4" (20.3 × 10.2 cm).
Collection of the artist.

Much of the texture in this painting was created by stippling wet glaze layers with a dry bristle brush, which picks up some of the color. In the background I stippled terre verte over Naples yellow. To create both the apple's red color and its texture, I stippled Holbein transparent red over cadmium lemon and white.

SCUMBLING

A scumble is any opaque application of paint that is made after glazing has begun. It can range in scale from very large, covering an entire area, to very small—perhaps just a few opaque impasto strokes carefully placed to define a detail.

Scumbling is almost inevitable in a glazed painting. As we have seen, each application of a glaze darkens a painting to a certain extent. This is why, from the very start, we strive to make our grisaille as high in value as possible. Still, it's only natural that with repeated layers of glaze, somewhere along the line things will get too dark. The scumble is how we restore a high value.

A glazed paint layer doesn't have much body. An oil painting composed of 100 percent glazes is not really going to work; it's not, after all, a watercolor. At some point it's going to need some "meat," some body, to make it convincing. The grisaille provides a lot of that substance, which, as you'll see, can be enhanced by introducing texture in the underpainting. But even in the course of things, we inevitably feel a "painterly" need to get into our beautiful glazed surfaces and add some small but densely opaque scumbles.

At the risk of being overly romantic, I'd like you to think of glazing and scumbling as something of a "dance" between transparent paint (the glazes) and opaque paint (the scumbles). Instinctively you will find them working together as opposite aspects of the same process. The finest examples of glazing and scumbling I can think of are the portraits by Rembrandt van Rijn, who carried the technique to perfection. The vast, dark and shadowed portions of his figures are all built from myriad deep glazes, while at the same time the expressive details of the sitters' faces and ornamental costumes are executed with full, rich, thick impasto scumbles. The combination of the two makes for a dazzling reality.

I should point out that the majority of scumbles are made from the color white, either alone or mixed with other colors in a fairly high proportion. White, of course—and this is true of all of them, including lead, zinc, and titanium—is a lean color because of its extremely low oil-absorption index of just 15 to 18 percent. When white, or a heavy white mixture, is applied over a glazed area as a scumble, it must be fortified with extra oil. With an underpainting the idea is to keep things as lean as possible, using no oil, but once glazes are applied, the viscosity of the painting changes.

In other words, the colored glazes are oil-enriched and viscous, so to adhere properly, any lean paint—in this case, white—that is to be applied over them must have oil added to it. In practice this means mixing into your whites some extra stand oil or sun-thickened linseed oil. Adding bodied oils to your white scumbles will maintain the high viscosity level of your painting and will guard against future cracking.

DEMONSTRATION

Scumbling is a way to restore high-value passages that inevitably become darker with the application of successive glaze layers. White (or a color mixed with it) is applied over glazed areas to bring some light back into the picture. White paint is lean, so oil must be added to bring it up to the viscosity level of the glazes it is going to cover.

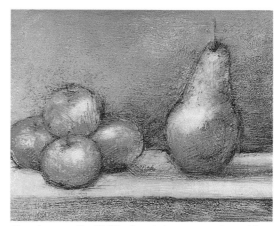

Here is a small still life already in progress. I would like to add some more glazes in lighter colors, but the existing colors on the apples and pears are already very dark, so I'll have to lighten everything up with an overall flat white scumble.

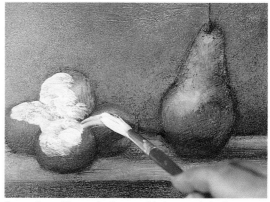

I use zinc white to do the scumble because it is the most transparent of the whites. I add a little oil to the paint and apply it with a soft brush.

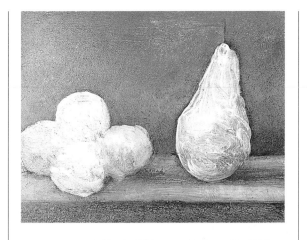

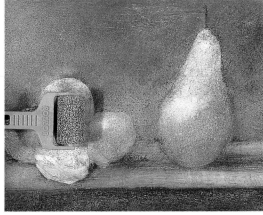

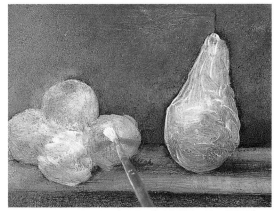

The illustration at top left shows you how the still life looks with the zinc white applied. Next, I smooth out the white paint with a stiff bristle brush and then use a small foam rubber roller to continue the smoothing and pick-up process. Below, the scumble is finished and has dried; I will apply more glazes over it until the painting is done.

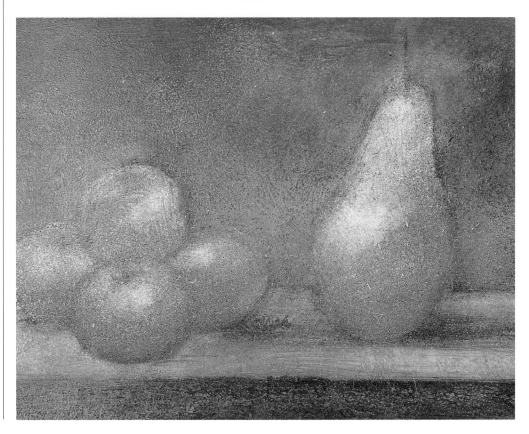

SCUMBLING

EGGS
Oil on canvas board,
8 × 10" (20.3 × 25.4 cm).
Collection of the artist.

This still life involved several layers of white scumbles. In a sense the color white was "glazed" many times to produce an eggshell smoothness.

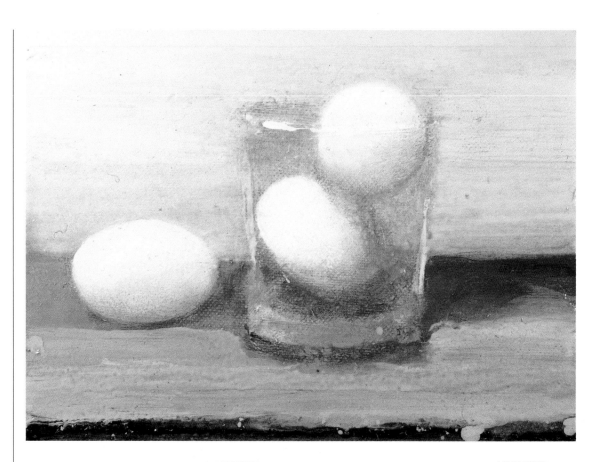

MACINTOSH
Oil on wood panel,
8 × 8" (20.3 × 20.3 cm).
Private collection.

The early steps in this painting were done in oil glazes and the details and final texture were made with smooth scumbles. Scumbles can be either smooth or rough.

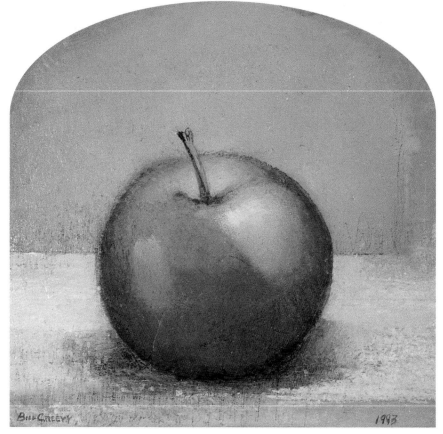

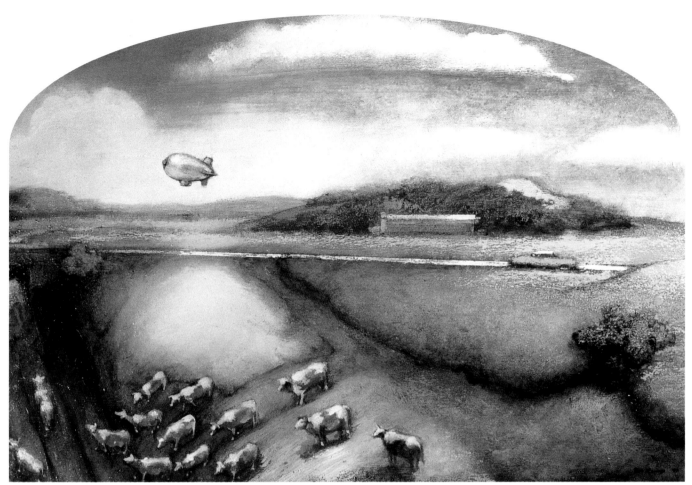

BIG DADDY COMES HOME
Oil and alkyd on wood panel, 12 × 18"
(30.5 × 45.7 cm).
Collection of Denny Levy.

This is a landscape with lots of richly textured details—all of which were made by using various kinds of scumbling techniques. The herd of cattle, the grassless ridge, the dried-up canal, and the blimp were all executed by scumbling over highly glazed passages. The field of high grass off to the right is an especially beautiful example of a combined glazed-and-scumbled passage.

UNDERPAINTING WHITE

One of the facts of life that oil painters had to live with in the past was that white is a slow-drying color, especially titanium and zinc white. This feature is not particularly troublesome when you're working alla prima, since the long open time gives you the opportunity to make changes and corrections. But in glazing, white's slow-drying nature can be problematic. Up until a few years ago the only solution was to use the ever-reliable lead white, the fastest-drying white of all, taking only a few days to dry depending on the humidity. It was, in fact, the only white oil paint available until the late 19th century. Lead white's rapid drying time made it ideal as an underpainting white. It permitted fast-drying grisailles, plus it had a tough, "stringy" texture that could retain brushstrokes, so it doubled as a texturizer. However, even as effective as lead white was (and still is), no doubt many an oil painter working before the 19th century wished that his white paint would dry just a bit faster—like in a few hours.

Today that wish has come true. One of the most recent technical innovations in oil painting is a modified white paint that is extremely fast drying and so heavy-bodied that it easily forms thick impastos and textures. This white goes under several different names but is most commonly called "underpainting white." All versions of underpainting white are basically the same. Chemically it is a titanium white made with a particularly strong-acting, fast-drying alkyd resin—meaning, in short, that it is an alkyd paint. Underpainting white's rapid-drying quality is the result of its alkyd formulation, eliminating the need to add metallic siccatives (cobalt drier is one), which darken whites.

Underpainting white shares the excellent film qualities that alkyd paints are known for. It dries not only fast but evenly throughout the film layer, and it remains flexible and does not brittle with age. Also, it can be mixed safely and directly into any other oil color, including traditional slow-drying titanium white. And because it is made of titanium dioxide pigment, it is nontoxic.

When underpainting white is used to create grisailles for glazing, it can produce spectacular effects. Sometimes referred to as "textured white," this type of paint can be applied with bristle brushes and palette knives to create sensual textures and surfaces. Since these thick passages dry fast, they can be glazed over instantly. The oily transparent glazing colors catch in the niches and grooves of the textured paint, producing sparkling, jewel-like effects.

DEMONSTRATION

For this demonstration I chose a highly textured subject—craggy rocks along the Maine coast—to illustrate the wonderful textural possibilities that can be achieved by using underpainting white with the oil glazing technique.

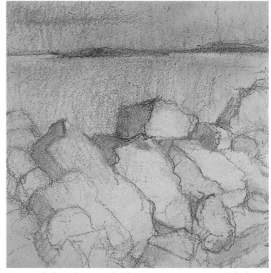

A pastel drawing on sized paper serves as a guide for the painting.

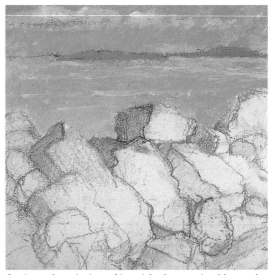

I mix underpainting white with ultramarine blue and apply it as the local color of the sky.

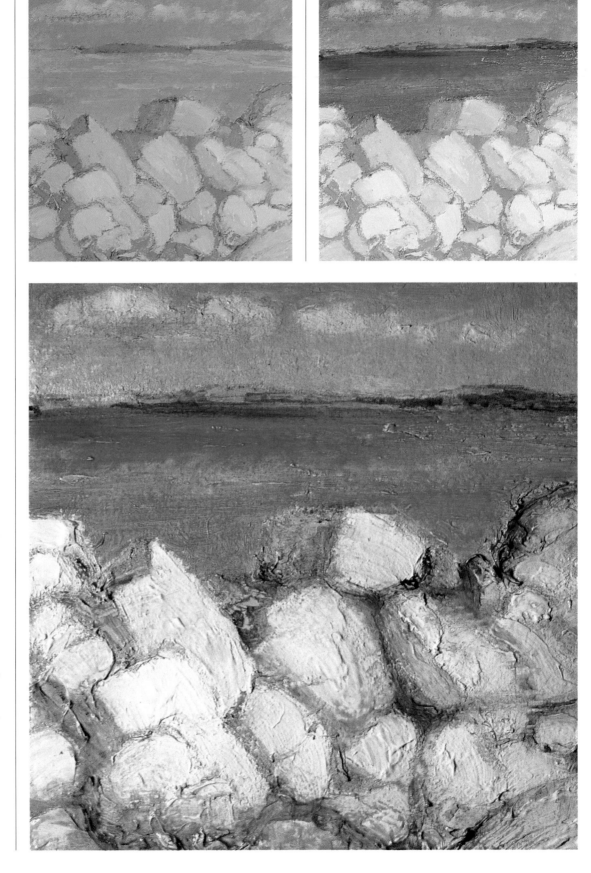

Pure, undiluted underpainting white is heavily applied to the rocks; I use some gray with it for the shadows. The rocks' texture is particularly exaggerated by the paint quality. Once the entire composition has been rendered in underpainting white, I leave the painting for about five hours until it is dry to the touch. Then I use manganese blue and ultramarine blue to glaze in the water. The underpainting white's texture creates the illusion of small ocean waves.

MAINE ROCKS
Oil on sized paper,
10 × 10" (25.4 × 25.4 cm).
Collection of the artist.

I glazed burnt sienna, transparent black, and transparent violet over the heavily textured rocks to finish the painting. These glazed colors created beautiful minuscule details where they caught in the texture of the underpainting white.

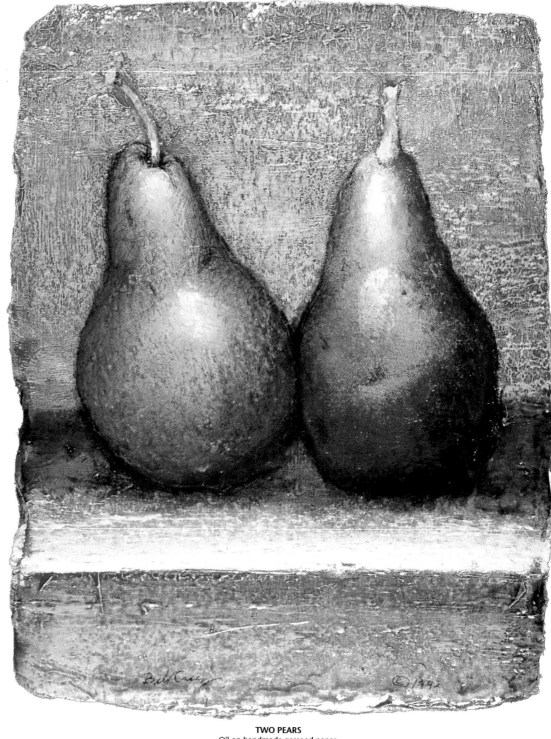

TWO PEARS
Oil on handmade gessoed paper,
6 × 4" (15.2 × 10.2 cm).
Private collection.

Both of these paintings were executed using underpainting white mixed with a touch of ultramarine blue in their initial stages, and both illustrate the beautiful qualities produced by glazing on top of a heavily textured grisaille. In each case I worked on handmade paper, whose inherently rough texture is made even more apparent by the underpainting white. What's beautiful about glazing on this type of surface is that the colors often work in unexpectedly lovely ways as they mirror the texture of the surface they're painted on.

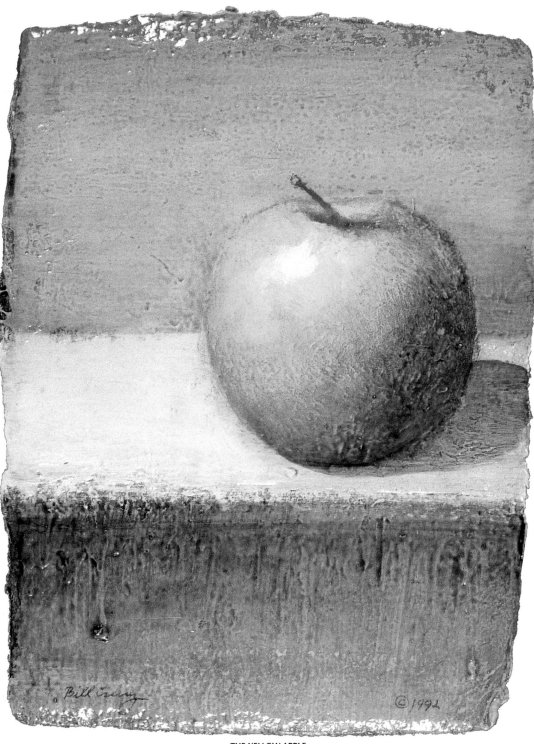

THE YELLOW APPLE
Oil on handmade gessoed paper,
6 × 4" (15.2 × 10.2 cm).
Collection of the artist.

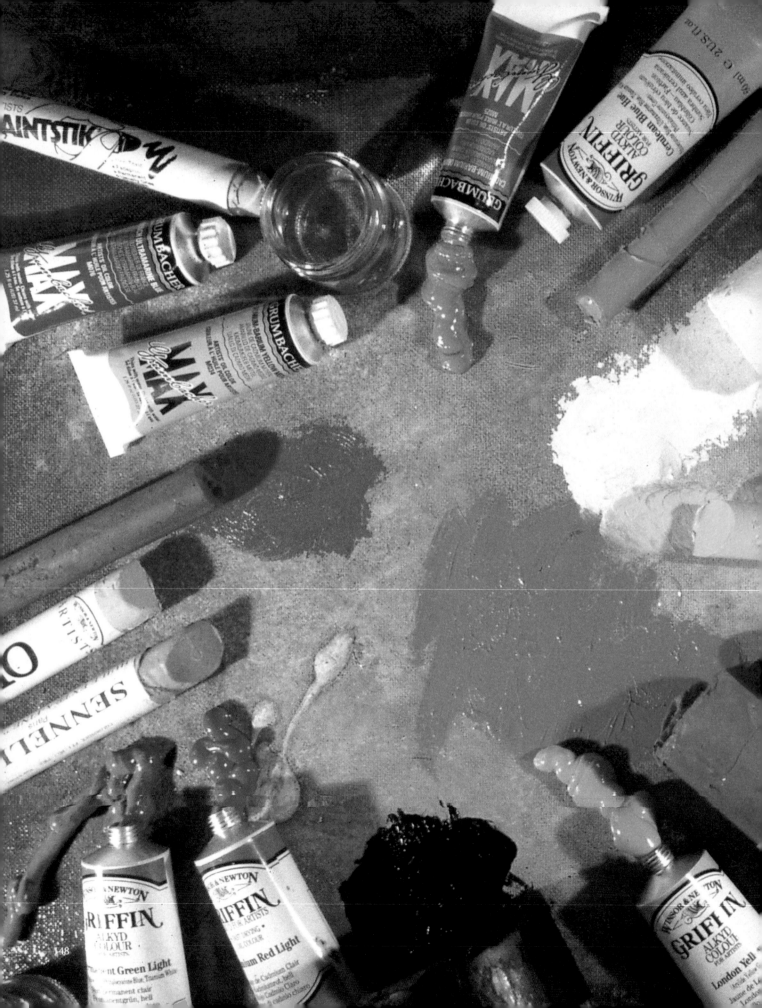

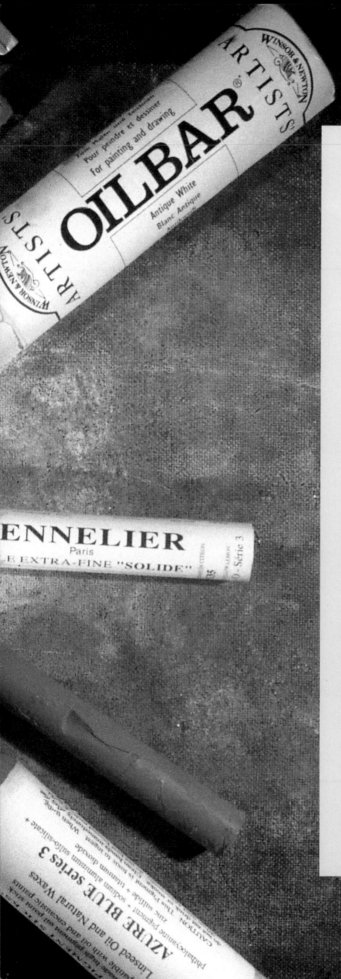

ALKYDS, OIL STICKS, AND WATER-MISCIBLE OILS

Throughout history artists have physically altered oil paint in various ways to meet their changing aesthetics, making it matte or glossy, thick or thin; its basic formula has always been flexible enough to accept change.

So it is not surprising that today several new oil paint variations exist. Especially worthy of note are three distinctly different forms: alkyd oil colors, oil sticks, and water-miscible oil colors, each developed to be an improvement over traditional oil paints and to satisfy the particular needs of contemporary painters.

Alkyds are oil paints made with a synthetic resin binder instead of a natural binder such as linseed oil. The result is paint that handles the same way oils do but offers interesting qualities, including improved drying and a stronger film. The oil stick is oil paint in a crayon form that allows the artist to draw and paint at the same time. Water-miscible oils are genuine oil paints that can be worked with water and/or traditional oils and solvents.

Alkyds, oil sticks, and water-miscible oils have long since gone past the mere novelty stage. They are high-quality, professional tools made by manufacturers famous for their devotion to producing superior materials. These products are here to stay, and point to future innovations.

ALKYDS

Alkyds and the development of alkyd chemistry offer some genuine improvements over the traditional oil paint formula. We all know that the basic recipe for oil paint is more or less the same as it was when developed in the late 15th and early 16th centuries: raw pigments ground and suspended in a drying oil, usually linseed or safflower, both of which are natural substances. Alkyds differ from traditional oil paints in that the binding medium is a man-made resin; the pigments are the same ones used in regular oil paints.

The word *alkyd* derives from the chemical combinations that make up the alkyd resin, namely polyhydric *al*cohols and polybasic a*cid*s—hence *alcid*, the original spelling of the term. For some unexplained reason the name alcid never caught on and was later changed to alkyd.

Invented in the 1930s, alkyds were first introduced as superior-quality wall paints, gaining a reputation in the 30s and 40s as the "Cadillac" of house paints. Alkyds would have been developed into artists' colors sooner had not the emergence of acrylic colors captured the interest of contemporary painters in the early 1950s. Thus, it is only recently that artists'-quality alkyds have been introduced. Winsor & Newton has pioneered their development, and today its Griffin oil colors are the leading and, for the moment, only true alkyd-based paints available. Other brands of alkyds have existed briefly, such as Shiva's Quick Dry oil paints and Talens Rembrandt's very beautiful, enamel-like "fluid oil colors." Unfortunately neither remains on the market, leaving only Winsor & Newton's Griffin line.

Alkyds produce a very strong paint film— stronger than traditional oil paint films. The alkyd paint film is also very flexible; it does not get brittle with age as traditional oil paint films do. Finally, alkyds dry much faster than regular oils. They are dry to the touch overnight and as dry as they'll ever get within just a few months.

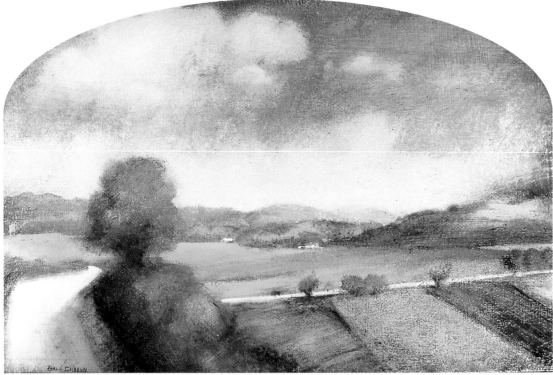

LAST DAY OF SUMMER
Alkyd on wood, 12 × 18"
(30.5 × 45.7 cm).
Private collection.

I completed this painting, which integrates opaque and glazed passages, in less than one day. I used Gamblin's Galkyd, an alkyd-based painting medium, because it gives a smooth, satinlike finish. The fast-drying action of the alkyd paints quickly set the earth-colored underpainting, allowing me almost instantly to glaze in the cool greens and blues.

Let's look a little more closely at the specific physical and working characteristics of alkyd colors.

FAST-DRYING OIL PAINTS

The usual response to the question "What are alkyds?" is, "They're fast-drying oil paints."

It's true. Alkyds dry rapidly. Paints made with natural oils that have not been altered with mineral siccatives such as cobalt driers take a few days to dry to the touch and months to dry thoroughly. In fact, the oxidation (drying) process may go on for years depending on how thick the paint film is. In contrast, all alkyd colors are dry to the touch the next day, and are dry enough to varnish in a month.

Alkyds do not dry as fast as or in the same way as acrylics, meaning that they can be blended and worked into each other just like any other oil color. In the time span of an average painting session, alkyds handle exactly like regular oil paint. The difference is, the next day they're dry to the touch and/or ready to be glazed or painted over. Acrylics dry much more rapidly than that and become as hard as a rock almost immediately, whereas alkyds can still be sanded and scraped as they reach the early drying stages.

ALL COLORS DRY EQUALLY

Another aspect of alkyd paints is that each and every color dries at the same speed. This is in drastic contrast to regular oil colors, which dry at different speeds. Titanium white, for example, stays wet three times longer than burnt sienna or raw umber. Obviously oil painters must take these varying drying rates into account. If a faster-drying oil paint is applied over a slower-drying one, the faster one may separate, resulting in cracks. It's like having dried paint on a rubber band that's being stretched—obviously the paint will flake off. The fact that alkyd colors are free of such variables in their drying rates is a real advantage to the oil painter. Any color can be applied on top of any other without risking eventual cracking.

WHITE CADILLAC
Alkyd on wood, 8 × 10"
(20.3 × 25.4 cm).
Collection of Jane and
David Copeland.

White Cadillac *is
a small, almost
hallucinogenic study
that later served
as the basis for a
larger painting. This
version evolved in
my favorite way:
while I was seated in
a comfortable chair
and working with
just a few earth
colors, white, and a
soft brush. Alkyds
are great paints for
daydreaming with.
They dry quickly and
evenly, but unlike
acrylics or gouache,
they remain blendable
for a relatively long
time. Here, I added
fine details with
colored pencil.*

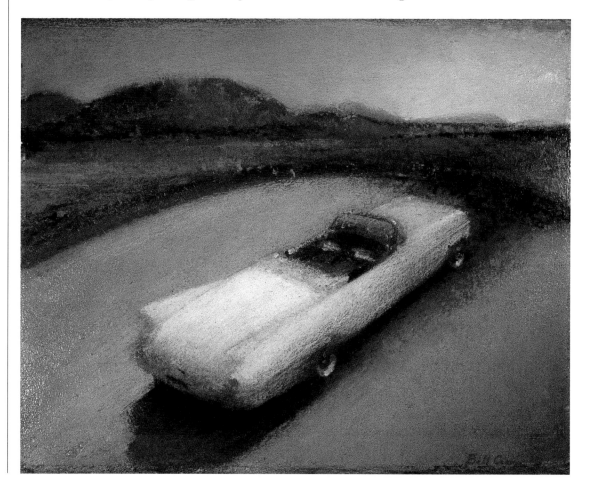

Moreover, all colors of the alkyd family look the same. That is to say, they have a more unified overall look than traditional oil colors, which can vary in the way they appear when dry. One color may look sunken in, while another may give off a higher gloss than its neighboring color, creating a patchwork or "suede" effect known as *dichroism*. Unlike oils, alkyd colors are free of any such dichromatic distortions, thanks to their synthetic resin base. Alkyds have instead something of the look of oils that have already been varnished. You'll notice this unified quality as you work with alkyds, and it is one of the special secrets to their beauty.

STRONG, FLEXIBLE PAINT FILM

With a synthetic polymer as its binder, alkyd paint resembles acrylic in the flexibility of its paint film, which bends easily without cracking. This is in marked contrast to oil paints, which become more brittle as they dry and begin to age. Also, the alkyd paint film is much stronger and tougher than a regular oil film, having less of a tendency to crack and chip.

BRIGHT, LUMINESCENT COLORS

Perhaps the best reason of all for using alkyds is for their brilliant color effects. Alkyd colors are definitely brighter and more luminescent than regular oil colors, having a deeper resonance and glow, a more jewel-like quality. To some extent the brightness is uncanny and almost surreal, with an enamel-like feel. Even whites and cream mixes have a shine to them, while the darker colors shimmer and glow. Alkyds always look fresh, a trait that, oddly enough, has little to do with pigment quality but is the result of the synthetic alkyd resin binder.

SUITABLE FOR MANY SURFACES

Alkyds are uniquely adaptable to a variety of painting surfaces, especially paper. There is a big controversy over whether oil paints should be used on paper or paper boards, since the slow oxidation of the linseed or other natural drying oil binder produces linotic acid, which can eventually corrode this support. With alkyds the problem is minimized by the rapid and permanent drying nature of the alkyd binder. Whatever acidic deterioration alkyds might cause to the paper support will be evident in the early life of the painting, because once completely dry the alkyd paint film becomes stable.

Alkyds can be painted safely on any other traditional support, such as canvas, Masonite, or wood. In addition, because their paint film is more flexible and less brittle than that of regular oil paint, alkyds adhere well to such unconventional supports as vinyl, plastic, glass, and metal.

CAN USE WITH TRADITIONAL OIL COLORS

Even though alkyds are made with a synthetic binder and regular oil paints are made with a natural one such as linseed oil, the two are nevertheless very compatible and can easily be used together in the same painting. There are several ways this can be done.

Perhaps one of the best possibilities is to use alkyds for an underpainting, and then finish the work in traditional oil colors. Alkyds are great for starting a painting because they dry so fast. They

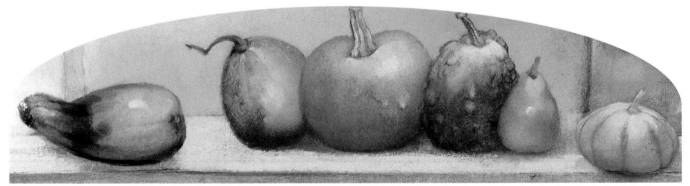

PUMPKINS, SQUASHES, AND PEARS
Alkyd on wood, 6 × 25"
(15.2 × 63.5 cm).
Collection of the artist.

Obviously for some subjective reason I prefer working on shaped wooden panels when I paint in alkyds. I think this feeling has a medieval source in the sense that alkyd color is so clear and bright that it lends itself easily to a luminist's mode of thinking. The glowing colors and "tight" consistency make me want to do paintings that resemble the jewel-like predellas of medieval altarpieces.

can be used either in a direct alla prima fashion or, as we have seen, to create underpaintings for traditional oil glazes.

Another way to combine alkyds and traditional oil paints is to mix the two directly together, which will accelerate the drying of the oils. However, care must be taken to mix them together *thoroughly* to avoid potential problems with separation caused by differences in drying rates.

A more typical approach is to combine alkyd mediums, rather than alkyd paints themselves, with traditional oils. Winsor & Newton offers three distinct alkyd mediums, any of which can be used with regular oil paints: Liquin, excellent for thinning paint and glazing; Wingel, for working wet-on-wet and alla prima; and Oleopasto, a stiffer compound for making fast-drying textures and impastos. Mixtures are intended to give traditional oils some of the advantages of alkyds—namely, rapid drying and the mediums' transparency. But here again, as when combining one paint type with the other, the safe rule of thumb is to make sure the traditional oils are well mixed into the alkyd mediums. This is a necessary precaution because of their different drying times.

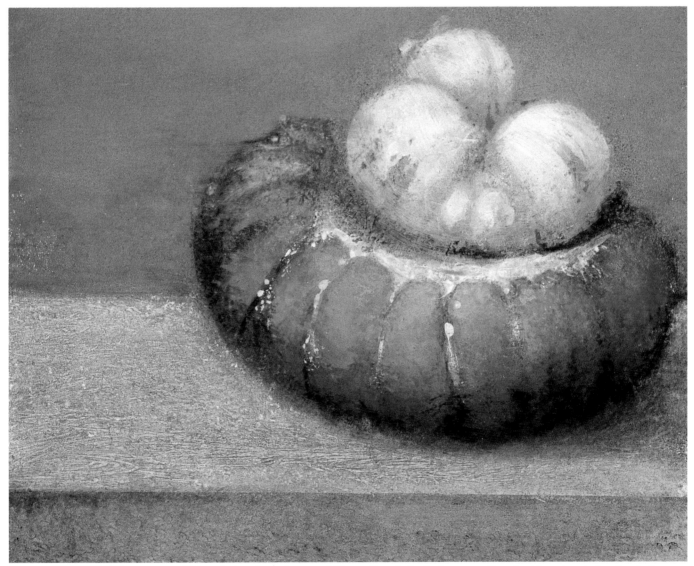

TURBAN SQUASH
Alkyd on wood, 8 × 10" (20.3 × 25.4 cm).
Collection of the artist.

This painting shows the enamel-like quality of alkyd colors, as well as the rich and varied surface textures they permit.

EXCELLENT FOR GLAZING

The ability to glaze with speed and confidence is probably the primary reason artists turn to alkyds. Alkyds are great for glazing. Two things make this possible.

The first is obvious: their rapid drying time. For viable results, the underpainting to which glazes will be applied must be thoroughly dry so that the glazed passages do not pick up any of this opaque layer. This is why so often in the past underpaintings were executed not in oils but in egg tempera, due to its shorter drying time. Alkyd underpaintings dry to the touch within a day. Furthermore, using alkyd mediums as glazing mediums (and they're all amazingly transparent) definitely accelerates drying time.

An artist working exclusively with alkyd glazes can successfully achieve several glazes in one day—approximately the same amount of work that would take maybe weeks to complete using only traditional oils.

Alkyds offer exciting possibilities for the future of the oil painting medium. They certainly seem to be here to stay, even though at the moment Winsor & Newton alone offers a complete line of alkyd paints and mediums. But I feel that other manufacturers will soon bring more variety to the alkyd direction. As it is, many of them do produce a range of alkyd-based painting mediums, Rowney, Grumbacher, Daniel Smith, and Gamblin, just to name a few, answering the needs of painters who more and more find them convenient and useful.

PEARS AND PUMPKINS
Alkyd and oil pastel on board, 8 × 8"
(20.3 × 20.3 cm).
Collection of Harriet and Milton Rosen.

This painting is a combination of alkyd underpainting and oil pastel details. I dipped the oil pastels into the thixotropic alkyd medium Wingel and applied them as a thick paste into the wet alkyd paints. The Wingel adds a glow and shine the oil pastels do not have on their own. The same technique can be applied even more effectively with oil sticks.

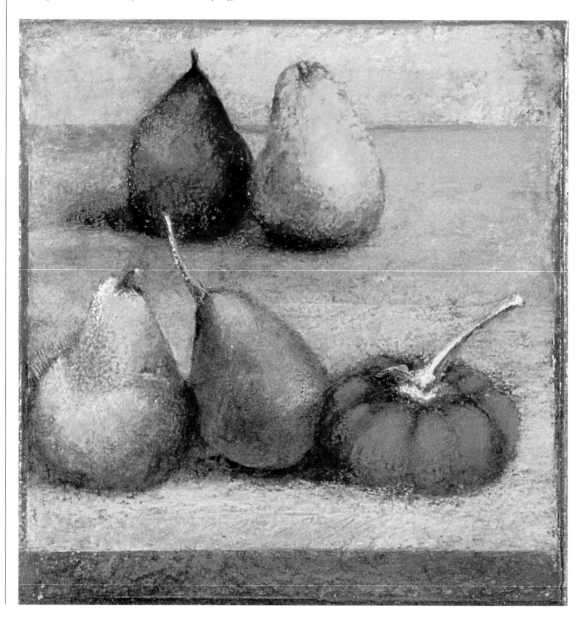

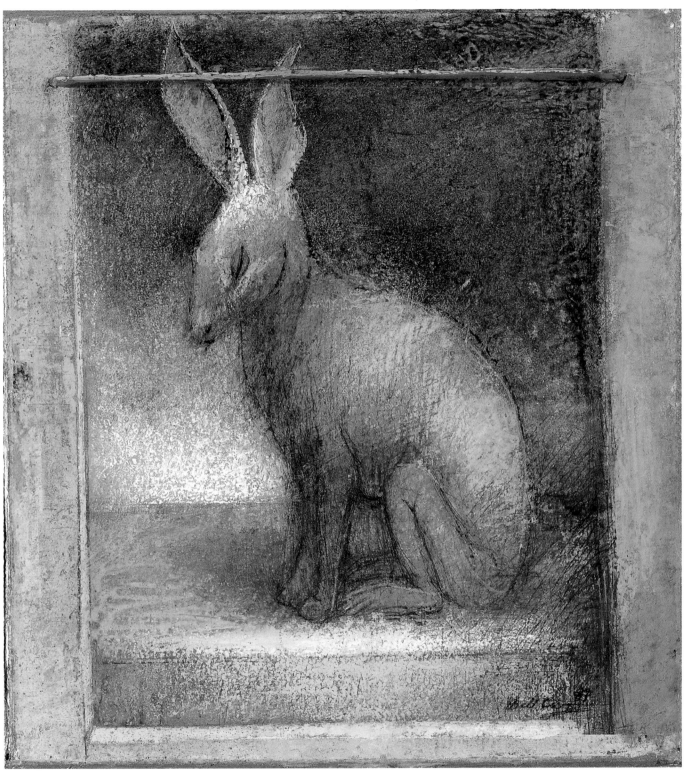

SLEEPING RABBIT
Alkyd, pastel, and oil
pastel on board, 12 × 9"
(30.5 × 22.9 cm).
Collection of
Marianne Perry.

This painting started out as a pastel pencil drawing of a stuffed rabbit I saw in New York's Museum of Natural History. Many days later, with layer upon layer of alkyd, pastel, and oil pastel, the final painting emerged. When spread over soft (chalk) pastels, alkyd mediums make for a beautiful and unique kind of glaze, one that is almost as transparent as watercolor but richer in gloss, texture, and color. The technique works best with dark, pure-pigmented pastels. For whites and light colors, opaque alkyd paints or oil pastels are better. (Photo by D. James Dee.)

ALKYDS

DEMONSTRATION

This painting, a still life entitled *The Racers* and executed in alkyds, features the two main characters of the fable "The Tortoise and the Hare." The support is a gessoed wood panel with a rounded top.

I set down the main components of the painting in a relatively detailed drawing in pastel pencil, fixing it with a spray of retouch varnish.

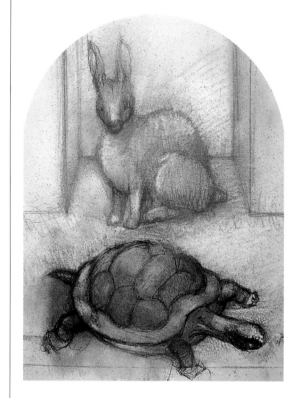

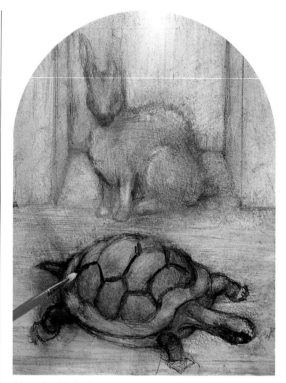

Next, I add dark outlines to the tortoise's shell, using olive green mixed with Wingel; then I leave the painting to dry for a few hours. Alkyds and alkyd mediums dry to the touch in about an hour or two if painted thinly.

I then cover the painting with a very transparent layer of terre verte and burnt sienna mixed with Liquin. This fast-drying, neutral color serves both as a beginning coat and as an isolating varnish.

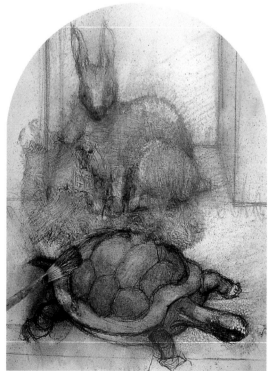

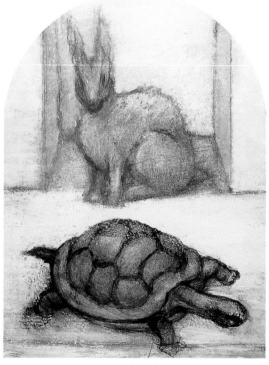

Opaque colors are added. Off-whites are mixed with Oleopasto and Wingel to give additional consistency and body. This opaque layer will be glazed over later.

The rabbit gets a heavily textured coating of titanium white mixed with Oleopasto and Wingel. The idea is to create the illusion of fur. I use palette knives to push the textured white paint around.

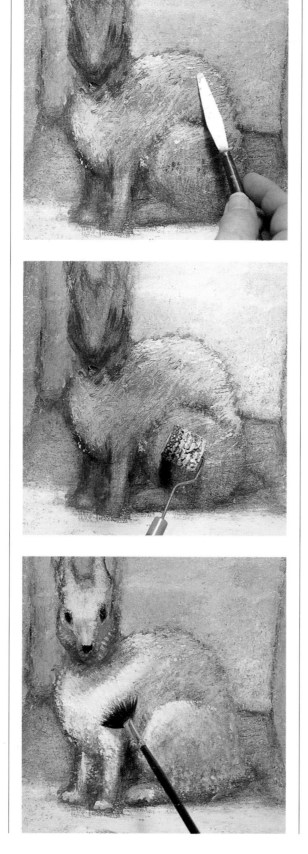

To further spread the textured white paint, I employ a foam roller.

I want the rabbit's breast to be smoother than the rest of his coat, so I use a fan blender in that area.

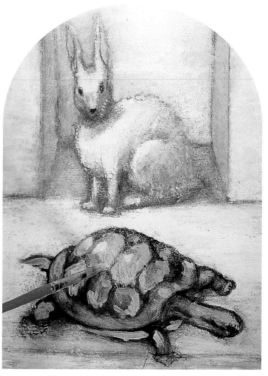

Opaque whites and yellows are added to the turtle's shell.

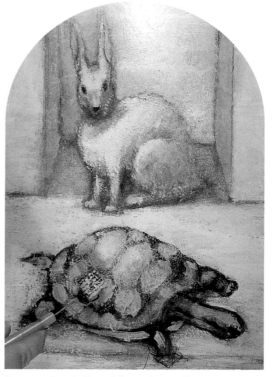

I use a palette knife and then a foam roller to exaggerate the texture of the opaque colors on the turtle's shell.

ALKYDS

The shell is now completely covered with thick, opaque white and yellow. When this layer dries, I will glaze over it with darker, more transparent local colors.

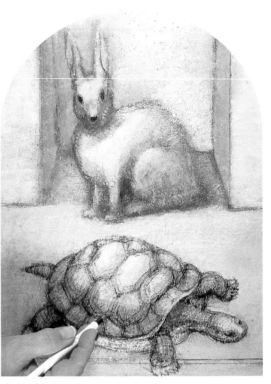

I apply an ultramarine blue glaze behind the rabbit as well as on the rabbit itself, wiping most of it off the rabbit but leaving a little bit to act as a neutralizer to the brown color.

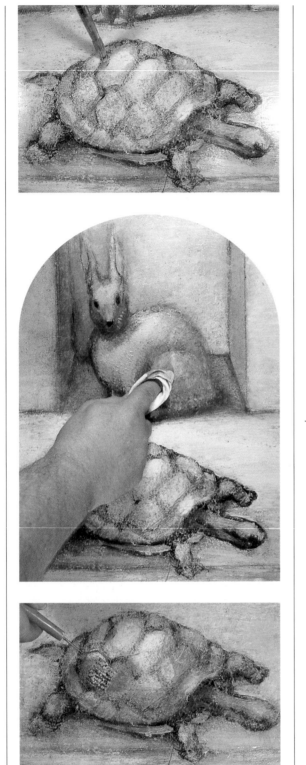

With a black ballpoint pen, I restore the graphic texture of the turtle's shell. Alkyds dry quickly to a hard-gloss finish, so it is easy to draw on top of them with pointed tools such as pens.

A heavy opaque coating of cadmium yellow and titanium white is painted around the base of the turtle. More of the same cadmium yellow is added to the details on the turtle's shell.

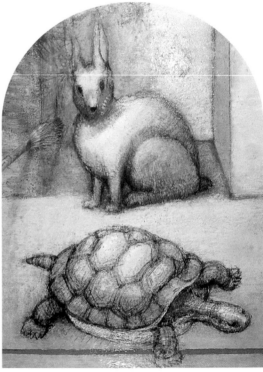

More ultramarine blue thinned with Liquin is added as a glaze to the niche behind the rabbit.

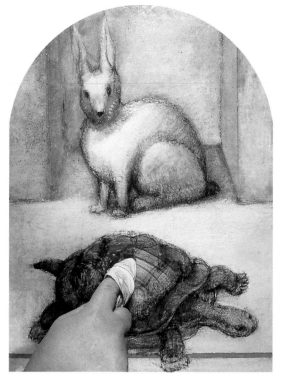

Next, I glaze ultramarine blue thinned with Liquin on top of the turtle. Then, with a rag soaked in Archival's "Fat" alkyd medium, I selectively wipe away portions of the blue glaze from the turtle's shell and body.

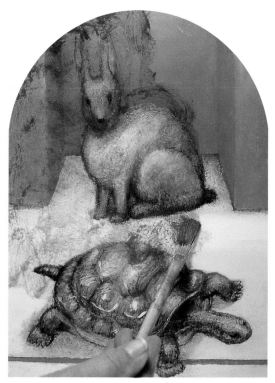

At this stage I cover the entire painting with a burnt sienna glaze. The idea behind this is to unify the composition with an overall warm, earthy golden brown. With a rag soaked in medium, I then wipe away most of the burnt sienna glaze, leaving traces on the yellow foreground and on the turtle but working some of it into the rabbit and allowing a slight haze to remain in the cerulean blue niche as a neutralizer.

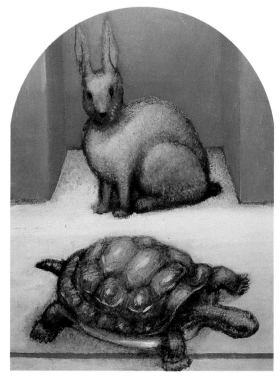

To make the background niche richer, I paint it in cerulean blue.

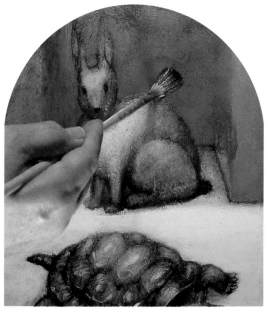

Next, I add ultramarine blue to the background to help define the shape of the niche as well as to enrich the intensity of this area.

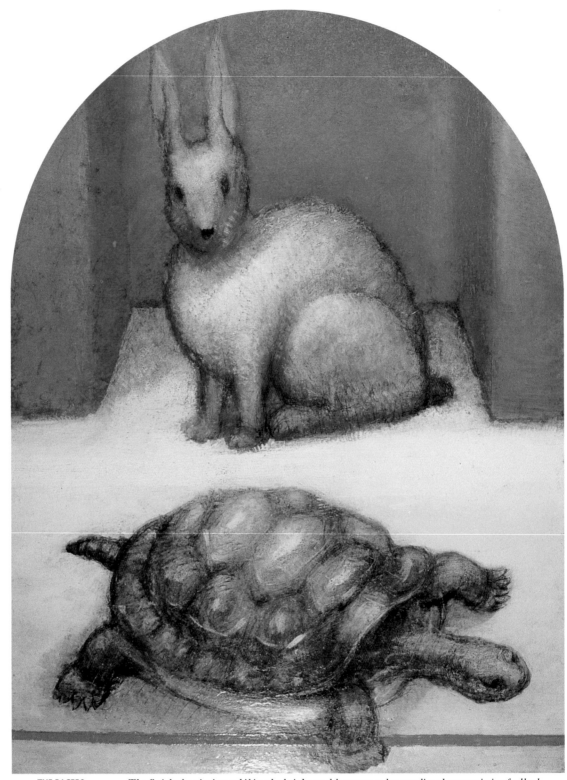

THE RACERS
Alkyd on wood,
20 × 12" (50.8 × 30.5 cm).
Collection of the artist.

The finished painting exhibits the bright and lustrous color quality characteristic of alkyd paints. The fast-drying properties of alkyds make glazing and establishing details very easy.

OIL STICKS

At first it would seem a gross exaggeration to call oil sticks *paints*. But in fact these crayonlike colored sticks are actually a combination of two distinct painting mediums: oils and the most ancient paint form of all, encaustic.

Encaustic, from the Greek meaning "to burn in," was the most common form of easel painting used by the ancient Greeks and Romans. This very simple and beautiful medium is based on colors made by suspending raw pigments (the same ones used in oil paints) in a binder of natural wax, usually beeswax. Rather than the solvents and oils that are used to make oil paints flow, heat is applied to convert the wax colors into a liquid paint. The encaustic palette is a hot plate of molten wax colors. While liquid, the wax colors are painted onto a solid support such as wood. Once the desired image is in place, the painting is fused with a final application of heat. When the hot wax cools and solidifies, the encaustic painting is considered dry.

Wax and oil are very compatible substances. In fact, encaustic colors are made with traces of oil in them to keep the paints more workable. Conversely, 16th-century Venetian painters would add a small portion of wax to the basic oil paint formula to give colors more body. Oil sticks are simply a modern modification of this ancient encaustic medium, the only difference being that they contain a larger proportion of oil than pure encaustic paints.

The principle behind oil sticks is that the wax and pigment they contain is made workable not with heat but by the action of the slow-drying oils in their formulation. Oil sticks are not liquid like paint; rather, they are a paste—oil paints in stick form. Their chemical formulation requires just the right balance of wax, pigment, and oil so that the stick is soft enough (because of the oil) to draw and paint with yet hard enough (because of the wax) to remain in crayon form. This hybrid medium is a highly responsive, versatile painting tool that allows the oil painter to draw and paint simultaneously, lending itself to fast and spontaneous execution. Working with oil sticks is oil painting at its most direct and immediate, sidestepping the palette and the brush altogether. Painting with oil sticks is very much like painting with only your hands.

DRAWING AND PAINTING DIRECTLY

Perhaps the most common way of using oil sticks is to draw and paint with them directly, thereby exploiting the convenience that is one of their chief attractions. In many ways oil sticks are as handy to use as drawing mediums such as charcoal or pastel. It's no problem to start right away on a picture with oil sticks. Just pull away a little piece of dried film from the tip of the crayon and you're ready to paint. All of your colors are ready to go in an instant—there are no tubes of paint to open and no palette to lay out. You can simply take your favorite color and start to draw with it, as freely and expressively as you wish.

The old separation of drawing from painting is no longer an issue with this medium. The fact that oil sticks do not need to be constantly loaded with fresh paint the way a brush does makes them an extremely fast medium to work with, allowing you to cover large areas of a composition in a hurry. Also, because oil sticks act a lot like a drawing medium, the quality of the lines and strokes you put down with them is noticeably different from what you get when you apply wet paints with a brush. Because of the wax oil sticks contain, the marks they make are not as fluid as regular paint. Color goes down more like crayon—that is, in more of a broken manner than a fluid one. In fact, oil sticks are great for working in a "drybrush" manner; you can create beautiful scumbles easily by dragging one color over an existing passage or the ground in such a way as to reveal both colors in a broken-textured way. Because oil sticks are paints in a paste form, their color stays on top of the painting surface rather than flowing down to fill the support's textural little nooks the way a liquid paint would. Thus, oil sticks mirror the texture of the surface to which they are applied, a trait you can exploit to produce some wonderfully beautiful effects.

Oil sticks can be worked with their tips like a crayon to draw lines, or they can be broken into shorter, "chubbier" versions and worked sideways to create an effect similar to that of a wide brushstroke. This approach works particularly well with the giant- or stump-size oil sticks. Wide strokes can give a very personal expressive quality to the textural surfaces of your paintings.

BLENDING WITH OIL STICKS

Oil sticks, like pastels and charcoal, are natural blenders. Their pastelike quality allows the oil painter to do masterful and sensitive blending that equals effects produced with traditional oil paints. Some artists, in fact, may find it easier to execute blending techniques with oil sticks. There are several methods for accomplishing blended passages in oil stick paintings.

Blending wet-on-wet. Oil sticks go down as a wet, creamy paste. Colors stay wet for hours and can be blended into each other very easily during a typical painting session. Blending wet-on-wet is the most direct approach, usually giving a kind of rough mixture. Also there is a lot of impasto buildup and visible evidence of paint strokes. With this method, it may be necessary to constantly wipe the oil sticks if you wish to keep your colors relatively clean.

IMPALA
Oil stick on Multimedia Artboard, 30 × 40"
(76.2 × 101.6 cm).
Collection of the artist.

Car paintings are always a chance for my imagination to take off—and oil sticks are just the medium to do that with. Oil sticks are fast and immediate, just like drawing. The model for Impala *was a tiny black-and-white ad in an antique car magazine for a 1959 Chevrolet Impala in California. The color, house, and ocean view are all made up, based somewhat on what I imagine it would feel like to own and drive a white '59 Chevy.*

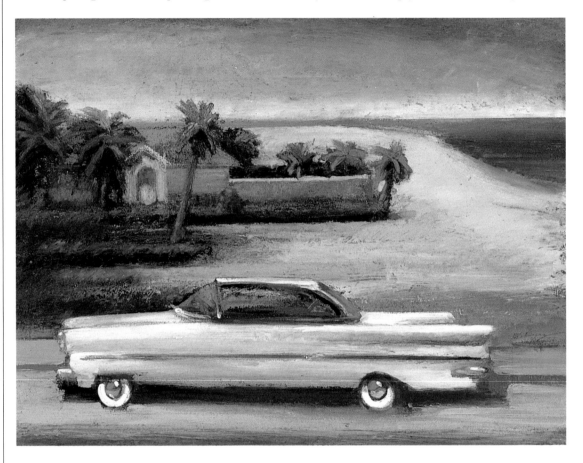

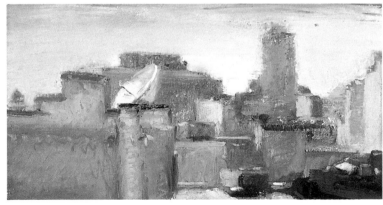

NEW YORK ROOFTOPS WITH DISH
Oil stick on Multimedia Artboard,
7 × 13" (17.8 × 33.0 cm).
Collection of the artist.

I had just bought a complete set of slim-size Winsor & Newton Oilbars—32 colors in all—and was eager to try them out. Oil sticks are very portable and are thus excellent for working outdoors—or in this case, from an open window in my studio. It was a rainy early spring day and I particularly enjoyed doing the TV satellite dish on the building across the street.

Blending with colorless wax sticks. All brands of oil sticks offer a colorless wax blender, which essentially is an oil stick with no pigment in it. Generally softer and greasier than pigmented oil sticks, colorless wax blenders are used primarily to blend unmixed oil stick colors together. They can also be used to extend color, giving it more body.

Blending with brushes. Just as in traditional oil painting, dry brushes, such as bristle fan blenders, can be used to blend unmixed oil stick colors. In fact, this is probably the best way to get really fine blending from oil sticks. Even color put down with the smaller-size oil sticks has a rough, uneven quality to it when first applied. Gentle blending with dry brushes can soften this effect. The fan blender is an obvious choice for this kind of work, but almost any relatively long-haired oil painting brush will do. The stiffer and shorter the brush, the less effective it will be when used dry. If you want highly polished, finely blended color, you can use a brush to apply a small portion of gloss medium such as damar varnish or Liquin to the area.

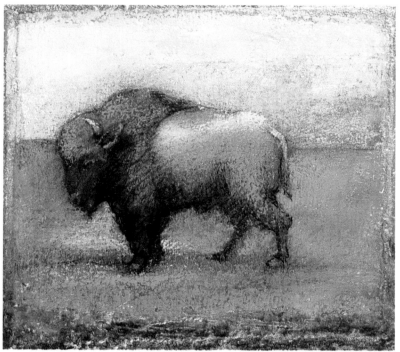

BUFFALO
Oil stick on handmade canvas panel, 6 × 8" (15.2 × 20.3 cm). Private collection.

This painting shows how beautifully oil sticks take to a rough surface. Several layers of thick canvas were glued together to make the panel. Much of the texture of this small piece was the result of dragging and scumbling thick oil sticks across the uneven surface. Later applications of pure Liquin deepened the effect.

SCRAPING AND KNIFE TECHNIQUES

Oil sticks can be worked with painting knives just like traditional oil paint that comes in a tube. Once applied to the painting surface, oil stick color remains soft and wet for a long time, meaning that it can be scraped and smeared around easily. Because it contains wax, oil stick color has a pastier consistency than regular oil paints, so that when moved around on the canvas with knives it tends to stand in high relief, leaving sharp ridges. The waxy, pastelike quality of oil stick color makes it resemble oil paint that has been allowed to stiffen a bit on the palette and is no longer fluid or syrupy. This makes it easier to control with painting knives.

Sgraffito effects are very easy to pull off with oil sticks. Any sharply pointed instrument, such as a blunt palette knife or a dental tool, can leave a sharp, incised line when scraped through a layer of fresh oil stick color. The line will be crisp and definite because the color that remains on either side of it will not fill in the exposed area as it would with fluid paint. Large metal spatulas or scrapers are great for making clean sweeps across fresh oil stick color to reveal a beautiful underpainted patina.

In addition to sharp tools, blunt implements can be used effectively with oil sticks as well. Common everyday items such as soup spoons can be pushed into wet oil stick colors to work them together wet-in-wet.

COMBINING OIL STICKS WITH PAINT MEDIUMS

As we know, various mediums are added to traditional oil paints to slightly alter the way they perform, making them thicker, glossier, or more transparent, or accelerating their drying time. These same mediums can affect oil sticks in similar ways. For example, simply dipping the tip of an oil stick into some turpentine makes the color more fluid, allowing a thinner application. Adding a heavy medium like Grumbacher's Zec or Winsor & Newton's Oleopasto makes oil sticks pastier, permitting heavy impasto effects and resulting in a faster-drying surface. Liquin makes oil stick color act like a transparent gel that dries relatively fast and has a high sheen. Combined with linseed oil, oil sticks acquire a more fluid, paintlike quality, making them resemble traditional oil paint.

COMBINING OIL STICKS WITH TRADITIONAL OIL PAINT

It goes almost without saying that oil sticks can be worked together with traditional oil colors just as they can be used alone. Perhaps the most common approach is to put the regular oil colors down first and then come in with the oil sticks as a sort of colored blender to push the paints around. It can also be done the other way around—that is, the initial color and design can be executed with oil sticks and traditional oil colors worked into them. Another idea is to do an underpainting in oil sticks and let it dry for a week or so, then glaze over it with conventional oil colors.

The advantage of working with conventional oil paints here is that the available color range is much broader than what currently exists in the various oil stick lines. Imagine the possibilities of using your oil sticks in conjunction with composite colors like those made by Holbein, or with Daniel Smith's wonderful new (and plentiful) interference and metallic colors. The potential combinations are almost infinite.

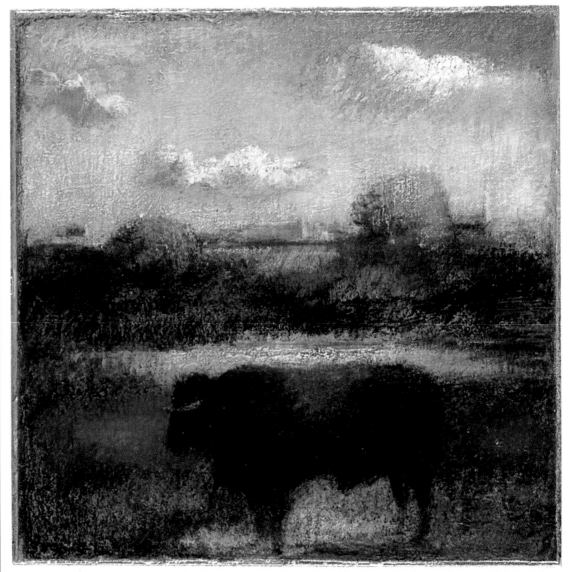

BLACK BULL
Oil and oil stick on canvas panel, 12 × 12" (30.5 × 30.5 cm). Collection of Edward and Gordana Dasaro.

Originally this was just an oil painting of the distant landscape; later I added the bull and the river with oil sticks and occasionally oil pastels, dissolving and working them in with varnishes.

DEMONSTRATION

I've chosen to execute this oil stick painting on tightly stretched, heavy-duty linen primed with a lead ground. Most oil sticks are soft enough to apply easily to stretched canvas, but rigid supports are more often used with this medium.

Oil sticks are very easy to draw with. Here I sketch in the basic lines for my still life with Sennelier Extra-Fine Oil Sticks, which I like for initial drawings because they are the smoothest and most controllable of all the brands. I start with just two colors: Sennelier brown and primary red.

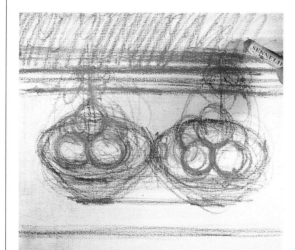

With a bristle brush soaked in turpentine, I spread the oil stick colors across the canvas, adding a touch of regular oil paint—a mixture of light red oxide and yellow ochre.

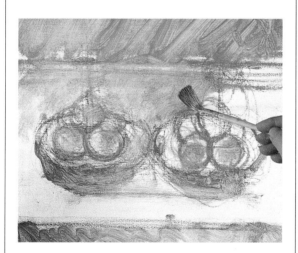

The canvas is now totally covered with paint. I let it dry.

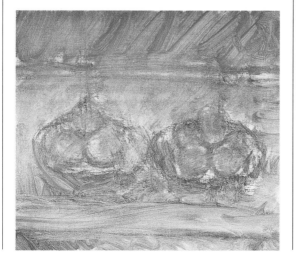

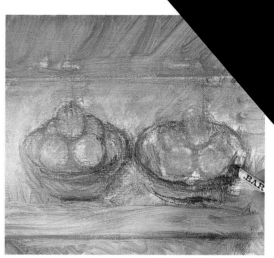

I reintroduce the drawing using Winsor & Newton Oilbars.

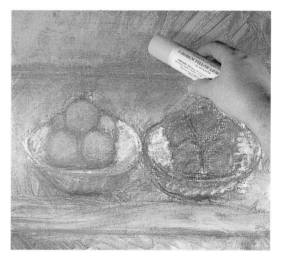

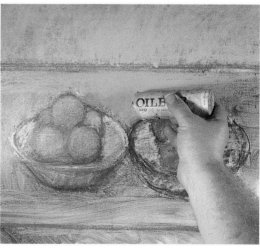

Now I apply pure basic colors heavily into various sections of the composition, using cadmium yellow light for the background and buff titanium and titanium yellow for the tabletop.

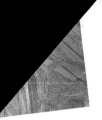

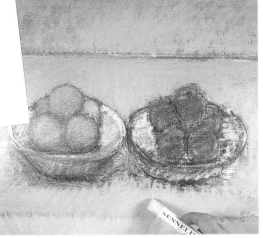

With a colorless blending stick I smooth out these freshly applied colors.

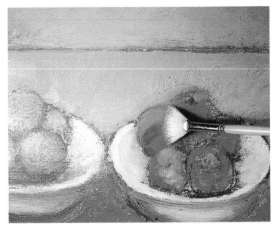

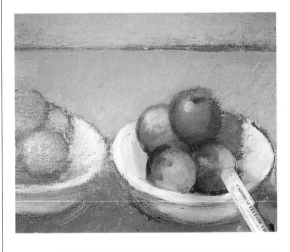

Using only R & F Pigment Sticks because of their maximum color intensity, I apply the final colors to the still life objects, then spread and blend the colors with fan blending brushes. One of the secrets to working sucessfully in oil sticks is knowing that brushes and other tools such as palette knives can be used.

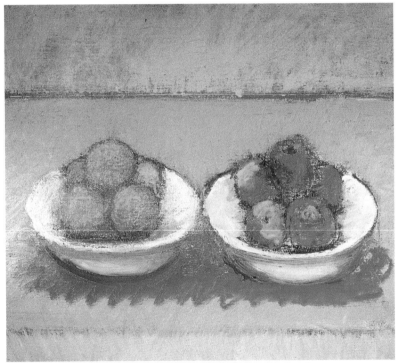

Here you can see how the painting looks with the basic colors in place.

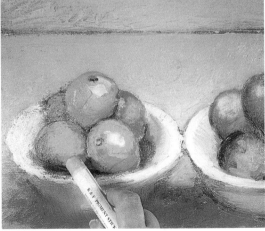

The final colors of the still life are heavily applied in an impasto manner. This creates the exciting textures oil sticks are famous for.

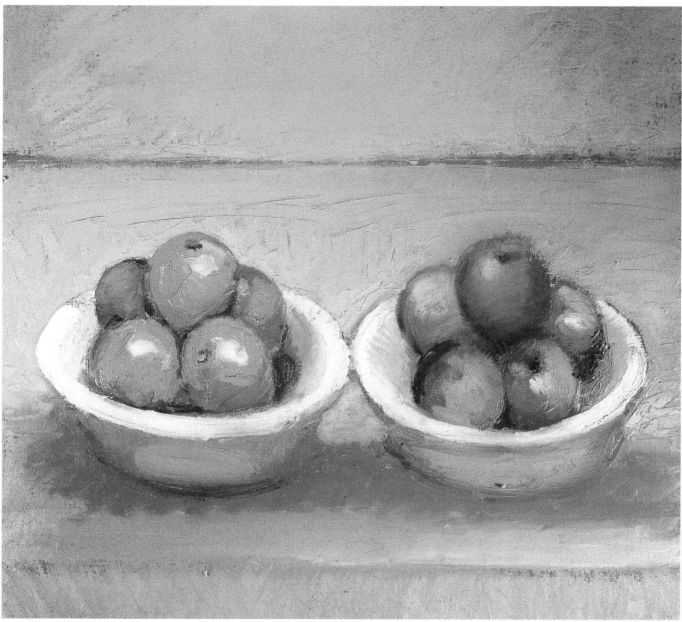

APPLES AND ORANGES
Oil stick on canvas, 16 × 18"
(40.6 × 45.7 cm). Collection of the artist.

The beauty of working in oil sticks is their directness and speed. They appeal to anyone who likes to work spontaneously.

Water-Miscible Oils

Who would have ever thought that water and oil would mix? Today, thanks to the prestigious American paint manufacturer Grumbacher, these two previously incompatible substances now work hand in glove. Grumbacher Max Artists' Oil Color, or Max for short, is the latest technical innovation in oil paint chemistry. Named after the founder of Grumbacher paints, Max is a genuine oil paint that is miscible with water. In other words, thinning the paints and cleaning up can be done with ordinary tap water instead of turpentine or mineral spirits. Max has made it possible to rid the oil painting studio of harsh, oil-based solvents with their irritating odors and potential health hazards.

This is not actually the first time that oil and water have been used together. Ever since the 15th century, oil and egg tempera emulsions have existed as a standard oil paint variation, and the milk-based casein paint has always been soluble in either oil or water. Egg and milk are natural emulsifiers, so it is not surprising that both

oil and water could be used with them in a paint medium. But Max is different. It is a genuine oil paint; water is nowhere to be found in its formulation. Instead, the chemists at Grumbacher have found a way to modify the traditional linseed oil binder to be "water-friendly." In all other respects, Max is identical to regular oil paints—except, as we've said, that it can be thinned and cleaned with just plain water.

This means that Grumbacher Max has the same brilliant, buttery consistency as traditional oil paints. It is made from the same pigments, has the same open time, dries at the same rate, and is subject to the same "fat over lean" rule that applies to regular oil colors. It is, moreover, compatible with all the traditional oil painting techniques and mediums. Max works with the same brushes and knives, supports and grounds, and varnishes and mediums as conventional oils. But when it comes time to clean and wipe your brushes, you stick them into a jar of water instead of turpentine.

Because Max is water-friendly, it has some unique characteristics. For one thing, it lends itself naturally to wash techniques, since water

STILL LIFE
Water-miscible oil on canvas panel, 9 × 12" (48.3 × 30.5 cm). Collection of Walter and Emily Luertzing.

One of the chief advantages of Max water-miscible oils is that they dry as slowly as regular oil paints but can be manipulated and thinned with water. To create this painting's smooth finish, I worked very close to its surface to blend color using soft synthetic brushes. Using water instead of turpentine made this close-up approach a lot safer and more enjoyable, since no solvent vapors were present.

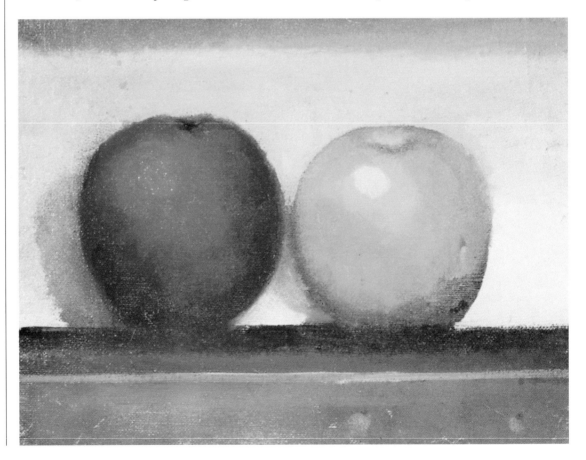

is so easy to use as a solvent to create thinned passages. (Just be sure washes contain at least 30 percent paint; if color is thinner than that, it will separate and bead up.) Also, because water is odorless, Max is a likely choice for executing details that require working physically close to the paint surface—not a great place to be if one is affected by solvent fumes.

Grumbacher Max can be a complete painting system unto itself, or it can be combined with other oil paints as well. There are 60 colors to choose from—almost as many as Grumbacher's traditional line of Pre-tested Artists' Oil Colors. With colors made from genuine mineral and synthetic pigments, the Max palette is a very balanced selection of opaque and transparent hues as well as neutral and intensely chromatic colors. There are two whites—titanium white and zinc white—but no flake or lead white. There are many brilliant and very lightfast synthetic-pigment colors: quinacridone red, gold, and orange, perylene red and maroon, dioxazine purple, indanthrone blue, and Grumbacher's exclusive Thio violet, to name a few. The cadmium colors are cadmium-barium mixtures, and there are many pure cobalts as well as a pure cerulean blue. All the earth colors are present, as well as the three major blacks: ivory, lamp, and Mars black. Also in the Max line are two specially formulated transparent mediums. One is a relatively slow drying, general-purpose medium called Max Liquid Medium; the other, Max Gel Medium, is a thixotropic alkyd-type medium that is fast-drying. Both are solvent-free and are miscible with water just as the Max paints are.

Max can be intermixed with any other brand of oil color or oil medium—and still retain its water-miscible characteristics. That means you can add your favorite Old-Holland, Blockx, or Sennelier oil colors to your Max colors and still have them be water-miscible. Or you can add Liquin, Venice turpentine, or damar varnish to your Max paints to increase their gloss or for glazing and not lose Max's water-friendly qualities. The trick is to keep the proportion of traditional color or medium in any mixture down to 30 percent. That is to say, if at least 70 percent of your mixture is Max in any form, the paint will remain water-miscible. If the proportion of Max falls below 70 percent, traditional solvents—turpentine or mineral spirits—become necessary. (It should be pointed out that Max is just as miscible with these as with water.)

For anyone who has been painting with traditional oils all along (which is most anyone reading this book), dipping a brush loaded with oil paint into a jar of water and watching it become miraculously clean is a strange and almost perverse sensation. Yet this is exactly what happens when you use Max. It takes a little while to get accustomed to using water instead of turpentine and to realize that nothing wrong is going to happen. But once you get over the initial feeling of strangeness, you gain a new sense of freedom working with Max.

This is especially true if you're in some way allergic to turpentine or mineral spirits. A lot of people are. While I've always sort of enjoyed the smell of fresh turpentine, I suffer from an itching rash on my hands after working with it for too long. It wasn't always this way with me, and in my case the reaction is only temporary. Certainly not everyone is affected by solvent vapors. But for some people the smell and the allergic reactions are not at all pleasant, and the potential for hazard is compounded in group situations such as classrooms. Already some schools have taken the drastic step of stopping their oil painting programs because of the concern over solvent vapors. It is exactly this type of situation that Max Grumbacher was designed to remedy—and it couldn't have happened at a better time. Thanks to Max, a whole generation of art students who may have been denied access to the experience of working in oils can now keep painting—thank heavens!

Grumbacher Max, of course, will not suit everyone, and certainly traditional oil paints are in no danger of being replaced by water-miscible variations. But it is reassuring to know that for those who want it, there is the option of leaving turpentine and mineral spirits behind forever and continuing on with free and odorless water.

The two works shown on the following pages represent two basic styles of painting that are easily executed with Grumbacher Max oils. One was done using a very loose approach, almost like painting a watercolor; for the other, I used smooth-blending techniques to create a porcelainlike finish. It is interesting that although the two styles of painting are very different, both were done using the same medium—ordinary water,which served to thin my paints and to clean my brushes. (The ease of rinsing brushes in water helps keep color fresh and clear.) Ironic as it may seem, no turpentine was used in any part of these oil paintings.

WATER-MISCIBLE OILS

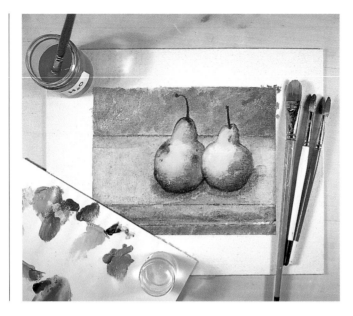

Loose handling. *Using soft nylon brushes and lots of water, I applied Max oil paints in thin washes much as one would when working in watercolor. The thin washes dried fast, so several layers were possible in one sitting. As each wash dried I would immediately apply a thin layer of retouch varnish on top of it as a sort of fixative. Since Max is an oil paint, it is possible to varnish it with traditional varnishes. After the retouch dried, I applied more thin color washes over it. To my surprise, the water-thinned oil washes were not affected in any way by the underlying varnish.*

The palette and brushes I used are the same as what I'd use with traditional oil paints. Both of the jars you see here hold nothing more than water—one container for washing brushes, the other for thinning paint.

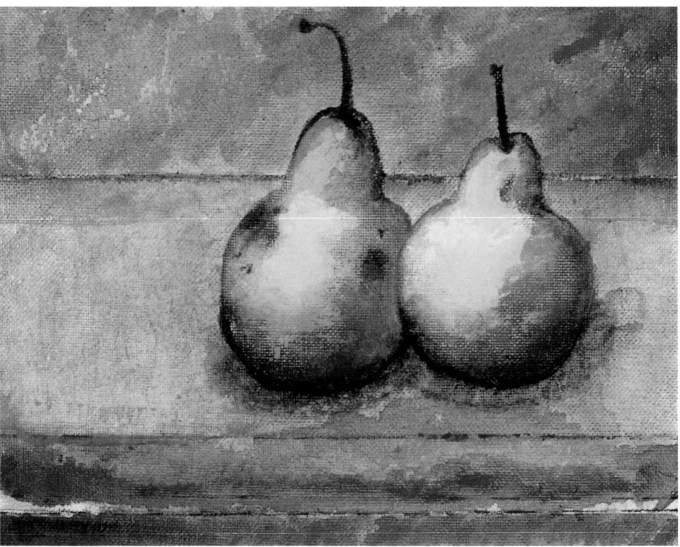

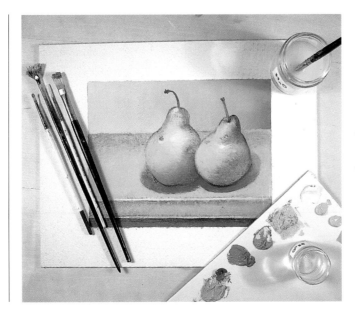

Smooth handling. *Here I used Max in a more traditional oil painting manner. I applied the paint in thicker amounts so it would stay open longer. With brushes dipped lightly in water, I was able to closely blend the wet color into smooth, subtle passages. Fan blender brushes were also used to achieve an even smoother, cleaner surface.*

Again, I used only water to execute this painting and to clean my brushes.

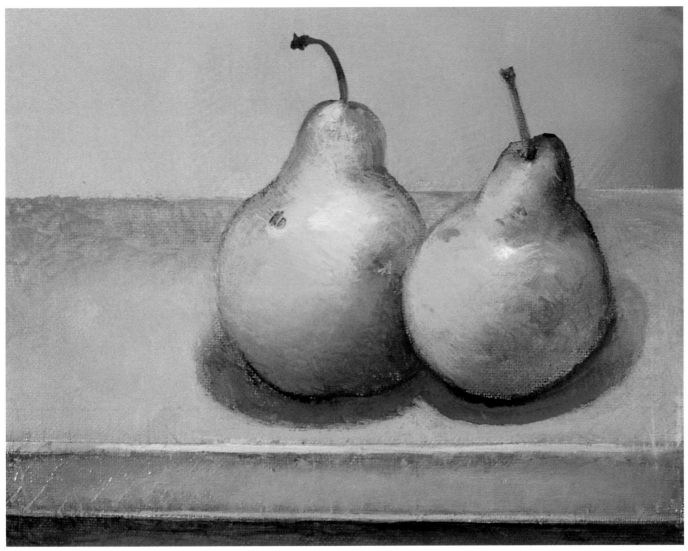

LIST OF SUPPLIERS

An obvious source for oil paints and just about everything else you need is your local art supply store. But if you want to find out more about the materials surveyed in this book and how to get hold of them, here is a list of dealers, including importers of products made as far away as Russia and Australia.

LARGE RETAIL OUTLETS AND CATALOGS

Daniel Smith Inc., 4130 First Avenue South, Seattle, WA 98134-2302. Toll-free: (800) 426-6740. Though it has a retail store in Seattle, Daniel Smith is perhaps best known for its beautifully illustrated catalog. Featuring a large assortment of European and American oil paints, the firm is also the exclusive source for its own very high quality brand, Daniel Smith Finest Oil Colors. The catalog carries everything else necessary for oil painting, including Daniel Smith's own product lines: canvases, solvents, mediums, brushes, easels, and painting equipment of all types. Prices are almost always discounted, and two-day delivery is offered.

The Jerry's Catalog, Jerry's Artarama, P.O. Box 1105J, New Hyde Park, NY 11040. Toll-free: (800) U-ARTIST. Chock-full of bargains, The Jerry's Catalog offers superlative oil paints and often hard-to-find materials at discounts of as much as 50 to 70 percent.

New York Central Art Supply Co., 62 Third Avenue, New York, NY 10003. In New York State: (212) 477-0400. Toll-free: (800) 950-6111. Famous for quality materials, New York Central carries most of the products mentioned in this book, including Windberg panels and Tri-Mar canvas stretchers. Call for a mail-order catalog.

Pearl Paint, 308 Canal Street, New York, NY 10013. Toll-free: (800) 221-6845. Pearl Paint is the world's largest art supply store, with branches throughout the United States. Most of the oil paints described in this book are sold at the main store in New York City, and many brands are available through the Pearl Paint Fine Arts Catalog. Selling a wide variety of materials at reduced prices, Pearl is a reliable source for sometimes hard-to-find European brands such as Old-Holland, Sennelier, Blockx, Schmincke, and Lefranc & Bourgeois. It also carries the Australian-made Archival and Russian-made Yarka oil paints.

Utrecht Art & Drafting Supplies, 33 Thirty-Fifth Street, Brooklyn, NY 11232. (718) 768-2525. Based in Brooklyn and with eight outlets across the United States, this large art supply dealer manufactures its own paint and sells it exclusively through its own stores and discount catalog. Utrecht is a particularly excellent source for high-quality linen at affordable prices. It offers discounts for buying in large quantities.

SMALL MANUFACTURERS AND IMPORTERS

Archival Oils, c/o Chroma Acrylics Inc., 205 Bucky Drive, Lititz, PA 17543. (717) 626-8866. Toll-free: (800) 257-8278. Contact Chroma Acrylics for help in tracking down these interesting but hard-to-find Australian-made paints. Pearl Paint in New York City is one reliable source.

David Davis Fine Art Materials, Inc., 148 Mercer Street, New York, NY 10012. In New York State: (212) 343-9277. Toll-free: (800) 237-0061. David Davis specializes in manufacturing artists' materials of exceptional quality, including an eponymous line of oil paints and such painting mediums (some of them rare) as cold-pressed linseed oil, triple-refined turpentine, and genuine Maroger Medium. David Davis is famous for its canvas stretchers (especially custom-made shaped ones), wood panels, and easels and other studio furniture.

Fostport, Inc., 65 Eastern Avenue, Essex, MA 01929. (508) 768-3350 or (508) 768-6164. This American firm is the exclusive importer of Russian-made Yarka art materials, including oil paints, linen, and sable brushes. Contact Fostport to learn where to find Yarka products in your area.

Gamblin Artist's Oil Colors Co., P.O. Box 625, Portland, OR 97202. (503) 228-9763. An artist-run business, Gamblin produces excellent oil paints and mediums at affordable prices. Call or write to learn where to find them locally.

The Italian Art Store, 84 Maple Avenue, Morristown, NJ 07960. Toll-free: (800) 643-6440. This is the best source in the United States for Maimeri oil paints and the full line of Maimeri products. The Italian Art Store offers greatly reduced prices, and features specials in its seasonal catalogs. Orders ship within 48 hours.

Lapis Arts, Inc., 1295 South Dahlia Street, Denver, CO 80222. (303) 782-0255. Made with rare pigments, Lapis Arts oils are handcrafted in small quantities by Erik and Jon Rieger. These paints may be hard to find in retail outlets, so send for the firm's handsome color chart and order form. Prices are extremely reasonable, and group discounts are available.

R & F Pigment Sticks, P.O. Box 248, Rifton, NY 12471. (914) 384-6403. These beautiful oil sticks are made in small quantities and are sold in only a few select stores, including Pearl Paint and Williamsburg Art Materials. They are also sold directly to individual artists.

Savoir-Faire, P.O. Box 2021, Sausalito, CA 94966. (415) 332-4660. Savoir-Faire is America's main importer of France's world-famous Sennelier products, including oil paints, mediums, and exquisite oil sticks, as well as Isabey brushes and Lana papers.

Williamsburg Art Materials, 266 Elizabeth Street, New York, NY 10012. (212) 219-9535. Toll-free: (800) 334-5278. Williamsburg makes unusual, extremely high quality oils at prices most artists can afford. These paints are available from the firm's New York City store, as well as through its catalog. Williamsburg is also a reliable source for R & F Pigment Sticks and Marvin Siegel canvas stretchers and panels.

PIGMENTS, MEDIUMS, AND PANELS

Hudson Highland Artist Materials, 18 Pine Grove Avenue, Kingston, NY 12401. (914) 338-8603. Hudson Highland is the producer of Solid Ground artists' panel, an ivory-smooth, archival-quality painting surface handcrafted of solid polymer. Perfect for oils, Solid Ground panels are indestructible; they will not warp or bend, are impervious to moisture and parasites, and need no special priming or bracing. They are available in five standard sizes as well as in larger and custom sizes. For the names of distributors in your area, call or write Hudson Highland.

Kremer Pigments Inc., 228 Elizabeth Street, New York, NY 10012. (212) 219-2394. FAX: (212) 219-2395. Toll-free: (800) 995-5501. This firm sells every kind of pigment imaginable directly to the artist through its New York shop and catalog. It specializes in rare pigments such as lapis lazuli, vermilion, and malachite, as well as in the highest-quality modern pigments. Kremer is the ultimate source for other artists' materials, too—mediums, grounds, waxes, resins, and the like.

Perma Colors, 226 East Tremont, Charlotte, NC 28203. Toll-free: (800) 365-COLO(R). A great source for pigments, Perma Colors also manufactures superior painting panels that are excellent for egg tempera and oil painting.

Pontifex, Inc., P.O. Box 598, Hollywood, MD 20636-0598. Pontifex manufactures genuine Maroger Medium, which is formulated according to Jacques Maroger's original recipes by one of his former students. Two kinds are available: "Flemish," which is smooth, and "Italian," a heavier wax version.

Tri-Mar Enterprises, Inc., P.O. Box 455, Port Washington, NY 11050. (718) 599-0300. Toll-free: (800) TRIMAR 1. Tri-Mar is an outstanding manufacturer of professional, heavy-duty canvas stretcher systems. The firm is especially well known for circular and other shaped canvas stretchers, as well as for Masonite panels. Custom work is available. Call or write for the name of a supplier of Tri-Mar stretchers in your area.

Windberg Enterprises, Inc., 1111 North IH-35, Suite 220, Round Rock, TX 78664. (512) 218-8083. Made of Masonite and grounded with acrylic, Windberg panels are excellent for smooth oil painting techniques and detail work. Call or write for a list of suppliers.

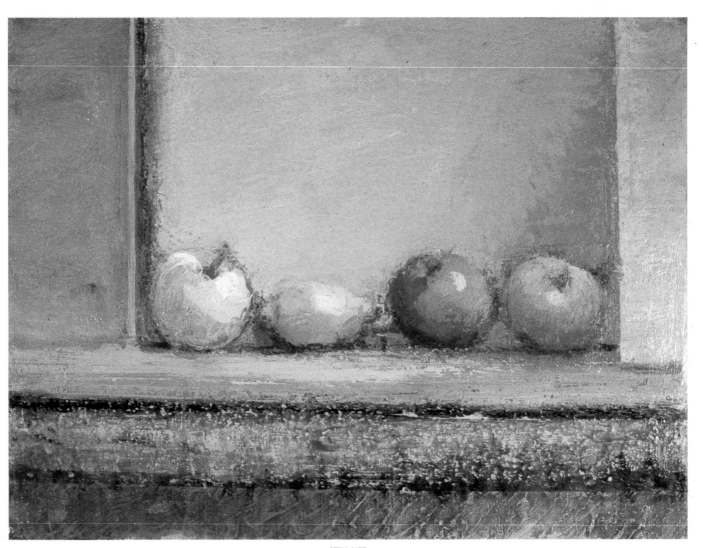

STILL LIFE
Oil stick on canvas,
12 × 16" (30.5 × 40.6 cm).
Collection of the artist.

Editors: Candace Raney and Marian Appellof
Designer: Areta Buk
Graphic Production: Ellen Greene
Text set in Caslon 540